C21049

CU00734734

Condition Notes 24/11

2 1 SEP 2016		
0 7 JUN 2018		
2 9 SEP 2018		

D&P/4261/4.12

 **Nottinghamshire County Council**

Please return / renew by the last date shown.

HANDY HINTS FOR HUMANS

How to get what you want and want what you get

Atalanta Beaumont

Matador
9 Priory Business Park
Wistow Road
Kibworth Beauchamp
Leicester LE8 0RX, UK
Tel: (+44) 116 279 2299
Fax: (+44) 116 279 2277
Email: books@troubador.co.uk
Web: www.troubador.co.uk/matador

ISBN 978 1784621 056

British Library Cataloguing in Publication Data.
A catalogue record for this book is available from the British Library.

Typeset by Troubador Publishing Ltd, Leicester, UK
Printed and bound in the UK by TJ International, Padstow, Cornwall

Matador is an imprint of Troubador Publishing Ltd

To my wonderful boys, Felix and Caspar
To my partner Ken
To my sister Ariadne
No words can express what you mean to me so this book is for you.

Table of Contents

Introduction

When I told my family I was writing this book to help people communicate more effectively, my mother said "Surely it's just a case of good manners." If that were the case all the polite people would be getting exactly what they want, be friends with everyone and never misunderstand or be misunderstood. Usually ultra-polite people will find that certain personalities will walk all over them and take advantage of their "politeness" in not complaining or showing up the person who is behaving badly. Polite people like the rules and tend to minimise awkward situations, accordingly they will find that personality types who enjoy flouting the rules and exaggerating will be an anathema to them. Firm boundaries, good negotiating skills and an understanding of our similarities and differences can alleviate these problems. But this book is not about good or bad manners, or solely about tricky personalities, it's about effective communication and developing an empathy and understanding for ourselves and in turn a better understanding and more compassion for what drives other people.

Language is the only way we have of communicating precisely what is going on inside us and yet so many of us fail to use it in this way. "He should have known I would hate that!" How many telepathic humans do you know? We constantly guess what other people are thinking "I know he thinks I'm an idiot." How? Did you ask him? "I just know." What? Now you're telepathic? We constantly misunderstand what is said to us and fail to communicate what we wish to say to others.

We all grow up with different values and different family norms but if we apply a few rules of communication we can change our language and behaviour and this in turn will change the responses we receive. Different personalities have different methods of communication, different expectations and will exhibit different behaviours. Once we understand this and stop believing that everyone "should" behave the way we do, we can tailor our approach towards the person we are addressing. They then will feel heard and understood and will respond in kind. Also key to effective communication is identifying what it is we want, what our boundaries are and what we will put up with and what we won't. We need to do this before we can even begin to ask for what we want or negotiate with others. So how to achieve this monumental ask?

Well, I am a transactional analyst which means I believe in Eric Berne's theory that all humans communicate from three different but closely related viewpoints. Depending on a situation and what past and present experiences the situation has conjured up we will adopt one of the three different positions from which to respond. These are Parent, Adult and Child. One of the main goals of this book is to develop an understanding of what triggers our various responses so that we can be proactive rather than reactive in our transactions with others. I believe when you understand how the influences in your upbringing still affect how you respond today then you have a chance to change your responses for the better. Whenever I use these terms, with capital letters throughout the book, these are to describe the three positions that are adopted by us.

Parent

The Parent part of our psyche is the repository of our own parental messages, the ones we received as a child from our carers. The Parent is built on old beliefs and messages that have been accepted wholeheartedly and uncritically as a child. The Parent has two parts, the Nurturing Parent and the Critical Parent. These are the internal voices we use on ourselves in times of stress or dilemma, either to soothe or castigate. "How could I be such an idiot!" or "It serves you right" come straight from the Critical Parent whereas messages we give ourselves such as "I did my best" and "I can do this" are our Nurturing Parent dialogue.

Our Nurturing Parent comes straight from the way we were looked after as a child and can encourage us or remind us to look after ourselves e.g. making sure we take care of ourselves when we are ill. Conversely our Critical Parent may drive us on when we are tired or unwell, ignoring the part of ourselves that wants to slow down in a replication of how we were treated or how we perceive we were treated by our real parents or carers.

Many of us base our beliefs and values on these messages from our upbringing, which is absolutely fine if the messages are reasonable and still function in the present day. However some of the information in your "Parent" will be outdated and irrelevant and will be holding you back in certain situations or driving you past your healthy limits. Our Nurturing Parent can keep us safe, champion us and support us but by contrast our Critical Parent can be judgemental and a very hard taskmaster to please.

The Parent part of ourselves holds our judgements and our prejudices, For example if you work in a multinational company and hold ideas that "immigrants" shouldn't work in your country you will have difficulties. If you have had fearful parents who continually told you to "be careful" you may be much more tentative than you actually need to be. You may lack judgement about what actually poses a threat and what doesn't. Additionally we tend to "flip" back into Parent or Child in times of stress or indecision and if we are not aware of this, it can lead to conflict within ourselves and with others when our response is inappropriate to the situation we find ourselves in because we are responding from a Child or Parent point of view and not from our Adult.

Adult

The Adult is the part of us that responds in the here and now, assessing situations, finding solutions and responding appropriately to current events. The Adult part of us rationally assesses the situation, works out what choices we have and then communicates this free from irrelevant and outdated past beliefs, prejudices and fears (Parent and Child). This part of ourselves is the most effective for communicating with others and if not contaminated by Child or Parent will help us make good, prejudice and fear free decisions.

One of the keys to being in Adult is to take time to respond. If you feel an instant response it is probably a "flip back" to a Parent or Child response. Taking your time responding allows you to work out your options and find out what works best for you. This does not mean the information in your Child or Parent is not useful. Much of the information passed on by your parents as you were growing up will be sensible advice and tested observations. You will have tried and tested beliefs which hold true, such as the need to look before crossing a busy road and these can be "integrated" into your everyday working Adult and be a very valuable source of information when assessing situations. You also need the Child part of yourself in order that you can be spontaneous, have fun and enjoy simple pleasures as well as being able to tap into your "intuition", which comes from your Child psyche. The Adult part of ourselves functions best when we include the useful and proven aspects of our Parent and Child, coupled with the rationality our Adult persona exemplifies.

Child

The Child part of ourselves is how we responded to adults as we grew up in order to survive and get what we needed from those adults around us. There are several parts to our Child. There are Adapted Child and Rebellious Child, our Free Child and also our Little Professor.

The Adapted Child is the child part of us that adapts to what we think adults may want from us; to be cute, to be compliant, to be quiet, to be clever etc. When faced with an authoritarian situation in adulthood, such as being interviewed by a learned professor for a place at university, some of us will automatically feel a need to be pleasing and to agree with the authoritarian figure – this is a "flip back" to Adapted Child, when, in our past experience, it was in our interests to be compliant. However in a university interview situation the professor could be looking for bright, argumentative students and your Adapted Child will get in the way of your Adult sussing this out.

Our Rebellious Child is part of our Adapted Child and is the part of us that wants to say "no" to the authoritarian figures we find around us but does not have the capacity to rationally disagree with the adult figures or may have fear of retribution. If you find yourself regularly doing things that "cut off your nose to spite your face" i.e. going for Pyrrhic victories – ones that cost you more than you gain – then you are probably acting from Rebellious Child. It is that feeling of "you can't make me!" which is not a particularly adult one! If you had very strong-minded parents or carers who were coercive when you were little you may have quite a lot of residual Rebellious Child. If you do not recognise this you may be constantly rebelling just for the sake of it. You will need to learn to engage your Adult in order to assess what is worth fighting for (see Choose your battles).

The Free Child is the part of you that is free from parental restraints. This is the part of us that allows us to take pleasure in rolling down a grassy hill as an adult or to twirl unselfconsciously on the dance floor. However it is also the part of us that may get drunk or high as the Free Child will disconnect from the Parent in order to be free and at the same time can decommission the rational Adult. The Free Child is both positive and negative and it is up to us to integrate the positive parts of our Free Child such as the ability to express our emotions and engage creatively and to eradicate the dangerous and irrational Free Child behaviours such as speeding along a busy road.

Our Little Professor is the Child part of us that retains our intuitive decisions and creative abilities that we relied on when we were a child and could not use rational Adult behaviours to assess situations. If we allow ourselves to return to the Child state we can tap into those creative intuitive abilities. Some of us have messages in our Parent that stunt our creative behaviours. We have been told that drawing or painting "is for kids" or that time spent imagining or daydreaming is wasted – tell that to the people who make small fortunes inventing video games or the man who invented the Rubik's Cube!

Some people grow up with parents who are skilled communicators and empathetic people, they teach their children the skills required to integrate all the useful parts of our Child and Parent and to discard those that do not serve us well i.e. to grow, to learn, to assess what works for us and what doesn't and then to adapt accordingly. However, many of us muddle through not understanding why it is we always fall out with the dental receptionist or why it is that so-and-so just never understands what we mean. Why we always get drunk and pick a fight at family parties. It is true there are a few obtuse or rude people out there but not that many. Most people just want to get their message across and understand what it is the other person wants. By understanding how we operate, by working out what works for ourselves as well as others and by recognising our triggers from the past, we can get the most out of life with the least conflict both within ourselves and with others.

This book is arranged alphabetically in order that you can read the sections you believe are relevant or interesting to you. It can also be read from cover to cover to give you a very comprehensive understanding of how we develop and learn to communicate, how different people with different experiences respond to different approaches and how to adjust your own style so you can integrate your Adult behaviour in order to achieve really top-notch communication. Or simply use the do and don't lists at the back as a quick MOT on communication and life-enhancing behaviours. However if you feel you are being constantly misunderstood or taken advantage of or would like to have more friends or a greater social life, or feel you are held back at work and you would like to be able to recognise some of the behaviours outlined under Parent and Child, then it may be a good idea to start at the beginning and work your way through to the end.

However you choose to use this book please believe that it was not written from a preachy position and that I am in no way judging the behaviours or lives of others. I have had my fair share of life's troubles and during my life as a psychologist and psychotherapist I have collected information on many things that could make life simpler, easier and better. Many people still believe telepathy is a valid means of communication! Many of my clients, when introduced to the concept of Parent/Adult/Child exclaimed "why did no one tell me this!" Some people have never had the necessity for firm boundaries explained to them and these have been a life-changing revelation. There are families who do not teach their children how to apologise or why they need to say "please" and "thank you". All of these are necessary for humans to get along in the world as are many of the other subjects included here. I am hoping that this book will help people to understand how they function, change what doesn't work well for them and to recognise outdated beliefs and dump them. Most of all I hope that people will begin to champion themselves so that they can get to the contented place that I now find myself in without having to have worked quite as hard as I did!

Adult

What does this mean? Well, transactional analysts (that's what I am) believe we operate on three levels Adult, Child and Parent. The Adult part of us is the most effective part for communication in that it rationally assesses the situation, the choices available to us and then communicates this free from undercurrents and past beliefs and experiences. If we are constantly responding like a child, either pleasing or resentful, or alternatively like a parent, admonishing or caring then we are hooked by the past into responding in ways we have grown up believing are expected of us. In child mode we politely accept drinks we don't want, we volunteer to help when we don't want to and become indecisive in our quest to be pleasing. The problem with this is that we can become resentful if we are always pleasing others or indeed forget what it is that pleases us. Alternatively if we act in Parent we will be monitoring others and judging them against an outdated, internal set of rules and regulations that we grew up with or else we will take care of them without being asked – this, in contrast to Child mode, leads to others resenting us.

A key ingredient for being in Adult mode is to take time to respond. Think about what you can and can't manage, what you would and wouldn't like. Instant responses often lead to committing to something that you later decide is not what you want to be doing – think about your answer first! It is perfectly OK to "get back" to people. This isn't about pleasing yourself 100% of the time – would that it were! It is about assessing what "makes sense". You may not want to help your spouse with a DIY task but it may "make sense" to if you want him/her to be able to come to the cinema later. Asking ourselves if doing certain things is the sensible option reduces the resentment that comes from "having" to do things and stops us slipping into Parent where we think people (including ourselves) "ought" or "should" do certain tasks or into Child where we experience life being lived by others' rules and as "not fair" – as my mother always says "No-one said it would be"!

So in order to operate from Adult: Assess the situation, take time responding, don't get "hooked" by yours or others expectations, ask what "makes sense". Then work out the end result of your response – and live with it. Well done! This is called "growing up".

What you might do (and shouldn't) to other Adults if you are not in Adult mode yourself

Try not to:
- tell another adult how they feel
- tell other adults what to do (outside a hierarchical work situation)
- wag your finger at another adult (try this and see!)
- ask them "Why did you do that?" Try "What happened?" instead
- use rhetorical questions – it's really annoying e.g. "As if anyone could have guessed that would happen?"
- say "sssshhhh" – Ask properly "Please could you be quiet I can't hear the film/play/music."
- finish people's sentences or punch lines.
- steal others' experiences – "Oh yeah, I felt just like that...." "John said he felt exactly the same..." "I know just how you feel".

In other words treat other people like adults. Think how you would like to be spoken to – even if it's something you know is hard to take – and then do your best to deliver the message kindly, factually and responsibly.

Acknowledgement and Appreciation

If you acknowledge the tasks that others have done on your behalf and show appreciation, others are much more likely to go "the extra mile" for you. This is true of almost anyone from the check-out person at the supermarket to your nearest and dearest. However much you think you are "owed" or that you deserve something – thanks are never wasted. Some people are not gracious at accepting praise or appreciation but that doesn't mean you shouldn't give it as the majority of the human race likes to be thanked. It is also important to acknowledge others' contributions to your life, at work, at home and in friendships. We are all connected to each other and an acknowledgement of this is fundamental to appreciating what we have and what we can give to others. So spread a little happiness and remember to say please and thank you and acknowledge all the people without whom your life would be infinitely harder.

Anger

Anger is one of the four available emotions and is as important as the rest. You have every right to be angry, on occasion and to express that anger. However it needs to be used sparingly and well to be effective. If you are permanently annoyed and shout a lot, people will just start to ignore you; this is "just how you are". Alternatively if you choose to express your anger effectively in a justified situation, notice will be taken of you. Anger does not necessarily mean shouting but it does mean a firm voice and a serious or annoyed expression to match.

Parents will recognise that smiling when telling off a child sends mixed messages – are you laughing or are you annoyed? This is

3

when you are not fully in Adult you have let the Child part of yourself creep in and "mix" the message. Most likely the child you are telling off will take the easy option and start to giggle. The same is true for adults. If you smirk when expressing anger or say it in a half-hearted apologetic manner you won't be taken seriously. You need to match expression and voice well so that you come across as fully Adult and committed to what you are saying. If someone has offended you, say so unapologetically but don't milk it..."You made me feel really bad... it affected my whole week...." This dilutes the emotion. You are in Parent instead of Adult and are trying to extract contrition by pushing the other person into Child. Concentrate on how you feel instead of what the other person has "done to you." Instead try a straightforward – "I'm really angry that you contradicted me in front of the children/Jane/Fred/my mother. Please don't do that. If you have an issue with me in the future, please talk to me about it." This is a three step approach to most verbal problems. Identify the problem and attach the relevant emotion – "I'm really angry that...". Say what you want to happen "Please don't do that." And finally explain a preferred approach – "If you have an issue..." Let people know by effectively expressing your emotions what does and does not work for you and you will find that others will start to respect you too. (See Boundaries)

Apologising

Apologising is an absolute necessity both accepting and giving. When you know that you have made a mistake and/or said something you shouldn't have, say so! If this mistake or comment has infringed on someone else, apologise. Apologise properly! This means saying you are sorry for what you have done and adding that you realise that... well, you realise you may have hurt their feelings, or you realise that your mistake has delayed something at work, or you realise that you were in the wrong AND that you are sorry. Saying you are sorry that they feel a certain way about what you did is a cop out and not a real apology at all. This is the rebellious Child part of yourself creeping in not really wanting to apologise or your righteous Parent part thinking "what's all the fuss about?". Apologising is an Adult business. It means acknowledging you got something wrong – get used to it, humans have about a 20% error rate so polish up your apologies to maintain good relationships and keep your friends – people who do not apologise are often resented and ultimately they are regarded as "small" people.

Accepting an apology is also important. Saying "I told you that it would go wrong... you shouldn't have done/said that." is not a good way to accept an apology – this is your Critical Parent chipping in. Saying "thank you, I appreciate your apology" is a great all-rounder statement and shows appreciation for the other person admitting their mistake – in other words you are behaving wholly as an Adult. This will also encourage an open atmosphere where people are allowed to get things wrong, learn by their mistakes, apologise and move on! This is particularly important when dealing with children. You gain nothing from apportioning blame or being self-righteous once someone has apologised, apart from a bucket load of resentment.

Learn to accept and give apologies and your life will improve dramatically. Teach your children this life skill and if you're already doing it – give yourself a pat on the back!

Assumptions

Just don't! Make assumptions that is. Once made these, have a cascade affect that can infiltrate the most robust of relationships. You assume that the foundations of your house are solid. You build your house. The foundations turn out to be sand – oops! The house is unstable, no one can be safe in it and your possessions are at risk. These are the possible consequences for a relationship when you don't check out something ambiguous early on. The relationship is unstable, built on dodgy assumptions and neither person feels trusted or trusting.

Much misery is caused by assuming things. You need to check things out and ask questions – you are not telepathic and cannot divine the reasoning of another individual whose upbringing and values are not the same as yours. Actually even if they are identical to yours, you still can't. You can make an educated guess but that is all it is – a guess.

Say you work in an office with a bunch of mostly friendly people. You guys have got into the habit of having a drink after work on a Friday before going off home. You find out through idle chatter that one of the group has asked just about everyone else to a birthday meal one evening but not you. You assume this person doesn't like you. You assume that the remark you made last week about their hair went down badly. You assume your failure to support their new enterprise in the boardroom last week caused ill feeling. You assume wrong and yet if you don't check this out, all your subsequent dealings with this individual will now be based on information that includes the "birthday party exclusion incident"!

It is perfectly normal for humans to look for reasons why events occur. This is how we make sense of the world and also how we predict future events. However, when dealing with other humans, rather than events, I cannot emphasise enough how important it is to check that your beliefs and assumptions are correct. Just ask!

Say you ask one of the birthday party invitees what's going on. You may discover that one of your assumptions was right. Good – your educated guess paid off. However that does not necessairly hold good for the future or for past information that hasn't been verified; you will still need to check out all future assumptions. Alternatively you could take the Adult route and say how you felt. You could mention that you were disappointed not to have been invited to the birthday meal. "I would have enjoyed going out with (whoever). It must have been fun." Also, it may be worth checking out that they are OK with the remark about their hair or the lack of support for their project in the boardroom if you have any suspicions that these were not received well. – "I just wanted to check you were OK that I didn't support your project?" However you may find that the reality was they could only invite six people and you didn't make the short list or that they had registered that you take your daughter to football on a Tuesday and the only night for the party was the Tuesday. They had made an *assumption* about your availability – annoying isn't it?

Making assumptions can poison relationships and having assumptions made about you leaves a feeling of misjudgement and injustice. So just don't do it – check it out, ask what's going on and make your life and everyone else's so much easier.

Autonomy

Autonomy is where the control of what we do lies within our own selves. It is where we make choices about what we will and will not do. Even within a constricted life where we need to work and need to pay bills, we can "choose" to work in a certain place even if we don't like it there because we have decided "it makes sense" for the time being – NOT because we have to. When we are in an impasse between Parent and Child, we become a victim and events "happen" to us. We have the frightened Child part of ourselves who is not being "nurtured" by the Parent but frightened and criticised instead. The Child feels put upon and "made" to do certain things either becoming passive and adapting or alternatively, becoming resentful and rebellious. The Parent part of ourselves bullies and cajoles instead of supporting – "You must, you ought, you should" instead of reasoning and supporting – "You can do this." "It's important for the time being to keep your job, even though it's not ideal." Seeing

7

the bigger picture here allows you to make Adult choices dependent on your needs and those of your family and "frees" you from the resentment of complying, essentially against your real wishes and desires. People who lack autonomy have often been poorly supported or ignored as children – change this by supporting and listening to yourself whilst at the same time doing things that "make sense" for you in your present circumstances.

People who lack much autonomy in their lives get sick! No, really. There have been numerous studies showing that a lack of autonomy can cause people to give in or give up (just as they did as children). In a study done in an old people's home (1) half the residents were given a plant to look after and were required to make choices about meals, arrangements of furniture and films they would like to watch and the other half had a plant looked after for them and all other choices made for them. The 'responsibility' group were found to be "more alert, active and contented" than the 'passive' group and eighteen months later the 'responsibility' group had suffered half the death rate of the 'passive' group. Being self-directed – which is what autonomy is – is vital to good health. So make choices for yourself. Explore what it is you really like and want and then (as much as is reasonably possible) make those choices – this is part of your self-expression and who you are. (see Boundaries and Responsibility)

(1) Tones, K and Tilford S (1994) *Health Education: Effectiveness, Efficiency and Equity*. Chapman and Hall, .

Balance

Balance is key to enjoying your life. When we are not in Adult and spend too much time in Child or Parent we become unbalanced. Remember one of the key Adult requirements is asking yourself "Does this make sense?" and the other is taking your time. It goes without saying that if you eat junk or eat on the go, stay up late, overindulge in products or activities which you know make you feel lousy and generally run yourself ragged (all Child behaviours) you will put your system out of balance. However there are other signs to watch out for. When we are out of balance we get irritable, tired, angry, depressed and sick. So how do you know that your life is out of balance? Well if you are in denial about being irritable, tired, angry, depressed or sick you can try the pie-chart method which I often use with clients to illustrate where they are putting all their time and energy and to see if this is how they want to continue.

Try using a different colour for each section as this highlights where you spend your time. Issue the following categories with a proportion of the pie (see illustration A for an example). Sleep should come up with about a quarter to a third of the pie, which is, of course, twenty-four hours or if that is not representative you can just do life in general over a set period of a week, a month or a year. The other categories to represent are Work; Leisure, Play, Friends, Family, Sports & Hobbies, Rest and Me Time (some people like to add Religion or Spirituality as a section if it is relevant). These categories are in addition to getting enough sleep to stay healthy. Incidentally, insomnia is one of the biggest indicators that your life is out of balance.

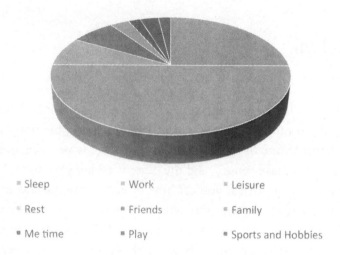

▪ Sleep	▪ Work	▪ Leisure
▪ Rest	▪ Friends	▪ Family
▪ Me time	▪ Play	▪ Sports and Hobbies

Whole pie = twenty-four hours

For the above pie chart the data was given as follows:

Work = 12 hours, Sleep = 6 hours, Leisure = 1 hour 30 mins, Friends = 1 hour 10 mins, Family = 1 hour, Play = 50 mins, Sports and Hobbies = 50 mins, Me Time = 40 mins and Rest = 0

In the above illustration the person is getting very little time with family and friends and sports and hobbies are minimal. This may be OK. For a single person who mainly socialises at work and loves their job this could be a very healthy balance but for a family person in their fifties there is not enough down time (leisure, sports, hobbies, rest) and for both parties not enough Me Time or Rest.

Me Time is time by yourself to think, meditate, take a long bath, practise yoga – whatever regenerates your batteries. Rest here does not mean sleep and is not covered by Me Time it means time in between activities to take a breather. Maybe a ten minute nap after lunch, maybe having a coffee after tennis or golf. Take ten minutes when you get in from work to change environments. If you find yourself rushing from one activity to another then you do not have enough Rest time. This differs from Leisure which I categorise as reading, possibly gardening or cooking, having relaxed people over for dinner, going to a movie. Play is having fun – chasing your kids round the lawn, playing monopoly, enjoyable sex, banter with friends, having a laugh – all humans have a great capacity for play and to stay healthy we need to exercise this. This is the Child part of you that needs to be exhibited as part of a healthy integrated Adult.

Friends constitutes enough time spent with your friends, maybe overlapping with leisure or sports, so that they stay good friends, enough time to talk with them so that they are invested in you and you in them (see Robert Weiss's "Social integration" in Depression). Work is work that you do in order to facilitate your life e.g. work to earn a wage, work to maintain a household, work to support another family member. Voluntary work does not fall into this category unless it is in the pursuit of a career path. Family is time spent with your family, interacting with them, helping them, being with them; it does not mean time when you are in the same place but pursuing entirely different activities. Sports and hobbies are pursuits you enjoy just for the pleasure of doing them e.g. Bridge, Golf, Tennis, Knitting, Painting.

There will be times in our lives when an optimal balance is not achievable or realistic as everyone who has just started a new business or just had a baby knows. However, I urge you to listen to yourself. Your body will let you know when you are tired, sick, overworked and underplayed. Your mind will let you know when you are low, fed up and unhappy. If you ignore this fantastic in-built early warning system, you do so to your own detriment. Classic signs of an imbalance are Irritable Bowel Syndrome, insomnia, being over or under weight, drinking too much, low mood, skin problems, irritability or angry outbursts. Catch these signs early, rebalance yourself (you can check with the chart how well you are doing) and put more energy into categories which bring you respite and pleasure and you have the key to a productive, enjoyable, healthy and hopefully, long life.

Beliefs

Knowing what your beliefs and values are is absolutely essential to living life well. So how do you do this? As children, many of us "adopt" the beliefs and values we grew up with. This is perfectly normal but as we turn into adults we need to check along the way to see if these are still valid. In an ever changing world many of our parents' beliefs will be outdated and these can hold us back. Out of date beliefs are like an Alsatian we have bought to protect ourselves who we find will no longer let us out of the door – they can become dangerous and limiting! Hanging on to beliefs or values that we have not checked are rational, valid and still work for us can be self-limiting – you will be basing the way you live your life on others' experiences and values and not your own. You will find yourself in the unchecked Parent part of your psyche. This is where parental ideas have been ingested without being checked for their value and validity.

Spend time thinking about what it is you value in life – your friends, your job, your environment? What human traits do you value in yourself? In others? Is it important to you that people are honest? Sympathetic? Emotionally literate? What have your experiences at school, work, home taught you? This will go some way to informing you of what your boundaries (see below) will be and what expectations you have. These beliefs will form the foundation of how you live your life and will help you to reach your goals. They will form part of your integrated Adult self – the part that holds Child and Parent ideas that have been tested and found to be of value and operates from Adult beliefs. If you know that you could never work for a company that exploits third world countries or workers, then you have ascribed to a certain set of values which others will recognise and will inform them (and you) of who you are. It is really worth taking time to decide what you do and don't ascribe to; after all, your beliefs and values define you. (see Generalisations)

Be where you are

This is a suggestion that you immerse yourself in the experience that you are having. So, if you are at the theatre, you are not texting. If you are watching a tennis match you are not reading the paper. If you are making love you are not mentally rehearsing your presentation/reliving that perfect golf stroke... etc.

When we distract ourselves by doing too many things at once, two things happen. One, we do not fully enjoy and/or experience what we are doing and two, we break up our ability to focus and concentrate so that we are captivated by smaller and smaller bits of information and find it harder to focus on long-term goals which require seeing through a (sometimes) time-consuming process. We can become easily distracted and by consequence, easily dissatisfied.

Abraham Maslow (1973) coined the ability to lose ourselves in something that was all consuming as being a "peak experience". He is referring to the sudden awestruck joy that humans can feel, bringing with it the feeling of wonder and belonging. The sort of things that might spark this are listening to music, watching a sunrise or working at a task which absorbs you totally. Or it can be generated by the flow of everyday life where you are totally absorbed and find yourself experiencing a sudden shift in consciousness, where you become wholly focussed and filled by the experience.

These experiences add to vital psychological energies and add value to life. They are believed to enhance creativity and add a spiritual dimension to one's life. However, they will not be experienced by someone rushing from pillar to post or by someone who fails to engage with where they are and what they are doing. Peak experiences are free, life enhancing moments which can be yours if you remember to be where you are and immerse yourself in the present. If that sounds too "airy fairy" remember that when you do not attend fully to what you are doing you "lose" from the experience and diminish your capacity to relax and enjoy what you are doing. So at the most basic level multitasking, when taken to extremes, can diminish your joy in the present, encourage you to disengage from your surroundings and leave you with a feeling of dissatisfaction. Something to bear in mind next time you feel you "must" check your phone or emails.

MASLOW, AH (1973) *The Farther Reaches of Human Nature*, Harmondsworth: Penguin

Birth (or arrival) of a child

The birth or arrival of a child is a momentous occasion and you should expect that it will change your life. If this is a first child then many things will be different once the child has arrived. Babies are demanding and time consuming and you will need to find your own routine and methods of coping that suit your new family. Babies often bring up unresolved issues that we have with our own parents and may highlight differences between you and your partner's expectations. An awareness of this will make coping much easier.

Mothers: A new mother has not only the new arrival to cope with but all the hormonal changes that accompany giving birth and the aftermath including the hormonal changes that accompany breastfeeding, if that is chosen. Be patient with yourself as you adjust to the demands of a baby and the new routines of your life and expect to be tired. There are many different ways to look after your baby and gradually you will find what suits you.

Remember to include your partner in all of this, his/her support will be vital and help bond you as a family. If you are appreciative of your partner's efforts they will be more inclined to help and their confidence with the baby will grow. Bear in mind that although you are a new mother you are still you and will need to see your friends, get out and have some leisure time and spend time with your partner. Take your time and remember you are designed to be able to manage but it is absolutely fine to have help of any sort that suits you. This includes alerting your partner or GP if you are constantly overwhelmed, tired and tearful and feel you are not coping. Most mothers feel like this from time to time but you may have post-natal depression if you feel like this for more than two weeks. Get help as this is easily resolvable.

Fathers: However much you were anticipating the arrival of a new baby it will probably be a surprise just how time-consuming this new person is. Your partner will be required to fulfil a very different role and you will need to be aware of this. You have two choices: be resentful or join in. Obviously I suggest the latter as this will bring you closer to your partner and the baby and will help consolidate you as a family. There are many things a father can do from changing the baby to comforting and talking to him/her and the support you can give your partner will be invaluable. If your partner thinks they are doing a good job their confidence will soar and the baby will be more relaxed. Take time also to be a couple and do the things you used to enjoy together. Even if the mother is breastfeeding it is possible to catch a movie or dinner between feeds. Remember it takes time to adapt to new roles and you will find your own unique way of accommodating this new person and enjoying your lives together.

Siblings: Be aware however reasonable your existing child(ren) that the arrival of a new baby is a shock. I think it is Penelope Leach who explains that if you introduced a new partner to your partner by explaining that you loved them so much you wanted another just like them, they would not be overly impressed. When you then go on to explain that they will need to share your attention, their toys and maybe their bedroom it will be hardly surprising if a sibling does not welcome a new baby.

It is your job as parents to make sure the other child(ren) in the family don't feel displaced. Interpreting the baby's gestures as smiles or waves at the existing child are good ploys. Wondering if the baby will be as smart or funny as the existing child works well too (flattery is always attractive!). My first son seemed quite accepting of his new baby brother. I left him colouring next to the baby who was in a carry seat on the floor. Five minutes later I returned and was puzzled to find the baby had green felt tip pen on his head. "What happened?" I asked my eldest "He's a Martian now so can you send him back to Mars?" was the reply – not quite so happily accepting after all! Be aware of your existing child(ren)'s feelings and be slow to tell them off and quick to praise them. Include them in changing and playing with the baby and let them make decisions "Shall we dress her in this T-shirt or that one?" Just as it takes time for you and your partner to adjust to a new arrival, so it does for a brother or sister, perhaps more so as the baby could be viewed as a rival. Be patient and everyone will adapt.

Your wider family may think that they have claims on your new baby. Grannies, Uncles, Aunts will all want to get in on the act. Be firm about how many visits you can cope with in the early days or you will be worn out. Ask people who are visiting in the first few days to bring some food over so that you don't have to shop or cook. Firmly emphasise the role you wish relatives to take and if you find too much advice offered or that you feel criticised by relatives, remember that 1) They are probably only trying to help 2) They may not realise that you are feeling sensitive about parenting your child 3) It is perfectly OK for you to refuse visits, help and advice – this is your child and you can do things any way that suits you 4) You may be extremely grateful for any help you can get 5) You will do better if you have a long and happy relationship with your relatives and so will your child.

Remember, above all, to enjoy your new baby. Talk to them, tickle them, laugh with them – you are your baby's first introduction to the world, make sure they feel welcome!

Blame

In a blame culture, either at school, home or work everyone will deny responsibility for fear of having the finger pointed at them. No one will volunteer for anything in case they get it wrong – nobody wants to be blamed! Blame comes from the Parent part of ourselves, which sees what ought or should be happening according to their (sometimes outdated) beliefs. Try instead to create an atmosphere of enquiry not blame. Ask "what happened?" not "What did you do, why did you do that?" If things have gone really awry, try asking "What made you think that (doing whatever they did) was a good idea?" Treat failures as an opportunity to learn and progress. After all if we never got things wrong we would never innovate. Bear in mind that if you think there is only one way to do things and it's your way then you are going to be largely responsible for carrying out those tasks. Embrace different approaches that achieve the same outcome, even if the route is not one you're familiar with. Remember if you act all Parental the response from the other party will be to act in Child. So encourage an Adult approach and remember: No blame = more help and more people willing to try out things. And the more things you try out the more likely you are to meet with success!

Body Confidence

Body confidence starts with recognising how much our body does for us on a regular basis and what an amazing biological entity it is. We have a peculiar habit in the West of dividing our body up into body parts – "Well I like my legs but my bum is too big." "I don't like my feet"… "My nose is too big"… "I would have liked bigger boobs." "I'm going to work on my pecs, my abs, my quads." This is a very unhealthy way to see your body, in terms of a commodity, rather than the wonderful receptacle for your persona that it is. It is very easy to find fault with our bodies if we break up our body into parts and compare them with other people's. Whereas viewing our body as our means to get about, see, hear, touch, feel, and smell the world puts it into some perspective and reiterates its use – it is the means by which we come into contact and get to know the world. It works as a whole, each part connected to and reliant on the other. It is therefore, essential that we take care of it.

We need to make sure that we get enough rest, feed ourselves well and that we avoid over-stimulating our physical selves with too much alcohol, nicotine, caffeine, sugar and drugs – both legal and illegal. There is a big rush to "fix" things when we experience ill-health and rather than treating the cause, we often treat the symptoms. It is important that if you know you get migraines when you miss meals that you acknowledge this and avoid illness by making sure you take care of yourself. Body confidence comes with being healthy and if we treat ourselves well and acknowledge our responsibility to keep ourselves healthy our confidence (and hopefully, delight) in all our body can and does do for us, will grow.

Get to know your body, after all it's unique to you. You may be particularly prone to headaches or have a predisposition to gain weight. Acknowledging how you can get the best out of your body will mean enhancing your enjoyment in it. Recognise how you use your body on a regular basis – walking to work, getting yourself meals, reading, watching, listening throughout the day – your body works hard and is an amazing asset. You can't change your basic dimensions and genetic inheritance – if you are 5ft 5inches tall, then you are. But you can be well fed, not over fed. You can be toned and fit. You can be well rested and energetic. All these things will add to your general enjoyment of life. If you treat your body well and enjoy all you can do with it, you will be rewarded with good health and an inner confidence and enjoyment which cannot be supplied by cosmetic surgery or drugs but comes from the knowledge that your body is a wonderful thing.

Boundaries

Without boundaries we have no solid, identifiable form both for ourselves and also as recognisable to others. Why does this matter? Your chosen boundaries are the limits that you set both within and without for how you are to be treated and regarded. Boundaries are a projection of how you view and value yourself. It is important that you set boundaries that suit you and you feel comfortable with – everyone's will be different. If you are too "parental" in your approach you may end up with rigid boundaries that may mean you are hard to get to know and have certain rigid expectations. If you are too "childish" in setting your boundaries you may find you get walked over and easily overruled; you may find yourself changing your boundaries depending on who you are with. You need instead to think about what is right for you, regardless of others' opinions and then test out your criteria and if they work for you stick by them.

Is it all right for people to ignore your suggestions? Overrule your decisions? Swear at you, take advantage of you? If not, how do you let other people know this? We must verbalise what we will and won't tolerate but more than just "talking the talk" we must "walk the walk". In other words we must live our beliefs in order to be taken seriously. So if you think it is not all right to have your suggestions disregarded then you must be careful not to disregard others' suggestions. It really is a simple case of "do unto others as you would have done unto you".

Boundaries are uniquely individual and not an opportunity to see what others' limits are and find them lacking when measured against yours. Your boundaries are only your business and in the same way others' are theirs. You cannot choose how others will bring up their children, respond to requests or live their lives and in this way one's choice of boundaries carries no judgement value.

Boundaries are our defining beliefs. They are the rules we

choose to live by and the expectations we have of how we will be treated by the world. However if you have been overruled, ignored or in some way abused whilst growing up boundaries will be hard for you to put in place. You will need to think carefully what works for you and what doesn't and how to express this to others (see Adult). If you have not done this before, go slowly. Follow the three step plan outlined in "Anger". Identify the problem and attach the relevant emotion to it. Say what you'd like to happen. Suggest an alternative.

One of the tricks for good solid boundaries is to stick by them. You cannot have a set of beliefs that suit you one day and not another – if you do not personify and own your boundaries others will not take you seriously and you will find that you get "walked over" or disregarded by others – especially children! It is important you understand why you have chosen certain boundaries and why they are important to you. This will help you to respect others' boundaries and will in turn help you to select better friendships and be a better friend and family member. Stick by your beliefs and you will find that others will like you for it and more to the point, you will like yourself.

A note of caution – if you have any form of addictive behaviour – smoking, over or under eating, drug or alcohol abuse, exercise abuse, OCD or a hugely controlling nature you may need professional help in setting your boundaries.

Bullying

To be a victim of bullying is really horrid. It means that you are out of Adult and into Child. The bully may be in Parent or Child but whichever they are in, when you return to your Adult self, they will lose their power. In this case this means neither accepting the role of "victim" or "persecutor" but just responding appropriately to what is happening to you and expressing how you feel about that. Bullies thrive when not confronted and only bully because they can get away with it. When you allow yourself to be bullied you are discounting your ability to stop the other person (see Discounting) and you are also crediting the bully with power that he/she doesn't have unless you credit him/her with it!

The solution is to confront them in as public a place as possible with as many witnesses as possible. Bullies thrive on fear and secrecy and any publicity robs them of this power. "Please don't do/say that to me. I don't like it/I find it offensive." If they claim innocence… "I don't know what you mean," then explain in minute detail exactly what it is you don't like and why. This is really a boundary issue, and as you work out your beliefs and boundaries (see above) and put these into place, communicating from your Adult self, people will be less likely to bully you. It will never get that far because they will have had early warning of what you will and won't tolerate.

If you can't tackle the bullying yourself through fear or intimidation, enlist help. It may be that your past childhood experiences mean that it is hard for you to respond in Adult and that the bully's tactics propel you back into Child's responses which leave you vulnerable to repeat attacks. At work contact Human Resources and remember to note dates and times of the incidents. For school contact the headmaster/mistress and after that contact the Governors of the school. Ask to see their bullying policy (by law every school must have one). For any form of intimidation or blackmail, go straight to the police. Bullying is never acceptable and relies on the bully counting on you putting up with their behaviour – DON'T.

Carers

If you find yourself in the position of a caring role there are several things to bear in mind. This is a very tough, time consuming and for a lot of people, stressful job. Many people have not chosen this role it has befallen them. You need support and friends in order that you can continue to have your own life as well as taking care of the other person. It is important that you have "time off" like any other job and that you spend time with friends having a coffee or seeing a film. It is not healthy for you or the person you are looking after if you are stressed and exhausted. You need regular meals, breaks and proper sleep. You are not solely responsible for the welfare of the person you are caring for; it must and should be a team effort, involving other family members, if possible, and professionals. If this is not happening you need to contact your local authority, a charitable organisation or contact your GP or health visitor in order to put respite care into place.

It is important to keep up with your friends and interests as there may come a time when you are no longer caring for someone and you will want to take up your life once more. This will be far easier if you have left a framework in place and have ensured that you have seen your friends and pursued some of your own interests. Try not to feel guilty about time for yourself, it is important that carers are well cared for themselves so that they can fulfil the difficult role that they have. If you strike the right balance a caring role can be very fulfilling, however if you do not it can be a very debilitating and demoralising role. There is a lot of help available but like many other situations you need to let people know that you need it; when you get help you will find life much easier, particularly if you allow yourself to accept it.

Child

This is about meeting the needs of the Child that still exists in you. It is also about acknowledging that some of these needs will never be met and letting go of the pursuit of them.

All of us have some remaining child behaviours which when integrated into our mature adult selves are useful and life-enhancing. For example getting excited about your birthday or Christmas is childlike and will enhance your enjoyment and maybe others' too. Mischievous jokes or pranks can also fall within the child enjoyment category as long as they are not repetitive and annoying to others. An impromptu snowball fight evokes the child in us as does a rollercoaster ride or a game with our children. Also our inner Child will let us know when we are tired and have had enough and is well worth listening too. If you find yourself constantly "pressing on" or "just getting on with it", you are probably achieving things at the expense of your inner Child who may have your health and well-being at heart – ignore this inner prompting at your peril particularly if you are the child of a very driven or successful parent as it is that internalised parental voice which is driving you on!

However, there are also negative effects of our inner Child. These can manifest as petulant and manipulative behaviours in order to get our own way. These will have been learnt in childhood when they were seen to be effective but are outdated and need to be shed as they are not part of a mature adult's repertoire. A more direct approach in order to get what you want is more in keeping with adult behaviour.

Other negative Child effects will be based on left over hurts from childhood resulting in unmet needs. It is important to address these although this can often be hurtful, reminding us of the things we wanted as children – more attention, love and praise – which may not have been forthcoming. If we still yearn for these as adults these "left over" needs will interfere with the way we relate to others particularly in family relationships such as marriage or parenthood. It will be possible for us to snap back into old behaviours, appropriate when we were children, but wholly inappropriate now, if others touch these remaining "sore spots" by bringing up past issues in their present behaviour which we have not yet laid to rest.

It is important to work out what your "sore spots" are. If you find yourself overreacting to others' behaviours then you have probably hit one of your "sore spots" from the past. Being excessively over-emotional in reaction is a good litmus test indicating that these are past needs that were not met. If you can identify these (sometimes with professional help) and lay them to rest you will be able to respond to the "here and now" rather than the "there and then" and form real relationships with people rather than repeating patterns learnt in childhood in order to try and fulfil 'past their sell-by-date' needs.

So first identify these needs. If every time someone mentions splitting the bill on a first date you find yourself becoming angry or thinking that this must mean the other person is incredibly mean then you probably have "left over" money issues which need addressing. If you find yourself at work hating the new girl whom everyone else thinks is wonderful you probably have "left over" attention needs. Once you know what your triggers are you can work on responding differently. One of the most therapeutic ways I have found to respond is to acknowledge that you didn't get what you wanted when you were little and that that hurt (and may do still) but then to separate the past from now and to choose to respond differently. Then you were little and vulnerable and there was nothing you could do to change things. Now you are an adult and can get things you need by being open and asking for them. This is how we can lay past ghosts and go forward getting more of what we want and need in an appropriate manner.

So nurture your inner Child. Lay past hurts to rest, enjoy

impromptu fun, have a giggle and be "silly" now and again. Also use your inner Child to warn you when you are "pushing on" too hard or ignoring needs that you can properly fulfil as an adult – like more attention and praise or time off to just do nothing. Learn to harness your inner Child in these ways and you will lay your past ghosts and flourish.

Children

I am not about to tell you how to parent your child. However I am going to suggest that that is exactly what you do. Almost all the real problems I have seen with parents and children have stemmed from the parent wanting to be "friends" with their child. Most children will have plenty of friends *of their own age*. Your job is to be their parent. After all they only have one set of parents. It is your job to say no, to show them how to be kind, polite, helpful, work hard, have fun, tell a joke, kick a football etc. and then to let them get on with it in the company of their friends. Being a parent is the hard 24/7 tough option; it is also the greatest gift you can give your child. So don't duck it and opt for the "friends" version where you opt out of modelling for them your standards, beliefs and boundaries – show them how it's done!

The following was sent to me, I don't know where it comes from but in terms of tolerance and using encouragement rather than criticism, I have found it to be a fabulous aid to parenting which, after all, does not come with instructions!

If a child lives with criticism
    He learns to condemn
If a child lives with hostility
    He learns to fight
If a child lives with ridicule
    He learns to be shy
If a child lives with shame
    He learns to feel guilty
If a child lives with tolerance
    He learns to be patient
If a child lives with encouragement
    He learns confidence
If a child lives with praise
    He learns to appreciate
If a child lives with fairness
    He learns justice
If a child lives with security
    He learns to have faith
If a child lives with approval
    He learns to like himself
If a child lives with acceptance and friendship
    He learns to find love in the world.

Choice

Some people believe that every decision we make involves choice. I am not of that ilk and believe that in the real world there are many constraints present when we are balancing our need for employment and providing for our dependents. Sometimes we cannot throw in a job or walk out of the house because of the consequences, however much we would like to. However, in most situations, there will be some element of choice and as we become more aware of ourselves and how our decisions affect us and those around us, so we become more aware of our choices and what they might mean.

However in some circumstances, there are people who choose to believe they have no choice as a way to opt out of responsibility. These people are opting out of Adult behaviour; once you realise that you can choose, so the responsibility when things go awry becomes yours. However, do not be put off by this as the real gains from exercising choice are enormous. No longer do you become "compelled" to do things but can choose – sometimes as a necessity – what you will and won't do, do and don't like, will and won't tolerate. Sometimes it will "make sense" to tolerate situations that normally you would not choose to put up with and in acknowledging this you are also exercising your element of choice.

As mentioned in Autonomy (see section A) people who decide things for themselves are happier and healthier and suffer less from depression. It is when we believe we cannot influence our situation that we become despondent and may give up. If we have been ignored as children or not had our needs met, then as adults we can decide (subliminally) that nothing we do or choose makes any difference. That was then and this is now. As an Adult you need to recognise that there will be some element of choice in each decision you make i.e. how you do the job you would actually like to give up. You can weigh up the pros and cons even in small decisions and then exercise your choice. If things go wrong you will learn from this and consequently will make better and better choices. But to make no decision at all and exercise no element of choice leaves you on the sidelines of life with others playing the role of the director – be brave, choose; once you're in, the water's fine!

27

Choose your battles

This is a really important life lesson. You cannot fight every injustice, every annoyance, each time something is not how you would like it to be. In order to be taken seriously and also not to be exhausted, you need to be selective. Some things are really important and need to be dealt with and challenged – they will matter in six months' time. Other things really don't matter and you won't remember the details by the end of a week. Learning to differentiate between these two scenarios is really important. If you rise to every tiny annoyance you will not be taken seriously when something really big happens. People will be too used to you "sounding off" at the smallest provocation and will take little or no notice when an important issue is at stake. Be selective and you will find out the issues that really matter to you (see Beliefs) and will end up having more success when persuading others to see your point of view.

If you find that your "buttons are easily pushed" then you will have found your "sensitive spots". You need to address these yourself so that you do not bring your own personal childhood issues into every adult encounter. If you are particularly sensitive about certain issues then let your close friends and family know so that they can avoid them. With people you don't know you will need to learn to let things go and not "engage" in the disagreement or discussion.

Also try (within reason) to learn to fight your own battles and leave your partner, children and friends to fight theirs – this is a good life skill to learn and means you will only take on issues that matter to you. By this I don't mean to imply that you selfishly ignore others when they need you to help them but that you don't wade in between others and put "your oar" in when it is not appropriate. If your partner is telling off one of your children it is not necessary for you to take part. If you disagree with what your partner is saying you can address it later in a non-confrontational moment. Adults will ask for support and help when they need it and that is when your input will be welcomed. Children are a different issue and obviously as a parent there will be times when you need to intervene on their behalf. Be careful, though, not to deskill your children by acting too early in situations where they are handling things well themselves. You can be supportive and help them "review" how they managed the situation, rather than taking over. In this way they come to believe that they have all the necessary skills whilst still benefitting from your support and greater life knowledge.

Commitment

Be careful to what or to whom you commit yourself but when you have done so, do things wholeheartedly. There is little point once you have agreed to do something, in doing things badly or half-heartedly. This undermines you as a person and shows little regard for the people or project that you are letting down. For instance if you are employed and paid for your job, do the best you can in that job. It is not all right to call in sick, if you are not sick – you are effectively stealing a day's work from your employer. If you say you will do something for someone then do it. If you agree to meet someone then be there. Of course there are situations when you cannot do what you have agreed to. In these situations be prompt and honest in your explanation of why and don't forget your apology if you have let someone down. Try to make amends if possible and avoid repeat behaviour. As a general rule let what you do be a measure of who you are.

Compassion

Compassion for others is really about recognising that others find themselves in a tough position and empathising with them. It does not mean that you have to know how they feel (how could you, you're not them?) or that you have to have been through a similar experience – it just means recognising where they're at and their humanity and vulnerability. Offering appropriate words is helpful if someone is experiencing a loss or a particularly difficult time. If you don't know what to say a very good (and kind) standard phrase is "That sounds tough." Alternatively admit that you don't know what to say and ask them how they are.

Compassion extends beyond the personal, too. In coming into contact with people every day we can extend to them the "benefit of the doubt". By this I mean that we assume we know nothing of their lives and in this capacity we are compassionate. So that when someone cuts you up in their car you just assume they're having "a bad hair day" for all you know it could be something much worse. This also means that when random things happen or are done by strangers to you, you are less likely to take them on a personal level. This is much healthier and of course much more likely to be the case. If someone doesn't know you they are hardly likely to be out to get you.

A little bit of compassion goes a long way. As Atticus Finch says in *To Kill a Mocking Bird*, "It's about walking around in someone else's shoes". Of course this does not mean ignoring very rude people (that's a boundary issue) or taking any old behaviour on the chin. It does, however, mean not rising to any little perceived insult and, as above, "choosing your battles" as well as recognising the fallibility of us all as humans and extending to others something we very much like to have ourselves – the "benefit of the doubt".

Confrontation

Sometimes you need to address a situation head on to resolve it. However direct confrontation, coupled with any form of accusation is very rarely effective. As with all situations, a little time thinking about what you would like the outcome to be, is time well spent. If you wish to resolve the issue and have a chance of your side being heard, as well as a chance at changing the situation, you need to go carefully and openly.

Being open when you approach someone means that you have not already made up your mind about what has been going on and how "they" can resolve it. If you can resist being drawn into the "them and us", "she/he and I" mentality then you have more chance of success. A good way to approach someone is to let them know you need to talk about something important, give them a time frame (so they can't avoid meeting with you) and ask when it would be convenient to discuss it.

When it comes to the actual discussion itself, one of the best opening line is to state what you believe. "I believe that there is some talk of moving managers to a different office...." And then to ask the other's views or thoughts on the situation. "I wonder if you could give me your thinking on this situation." This allows you to be gracefully wrong. "Actually there are no plans to move the managers to a different office." You can then withdraw saying "Oh, thanks for clearing that up, I was worried." However if the situation is as you believe it to be, you then get the other person's thinking and viewpoint on what is happening (whatever it may be) and this gives you a chance to assess the reasonableness of what they are doing, their beliefs (as opposed to yours) on the issue and how best to tackle the situation and get what you want.

You can counter what they are saying by putting your view. "It's interesting what you are saying, but my take on it is... and that has got me worried/annoyed/feeling ignored...." Having an open discussion and expressing the emotions that go with your beliefs about a situation is far more likely to get the other person to listen, to understand the effect of what they are doing/planning is having on you, and be willing to alter their decisions or views. A direct confrontation or accusation: "Your son is bullying mine in school." Will illicit an immediate defensive response in all but the most relaxed or laid back of people; worse, it will close down the conversation. In order to resolve conflict you need for all parties to be able to express their views and beliefs. If you can attach an emotion to the belief you have about the situation they will be much more likely to, one, listen and two, be willing to consider an alternative solution.

Be wary of using any of the following Parent words – ought, should, must – these often have the effect of putting the other person's back up and because they are words associated with being parental they can often cause the other person to revert to Child behaviour which is almost certain to result in an inability to resolve any conflict. Instead try to stick to Adult behaviour and language, avoiding blaming and being sure to ascertain the other person's viewpoint.

You will not always be able to resolve any conflict but with the above method you will have a better chance. If you cannot resolve your differences, try to agree to differ. You are both entitled to different views and opinions; neither has to be "right". Be gracious in defeat and you will be a person that others are willing to be more open with and happy to try and resolve differences with and that, of course, raises your chances of getting more of what you'd like.

Courtesy

"Manners maketh man." Whoever said that was working along the right lines. As a human being it really is important that you thank people when they do things for you – it's about acknowledgement and courtesy or politeness. It is not all right to accept a deed from another without acknowledging it in some way. Recognition is a human need and when we recognise others' contributions they will be much more likely to want to do things for us. The more specific you are the better. So don't just say "Thanks for your help." Be more precise and say "Thank you so much for those cupcakes you made; you really have a light touch with sponge and you saved me a lot of time." Or "The work you did on rewriting the project application was spot on. Thanks for that, I'm sure it's a large part of why we got the contract."

I would also include under courtesy, the need for acknowledging the situation you find yourself in. By this I mean that, when you are visiting your grandmother you will obviously choose different clothes and use different language, than when you are out on a date. It is about matching your behaviour to the culture, or age, or experiences of others. This is about "appropriate" behaviour for the situation in which you find yourself and is considered part and parcel of courtesy.

The same is true if you inconvenience someone, say excuse me or sorry (see Apologising). This just makes the world go round a little better as people who are treated with courtesy tend to treat others well. Don't forget to use "please" either. When asking for something use "please" or a suitable euphemism such as "I'd really appreciate it if…" Regardless of whom you are asking, a child, an employee, your wife, your son, a policeman. Politeness has a "feel good" knock-on effect and the sooner you learn this as a person the happier your life (and that of those you come into contact with!) will be.

Death

Whether we like it or not one of the only sure fire things in this life is that we and everyone else on the planet are going to die at some point. Each of us will experience and handle the death of another in our own unique way and of course it will depend hugely on what that person meant to us when they were alive. There are many different and equally valid ways of coping with grief. There are widely believed to be several stages to the grieving process but I personally believe they can come in any order and all stages can be experienced alongside each other so you may be feeling several contrasting emotions at once. It is possible both to hugely miss the person and be furiously angry with them too. There is no accepted time frame in order to come to terms with the death of someone – it takes as long as it takes. You do not "get over" the death of someone but you do, in time, learn to live with their loss. The fact that you miss the person is an indication of the part they had in your life when they were alive.

Elisabeth Kübler-Ross outlined the five stages of grief and they are worth reading just so you can know what to expect in very general terms. As I have said above each person is different and these are not hard and fast rules.

1) *Denial* This is not happening to me. Sometimes people continue to act as though the deceased person is still alive. An expectation that any minute they will walk through the door and life will continue as "normal".
2) *Anger* Why me? How dare the person die, leave me? A feeling of rage that this has happened.
3) *Bargaining* Please don't let my loved one die… I'll be good forever. If only they hadn't died. Pleading, wishing, bargaining with a higher power.
4) *Depression* Hopelessness, frustration and bitterness sometimes

leading to thoughts of suicide (see Depression and Suicide)
5) *Acceptance* This is not resignation to the death of the person but acceptance. An ability to look forward and enjoy your own life whilst remembering happy times with the deceased and recognising that life goes on.

Several things may help when dealing with the death of a loved one: Being able to tell at least one person exactly how you feel. Getting out and seeing people. Taking up a new interest or hobby (when you feel able). Taking time to remember the person you have lost, acknowledging the gap in your life and maybe visiting their grave, or planting a tree in their memory.

It is not always acknowledged that for some, the death of another can be a relief or can be welcome in some way. If the relationship has been difficult or complicated or there has been a long illness, death can put an end to this and be very welcome. There can be strong feelings of guilt if your feelings towards the person who has died are ambiguous or if, in some way, you are pleased they are dead. These are also normal feelings but can often be unacknowledged or left unsaid, particularly in literature that deals with grief.

Each person will have a unique way of dealing with death but the one thing you can do for yourself is to be kind to yourself. Grieving takes time and you need to allow yourself that time; you may have mixed and complicated feelings about the deceased. Remember to eat well, choose foods you like and that are easy to prepare. Take exercise; this can ward off depression and lift the spirits, even a short walk to the shops. See people you like and trust this will take your mind from your sadness even if only for a short time. Most of all grieve in your own way, take the time you need and remember you are still here and in honour of the person who died, you can live well.

Delegation

This is absolutely necessary in order to survive. In a business, a family or a social group you cannot do absolutely everything yourself. If you try to you will become exhausted and resentful. Good delegation involves letting the person you are asking to fulfil a task you would normally do, know exactly what you would like to be done. In a family or social situation it also allows the other person to do the task "in their own way".

Often people who fail to delegate do so because they are perfectionists and either believe it will be quicker to do it themselves (in the short term this is true but in the long term this is madness!) or that the way they do the task is the "only" way to do it – big mistake! It is patently not true that you are the only person who can fulfil any tasks – if you dropped dead the task would either get done by someone else or else it wouldn't, in which case it wasn't that important anyway. There are plenty of different but effective ways to complete any given task. The exception I make here is in the workplace – I'm sure there are certain things in some environments that absolutely have to be done in a certain way – the trick when delegating is to show the other person this "exact" way and let them know why it is so important.

Remember not to take advantage of others' subordinate position or kindness by delegating tasks you cannot be bothered to do yourself or you merely dislike. In order to maintain good relationships around you, you will need to be seen to be working equally hard or harder than those you are delegating to. If you are on the receiving end of someone who seems to be passing their entire workload over to you, you will need to refer to the Boundaries section and to register your discomfort or unease.

The final act to complete the task of delegation and ensure that people will enjoy taking over tasks from you is to compliment them on what they have done and to thank them properly. This is particularly important when getting children and spouses to participate in the running of a home! Don't correct the way they have done things (unless it was a total disaster and then be gentle) thank them and let them know how much you appreciate what they have done. Another good ploy is to let other members of the group/family know how good/kind/helpful they have been – be liberal and public with your praise and people will be queuing up to do tasks for you.

Depression

Depression is an extremely serious illness that can lead to suicide however it is not the same as the occasional low mood. Before discussing how to keep depression at bay here is a brief outline of what constitutes depression.

If you have five or more of the following symptoms for longer than a period of two weeks you are probably depressed and should seek help immediately. The first port of call should be your doctor.

1) A depressed mood, feeling empty or irritable, crying a lot
2) A decreased interest or pleasure in almost all regular activities
3) Weight change, either quick gain or loss
4) Sleep disturbances or an inability to fall asleep
5) Agitation or inertia
6) Fatigue or loss of energy
7) Feelings of worthlessness or guilt
8) A diminished ability to think, make decisions or concentrate
9) Thoughts of death, particularly suicide

There are several available routes to take if you have depression. Undoubtedly if you have thoughts of suicide which include collecting enough pills to do yourself harm, or looking for times when you will be alone and can harm yourself, you should probably take anti-depressants if they are offered to you as they may save your life. However this is not a long term solution and other steps need to be taken in conjunction with medication to ensure that you get better and do not have a repeat episode. Some sort of talking therapy should be sought. Cognitive behavioural therapy and transactional analysis have a very high rate of alleviating depression and in some cases are more, or as effective as anti-depressants – which only work for about 60% of people who take them. Depression and its cures has been very well-researched and in most cases a two-pronged approach involving both medication and a talk therapy has been found to have the best short-term and long-term outcomes.

There are several steps that will help if you have depression or low mood. The first step is not to blame yourself. If you had a broken leg or the flu you would not blame yourself for having them. Depression is one way that humans express when things are not right for us. Depression is almost always a sign that your life is out of balance (see Balance). It can be an expression of grief over the end of a partnership, through death or divorce, the loss of a job, or as a result of illness. There are also some prescription medicines that carry a risk of depression as a side effect and you should certainly make sure that this is not the case before exploring other reasons for developing depression. Long term disability or illness can also, in some cases, lead to a depressive episode.

The good news about depression is that even if left untreated it usually only has a cycle of eighteen to twenty-four months. I know this seems forever if you are currently experiencing depression but it will pass. The exception is if you have bi-polar disorder where you experience extremes of behaviour involving both deep depression and manic euphoria. You will certainly need medical intervention to stop these cycles of depression and euphoria. There are also some people who appear to have a chemical imbalance which causes life-long depression and these people will also need to be on life-long medication. Be patient if you fall into one of these categories which will need life-long medication. It can often take several months and an experienced psychiatrist to get the medication that is required properly balanced so that it is its most effective and least debilitating.

There are many things you can do to help ease a depressive episode.

1) Take some sort of exercise. Exercise has been shown to alleviate depression, sometimes as much as taking anti-depressants. You need to take about thirty minutes brisk exercise. If you have a disability try to find something you can do, such as wheelchair sports, swimming or armchair aerobics.

2) It is important not to drink alcohol as this is a natural depressant and will exacerbate symptoms.

3) Smoking and eating poorly will also exacerbate feelings of depression. It is important to take care of yourself just as you would if you had any other illness.

4) Try to get out in the daylight every day. This helps regulate your time clock and primes your body for sleep when darkness falls.

5) Try to socialise (I know this is the last thing you feel like doing!). Mixing with others, particularly friends who know you, will lift your mood and help you "escape" your depression for a little while. Then these "escapes" will become longer and longer periods and the depression will start to recede.

6) Listen to music you like and go and see funny films – *Fawlty Towers* is very therapeutic! Do not go and see dark, depressing films and do not watch the news too often.

7) Try to get some routine going in your day. If you are working, be open about your condition and enlist some help. You cannot be sacked for having depression! (Some employers may try in which case you will need to enlist some help.)

Incidentally, people who own a cat or dog have a lower incident of depression as do people who belong to an organisation that meets regularly such as a church, a singing group, a sports group, painting or bridge lessons.

Depression can be viewed as anger turned inwardly. If you have been brought up to believe that you are responsible for all that happens to you and you have lacked support and help and consequently find it difficult to turn to others for help, you may well be more susceptible to depression. If you have been on the receiving end of poor parenting, for whatever reason, you may well turn your anger in on yourself. For instance, if you are left by a partner, instead of being really angry with him/her, you will blame yourself. If you lose a job you will attribute the loss to your personality rather than a need for the company to cut down on staff. This personalisation of events can contribute to a higher incidence of depression in those with this thinking style. Some other psychological issues that contribute to depression seem to be poor boundaries (see Boundaries) lack of clear beliefs (see Beliefs), lack of autonomy (see Autonomy) and a high incident of discounting (see Discounting).

Robert Weiss (1974) believes there are six major provisions for social relationships and I believe a lack of any of these can also contribute to feelings of low self-esteem and depression and that such a lack should be addressed. They are outlined below.

Attachment is the feeling one has intimate bonds that provide a feeling of security and place.

Guidance is the provision of directive communication and advice and is provided in relationships with a trusted person

Opportunity for nurturing is found in relationships where a person feels responsible for the well-being of another.

Reassurance of worth is obtained from people who provide confirming information about one's competence and skills.

Reliable alliance is a sense that one has others who can be depended on for assistance and material aid.

Social integration stems from relationships in which participants engage in social communication with others who share similar concerns, interests and activities.

Remember throughout history some of the most creative and inspirational people have had depression; Churchill, Spike Milligan,

Stephen Fry. Depression is not a "fault" it is an illness and nothing to be ashamed of. A quarter of all adults will have had some sort of depressive episode in their lives if they live to sixty-five. Please, if you have thoughts of suicide, remember this. Suicide is a permanent solution to a temporary problem. There is a lot that can be done for depression and depression is not terminal!

Different Strokes

Just a reminder; there are many ways to accomplish a task. If you adopt a "my way or the highway" approach you will find that several things happen, depending on the person you are dealing with. People adopting the same attitude as you, will clash with you – after all they want their way at all costs. Less confrontational people will avoid you or do things their way behind your back or do things your way and resent you. Almost certainly you will not be a person who is offered a lot of help; after all you know the best way to achieve everything!

People with one way of doing things are also very vulnerable to change and can become depressed or irritable if made to deviate from their learned patterns. These are usually people who have grown up with relatively intolerant and/or perfectionist parents who generally think they are right and demand the same mind set as themselves from their children. Try to free yourself from this sort of rigid thinking. If you can adopt a flexible, tolerant attitude and realise that you will learn many things if you let others demonstrate their abilities, life will be much easier. There are many different, useful and interesting ways to do things and knowing several approaches will stand you in good stead, especially when things do not always go to plan. An open mind and tolerant attitude will gain you a much easier ticket through life, so if you are not as flexible as you could be, ease up and start to enjoy yourself more.

Discounting

Discounting can go on at many different levels. It can be done to you and you can do it to yourself and to others as well as discounting the situation you are in. Whatever form it takes it is very destructive and gets in the way of us being truly autonomous and integrated as a person.

So what is it and why does it matter? Discounting is when we behave in a passive manner towards the solution of a problem. It is where we dismiss the information and available solutions to fixing a problem. Often we will not be aware of doing this and our reasons for this will be based on past experiences and beliefs, some even stemming from childhood. However if we continue to do what we've always done, we'll get what we've always got. With passive behaviour what you will get is precisely nothing.

Imagine I am sitting in a railway carriage where there are several other people and the window is open. I feel cold. I shiver ostentatiously and pull my coat closer whilst frowning at the person nearest the window. What am I hoping to achieve? I am "discounting" my own ability to 1) Close the window 2) Ask someone to close the window. Simultaneously, I am instilling the person nearest the window with telepathic powers and giving them the power to decide whether to acknowledge my discomfort or not. There are many reasons why I might behave like this – maybe I have been brought up not to ask for anything. Whatever the reason, if I continue this behaviour I am going to be uncomfortable a lot of my life! The first steps towards stopping discounts are to recognise them:

The four passive behaviours which manifest as discounting (Stewart and Joines 1987) are:

1) Doing nothing – where we literally do nothing
2) Adapting – where we adapt our behaviour to that of another

person; doing what we think they want without even checking or with any regard for our own wishes. For instance if the man I frowned at in the railway carriage closed the window without asking if I would like the window closed, or if I was cold, he would be "adapting" to his belief about my wishes.

3) Getting agitated – in the above example this is the frowning and shivering. It could be sighing or drumming my fingers.

4) The fourth behaviour is violence or incapacitation – smashing things or kicking a door would be violence and becoming incapacitated by becoming ill, fainting or getting drunk would be good examples of incapacitation. In the railway carriage I might leave the carriage slamming the door behind me (violence) or I might start to develop "Hyperthermia" (incapacitation).

All of the above behaviours have one thing in common – they discount our ability to fix our own problems or ask someone to help us to fix them. Martin Seligman identified this as "learned helplessness". (Seligman, M, 2006) He saw that either there was adaptation where people might become docile, such as in an old people's home where they would then be better liked by the staff or conversely, people did nothing because they had learned that absolutely nothing they did changed their situation. Most interestingly of all, he found that "learned helplessness" contributed towards depression (see Depression).

The trouble with these passive behaviours is that it is a wild generalisation for humans to make that they cannot affect their situation. Of course there will be situations you can do nothing about but once you are an adult, in almost every situation you can have some effect or can make an attempt to have an effect. So first of all you need to recognise when you employ these passive behaviours and secondly you need to find alternative ways of behaving which result in solving the problem. Start slowly and practice in relatively safe situations (where you know the people) by changing what you normally do and acting to solve the problem.

A very useful reminder I have found is that whenever I believe I can't do something I substitute the word "can't" with the word "won't" or with the phrase "I don't want to". This reminds me that my behaviour is mine alone to control. Whatever you decide to do remember "discounting" behaviour ensures you stay stuck and get nothing of what you want!

Above shows how you discount yourself. However there are also the instances when we are discounted by another or indeed, we discount another. You will know if you have been discounted by someone; you will either be non-plussed by their response, or you will up your behaviour in order to get the response you want, or you will feel let down, or sad or in some instances angry. Being discounted by someone means that your feelings, opinions or needs have been "dis-counted" i.e. marked down in value and not given their proper due (according to your perception). If this happens to you, you need to let the other person know what they have done using the "I/You" statement. For instance if you have hurt yourself and someone says to you "Oh, you're all right," you may well feel discounted. Perhaps you don't feel all right, perhaps you are really hurt and would like some attention and sympathy or perhaps you just need confirmation that they care about you. Whichever is the case this is a boundary issue (see Boundaries) and you need to make it clear how you feel and what you would like them to do instead. Being constantly discounted and not doing anything about it will make sure you feel you don't count.

Try not to discount others, either. It is important not to tell others how they should feel in any given situation – how on earth do you know how they should or shouldn't feel? Make gentle enquiries as to their feelings and if someone tells you they feel a certain way then do them the courtesy of believing them. This helps the other person to behave appropriately and makes them feel heard and understood – the opposite of discounting them. Also recognise if someone's behaviour becomes more and more exaggerated or they keep repeating themselves it will invariably be because they judge the response you are giving to be unsatisfactory to them. For instance, if someone tells you they have just graduated and you respond in a certain way and they then repeat what they have told you, just in a different format, then take note. You need to up your eye contact and warmth and really mean it when you congratulate them or enquire about what this means for them. Discounting leaves a bad taste in the recipient's mouth and can build resentment, so try not to do it.

The other form of discounting which is worth mentioning is when we "discount" something once we have achieved it. So we may attach a lot of importance to becoming the CEO of our company but once we have achieved it we dismiss its importance and slog on to the next goal. Similarly we can long for something, a piano, a trip, a new car but once we have it we no longer "rate" it as quite as valuable, therefore discounting its importance. This is a sure fire way to reduce your enjoyment of life and to raise your discontentment levels. Employ your Child ability for glee and enjoyment (see Child) and you will be less likely to gloss over the importance of all you have and all you have achieved.

Seligman, M 2006 *Learned Optimism*, Vintage Books, Random House, Stewart I and Joines V, 1987, *TA Today: A new introduction to Transactional Analysis*, Lifespace Publishing, Nottingham

Divorce

Whoever is the instigator of divorce, it is hard on both parties. Try to remember you once loved this person enough to go through a marriage ceremony with them. Don't rush into any immediate decisions and if you have the resources try to get some kind of couple counselling. Friends are good to confide in but not great for advice, they will have their own viewpoints and a different agenda from you.

If you have children you must remember that your primary function is as a united parenting partnership. Whatever your differences it is important not to bad mouth the other parent. Don't forget your child knows they are half of each of you, if you bad mouth one parent you are saying half of your child is not OK! Try to make decisions about the children's futures together, such as which school they should attend and certain rules that they need to stick to. Do not overrule decisions that one parent has made without discussing it with them first. Children will always sense a divided front and will manipulate you both to their own ends – beware!

Divorce is tough so be kind to yourself. If you did not want the marriage to end you may be experiencing feelings of anger and grief akin to losing a loved one (in effect that is what has happened). You have also lost your planned-for future together and you will need to come to terms with this. If you have children they may be experiencing grief as well and school work and behaviour may suffer. Talk to your children about their feelings; let them know it is normal to feel the way they do. When your child visits the other parent let them enjoy their company, don't pump them for information and let them decide what to tell you about their day.

However distressed you are try to get good, independent legal advice. If you have no resources the Citizens Advice Bureau can help. Each divorce is very different and you may be able to sort things out with your partner to the satisfaction of you both but remember you are no longer a unit working for the good of each other and you need to know what is fair and just at the end of your marriage. Once you have made an agreement it is costly and time consuming to go back and alter it so make sure you know the implications of anything that you sign. Once you have an agreement, accept it. It is debilitating for both parties if you keep trying to "modify" the agreed conditions and means neither of you can move on.

Emotionally it will take time to get over a divorce even if you are the one who initiated it. Let yourself come to terms with your loss and start to look for ways that you can enjoy yourself that show your individuality; things that you particularly like to do and hobbies that interest you that you may have neglected. Gradually you will be able to view yourself as a functioning individual again instead of part of a partnership and you will be able to look forward to the future. The end of a marriage is hard for everyone involved but almost everyone goes on to have happy fulfilled lives with new relationships which are made much easier if you have dealt with your previous marriage with integrity.

Don't

Don't what? This isn't something you shouldn't do, these are messages that some people receive when they are growing up. Most families have their own "codes of conduct". These are the parameters within which the parents feel comfortable and may encourage their children to stay with verbal and non-verbal "don't" messages. These are how parents pass on their own limitations and fears to the next generation which is why you may get generations of people behaving in the same self-limiting ways. Each family's set of don't will be different and they may well be different don'ts for different children within the same family. And of course some families don't bring up their children using "don'ts" but an awful lot do.

For instance, in some families achievement is not well regarded and there may be unspoken or verbalised messages "Don't blow your own trumpet" "Don't be big headed" "Don't be successful" "Nice girls don't win". There may be mixed messages such as "Work hard at school/Don't show off." So if you work hard and don't get noticed that will be fine but if you get noticed for working hard you may get additional messages which are more subtle "gentlemen don't need to be the best at everything" or "you're so pretty you don't need to worry about maths". These messages cause real difficulties if they are absorbed at subliminal levels. If you work hard but never seem to achieve the top position you may want to look at the subtle or less subtle messages going on in your family. Look carefully at the way you felt you needed to behave in order to be accepted.

The way to identify if you have been on the receiving end of any don'ts is to think of the things you would like to be happy or successful in but so far are not and then to examine your beliefs around these areas. (See Beliefs) Left over beliefs belonging to your parents will frequently include "don't messages". They could be "Don't be happy", "Don't be successful" "Don't grow up"… if you have ever thought about suicide you could have a "Don't exist" message. All of these messages can be tempered e.g. "It's OK to exist if I…." "It's OK to be successful if I…." If you have had problems with your sexuality you may have had a message which is "Don't be a girl" or "Don't be a boy" where you are not the sex of child that the parents either expected or wanted.

Other messages are "Don't be well/sane", "Don't belong", "Don't succeed", "Don't be close", "Don't think", "Don't feel" "Don't be important" and "Don't do anything". All of these various messages carry their own problems and only by examining your own behaviour can you work out which might apply to you and set about challenging these archaic and unhelpful messages. If you are someone who feels "stuck" or keeps sabotaging your own success it may well be worth you reading the chapter on Injunctions and Decisions in Stewart and Joines *TA Today* where they describe each injunction in more detail and how you may have received these messages. When you have worked out which apply to you, you will be able to challenge their veracity and believe that you can be how you want to without "conditions" attached. Very few parents, however good they are, manage totally unconditional love. As adults we can recognise this and choose our own "conditions" to live with and chuck the out-of-date ones on the rubbish heap where they belong. In this way we can leave the self-limiting messages behind and set about becoming the best we can be.

Duty

Beware the word "duty". Whose is it? Usually the use of the word duty is employed in order to coerce another into doing something they would not normally be willing to do and it is usually something that involves self-sacrifice. It is fine to do something noble and self-sacrificial if that is what you want to do but nowhere does it state that you are morally bound to do your duty. What is your duty? Who decides what it is? Surely only you know what your duty is having worked out your own moral and ethical boundaries and beliefs (see Boundaries and Beliefs). Do not be conned by someone else's, often out-of-date, concept of duty. In my experience I have found that this is a word often used by parents towards reluctant children (at any age) – you have been warned!

Education

There is a reason why people in third world countries are prepared to travel four to five miles on foot to attend rudimentary schools. Knowledge is power and education is freedom. If you do not have particular academic abilities or the school which you attend is poor – underfunded and badly staffed, try at least to become literate and numerate.

Being able to read unlocks a whole world. You can read street signs, information and instructions but most of all you can then go on to read about anything and everything else that interests you. Being numerate is essential in order to make sure you are not being short-changed, your ten per cent discount really is ten percent or that you can apply for the best loan or mortgage deal. Fundamentally to be successful you need to know how best to manage your funds.

If at all possible try to pursue education to the level where it is certificated. In most countries this is around fourteen to sixteen when you are able to "graduate" with recognisable qualifications. Even if these are not the best in the world they are proof that you are educated to a reasonable level and they will let you continue your studies at a later date. These are "bankable" qualifications that can never be taken from you.

Do not be afraid to ask for help (see Help) or to let people know that you do not understand. There are many people with learning difficulties and there are now many solutions available to tackle these but if teachers are unaware that you are having difficulties they will not be able to help. Fortunately a lot of teachers go into teaching because they love their subject and want everyone to understand it; if you ask for help most teachers will be only too delighted to give it. If you clash with certain teachers remember they are a resource and you need to get on with them well enough to have access to that resource.

Higher education is not the be all and end all but it certainly is a stepping stone to greater opportunities in some fields. There are very few people who regret getting their degree and learning for learning's sake is a very valid pursuit. I believe that no knowledge is wasted. However there are different sorts of learning and emotional literacy and social intelligence are probably more valuable than any amount of exams. Nevertheless if you are given the opportunity to go to school, in a world where many are denied this privilege, please try to use it to its fullest extent and get the most you can for yourself and your future.

Elephant in the room

The "elephant in the room" is a euphemism for the subject that is glaringly obvious and is not mentioned. If you do not address the "elephant in the room" it will trumpet and blunder around causing all sorts of trouble. Fundamentally this is about addressing the most pressing, difficult, subject that you would much rather avoid. However, it is this avoidance which causes all our subsequent interaction to be distorted as we carefully avoid mentioning what both or all of us are thinking. For instance, if you go to visit your friend who has terminal cancer and you never talk about the fact that he/she is dying and has terminal cancer, then that is the elephant in the room. This avoidance will cause you to pussyfoot around subjects and to be "careful" when with your friend. You will cease to be the friend that you were and you will become the friend avoiding the most obvious, pressing, difficult topic.

Addressing difficult topics is, by their very nature, hard. It needs to be done, though, unless you wish to appear cowardly or patronising. It is also near impossible to have an authentic, meaningful dialogue where some large, tricky topic lies between you. In the case of terminal cancer, your friend knows they are dying. It is OK for you to talk about this; they can let you know if the subject is not a good one. Obviously timing is important and sometimes you need to let the elephant go on its way if the timing is not right or maybe you missed your "time slot". Be sensitive and use your common sense. It is not a good idea to tackle "elephants" with unbalanced or erratic people or someone who may have power over you and enjoy wielding it.

Humour and honesty are good characteristics when addressing difficult or sticky issues. If you run into someone you have behaved appallingly to in the past, then address the situation – be honest, apologise, do whatever you need to do to get back on stable ground. Similarly if you run across someone you believe owes you an apology then let them know what you expect and then move on. Clearing the air in this way leaves you both on an even keel and makes way for Adult to Adult conversation and room for honest interaction and intimacy if that is what you want. Try not to leave huge elephants blundering around your life, they have a horrible way of treading on things that matter and breaking things you value; address them and they will vanish into thin air.

Empathy

Not everyone automatically has empathy which is the ability to understand and care how another person might be feeling but we can all develop it to some degree. Obviously you cannot know exactly how the other person feels but an empathetic person has a good idea to start with and will ask questions and respond in ways which the other person feels to be appropriate and caring. Empathy is a hugely important skill and a lack of it leads to discounting other people (see Discounting), loneliness and a lack of any real intimacy.

People who lack empathy, ironically feel misunderstood and are often isolated. Even if you are unfortunate enough to suffer from some form of social disability, empathy is still something you can learn.

Empathy starts young with parents and carers pointing out to their children when they have had an emotional impact on someone else. "Look she's crying. You made her sad when you hit her." Or alternatively, pointing out when people are pleased "Look how happy granny is, she has a big smile." If these early interventions don't occur it is hard for children to pick up cues on other people's feelings and responses. However, it is never too late to learn.

If you are not sure how people are feeling – ask them. "I think I might have upset you when I said..." or "You look really fed up today." Or, even "How are you feeling?" Avoid at all costs telling other people how they feel. You don't know and it cuts communication so that they then won't feel any inclination to tell you how they feel. "Oh you must feel really awful." Must they? Why must they? You have no idea how they feel and are probably projecting how you would feel in a similar situation. This is anything but empathetic. A feeler statement will give you a much better idea of how someone feels. "That doesn't sound too good." is a good feeler statement. The other person can then let you know. "Actually it's OK." Or "Actually you're right. I feel really upset about it." Feeler statements are very useful when you are learning to be empathetic towards others.

Empathy does not mean you have to be touchy feely and constantly asking people how they feel. It does however mean being aware of changes in other people's demeanour or manner which can alert you to their being unhappy with you or with situations you are both involved in. It means developing a warm and open manner when enquiring what is going on for them and not imposing how you think they should be upon them. It is up to you if you wish to take an interest in what is going on for other people and then respond – with friends, family and colleagues you wish to maintain a good relationship with, this is usually a good idea. Empathy brings its own rewards – warmer relationships, less misunderstanding a feeling of connection – what's not to like?

Empty Nest Syndrome

This is the rather pompous term for the feeling of loss and let down when your children "fly the nest". Nevertheless this is what you are working towards as parents from the moment you have your children. Your job is to produce independent, self-reliant, motivated adults. If you have done this well with a certain amount of good humour and well-defined boundaries, your children will naturally come home and visit you from time to time. What is not in the job description as parents is to create needy, dependent children so that they never leave you. With this in mind you will have a very good idea of when your child or children will leave home and you can prepare yourself for this event.

If you are lucky your child will go on to college or university and there will be a natural decline in your involvement of your child's day-to-day activities. You will still see your child during the breaks but they may start to want to take holidays with their peers and not with you. Some children attach themselves to other families when their close friend is a member of that family. So if they have a girl or boyfriend they may spend a lot of time round at their partner's family's house. Congratulate yourself that you have brought up a person that can adapt to their surroundings and is welcomed by others into their home. Accepting that there will be some feelings of loss is inevitable and you can plan for this.

Children who go straight to work from school may need time to save money and form friendships before they move out to share a flat or house with someone else. The same is true for children who have finished university and not immediately found a job. Also many parents will be quite happy for their children to return to the family home if things do not work out and they become homeless or jobless. This is all fine within clearly-defined boundaries so that all parties know what the new rules are in a house with grown-up children. Do they pay rent? What food can they eat? Can they bring friends back without permission? Is there a time limit on how long they can stay?

If you have been heavily involved in your child's upbringing it will be important to foster independence from you as they grow up. Just because you are in the home doesn't mean your child needs everything done for them. By the teenage years children need to be able to work the domestic machines in the house, cook a meal or two and have a set of chores that are their responsibility, otherwise when they come to leave home they will be bottom of everyone else's list for house sharing; no one wants a lazy house-mate. Also they will be de-skilled in the adult world and have a much harder time adjusting to being independent.

As they approach fifteen or sixteen it is now that you can regain some of your own independence. You need to gradually withdraw your support until you are only offering it when asked. Think about expanding your work, pursuing more leisure activities or volunteering. Perhaps you would like to spend more time with your partner, if you have one, or alternatively your friends. If you have any money left after bringing up your children (!) you may like to travel or take up a new hobby or sport. Your children need to feel that you expect them to leave (eventually) and that they are not required in order for your marriage to function or, if you are a single parent you do not need them to prop you up. The main aim of parenting is to produce a fully-functioning adult at the end of the process, one that you are happy to see when they return to visit you but also one who is free to pursue his or her own goals and life with hardly a backward glance. It is inevitable that you will miss them and feel some loss and sadness but each of you will be entering a different stage which, although you are their parent, involves an adult-to-adult relationship. So pat yourself on the back for bringing up your child and move on to your new, much less arduous and less expensive, relationship.

Enjoyment

The ability to take pleasure in events and occurrences large and small is really what enjoyment is all about. In our western society we have become more and more connected to what we can have rather than what we can enjoy. These can be the same but, crucially, not necessarily. You can both have and enjoy a car. However it is perfectly possible to get great pleasure out of seeing a robin or a cardinal fly by as you walk along. Or feel pleasure at the first snowdrops or at your son offering to take the dog out so that you don't have to. Be aware of the many free available pleasures in every-day existence and your well-being will soar. It has been found that possessions do not bring the same pleasure or satisfaction as experiences and Oliver James has written about this in his book, *Affluenza*. He reports how the ever-increasing pressure of our commercial environment encourages us to "keep up with the Joneses" by buying things we either can't afford or which bring us little satisfaction.

For our well-being we need to invest our time in interactions with other humans and experiences. If you are not particularly good at this make a game of it. How many things can I take pleasure in on my journey to work, during walking the dog, sitting in the park? It's up to you but the more you practice the more you will take pleasure in every-day things and enhance your life for free. This way of interacting with the world also frees you from some of the commercialism that we are exposed to in every day Western life. If possible pass on this gift for childlike enjoyment in your every day experiences and surroundings to your children – unlike most store-bought items this will last a lifetime, get better the more you use it and never wear out.

Oliver James, *Affluenza*, 2007, Vermillion

Emotional expression

This is the ability to match your tone of voice, words and expression to the emotion you are feeling and wish to convey. It is surprising how many people can relate something really bad that has happened whilst smiling. Inappropriate facial expressions cause huge miscommunication between people. It is particularly confusing for children who are trying to learn the repertoire of emotions available, if an adult laughs whilst telling them off or conversely, keeps a grim face whilst saying how pleased or happy they are.

Many people are guarded about showing their emotions and that is fine. But when you are communicating with someone that you want to know what it is that you are saying or feeling then your signals need to be clear. When you are angry, look and sound angry. This does not mean shouting but it means an "authentic" feeling being expressed instead of a "fake" one. Many people pick up on fake emotions and are then confused by the ensuing events as the emotion being expressed does not match with the body language or subsequent behaviour of the person expressing themselves.

If you are known as a "closed book" or someone with a "poker face" make sure this is because you want and need to keep your emotions private and not because you are expressionless on the surface whilst seething inside. If this sounds like it might be you, practice authentic voices to go with each emotion and try and really "feel" what it is that you are experiencing. Then, when you come to convey to another what it is that you are feeling, your genuine feelings will shine through and the other person will be able to respond to you appropriately.

If you feel you are on the receiving end of an emotionally "illiterate" person let them know. "I didn't know you were annoyed because you were smiling." Or "I didn't know you liked my present because you were shouting/frowning." This is good feedback and helps people to understand what cues you need to read their behaviour.

Alternatively if you come across a person who is emotionally "leaky" or "gushing" then it is quite all right to give feedback that lets them know that this also gets in the way of you interpreting how they feel. A gentle joke may nudge them out of it "I thought you were going for an Oscar there." Or "You were crying and shouting so hard I didn't really understand what you wanted."

If you are in a partnership where one of you is emotionally closed and the other emotionally very open then you will need to adjust to the middle ground if you are ever to communicate effectively with each other. Bear in mind that some of the biggest misunderstandings come when we do not acknowledge that another may just be expressing themselves differently not necessarily badly and that we need to respect the different interactional styles each of us have. With tolerance and good feedback (non-judgemental) all can be resolved.

Expectations

We all have expectations. The problems only occur when our expectations are not met and we become disappointed or resentful. It is important to realise in a shared event such as Christmas or a party that there will be several different sets of expectations all based on individual experiences and beliefs about such events. Discussion is all. If it's not your party or you are not the host then discuss with others what the party/event is going to be like. Ask questions. Will there be dancing, what are people expected to wear? If there is something you regard as essential to the event i.e. crackers at Christmas or champagne for a birthday, then a simple solution is to offer to bring them. If you are the host then the key is to be organised and let people know well in advance what is expected of them. On Christmas Day are they expected to arrive early and muck in or turn up half an hour before kick off and be liberal and admiring in their praise? Assigning people roles and tasks for big family events can take the pressure off the organiser and help everybody to have some of their expectations met. It is also a good way to get everybody emotionally invested in the end result and keen to help.

With people, there is a theory which I have usually found to be true. You get what you pay attention to. So if you are constantly expecting the worst or have labelled someone as "difficult" or a troublemaker" that is the only behaviour you have planted seeds for. This is why it is quite possible for someone else to get completely different behaviour from the same person. If someone constantly does something you find unhelpful or dislike it can be useful to say "that is not really you, I always see you as such a kind/helpful/thoughtful person". When we know others see us as something good we strive to become that – very few people want to be thought of badly – this is particularly true of children and teenagers who will model your expectations, particularly the bad ones!

If you are constantly disappointed by events or people then I suggest there is a serious lack of communication going on. In personal relationships it pays to be clear about what you expect. So that when you are asked to dinner you need to ask are we being casual or smart? This will give you a very good idea of what to expect. If you want to go somewhere smart then an opening line is "I thought it would be fun to dress up and treat ourselves." This takes the pressure off the other party and lets them know what it is you like. Liberal praise is another good tool for when things are going well and encourages the other person to repeat their behaviour. Positive reinforcement is so much better than a negative response.

So the key to having your expectations met is to ask questions, check out the event and the other person's expectations and offer to do the things which are important to your enjoyment of a situation. With people it is important to expect the best and to ask for it when it isn't forthcoming. Other than that, try to relax and go with the flow. Sometimes the occasions we don't organise and don't expect and that are completely unknown to us, turn out to be wonderful experiences. Sometimes the way someone else solves a problem can be new and innovative. If you organise everything to meet your own beliefs and ideas sometimes you will miss out on others' interpretations and different, just as valid, experiences.

Family

You can't choose your family; where you end up is pot luck. Your original family defines who you are as you grow up; this is the first indication you have of your own worth. You may be over or under valued but whichever is the case, as a child you are completely vulnerable and may have to buy into a distorted or dysfunctional view of how the world works in order to survive. Alternatively you could be lucky and find yourself supported and nurtured in a way that enables you to develop into a balanced and contented adult. As a child you may not be able to choose how to live your life and what your values are but as an adult you can redefine your own worth and choose your own set of criteria by which you will live. These may include your original family's core values or they may not.

However there are certain constituents to family life that are unique and should not be underestimated. That each family is unique goes without saying; even more in today's society where you can come from a single-parent family, a divorced family, a step family, be brought up by two same-sex partners, have disabled parents or siblings etc, etc. The combination is endless but whatever the components that make up your family when you are small, this will be your "norm". As you get older and go into the wider world of nursery and then school you will develop an awareness that allows you to judge whether your family works for you, fits into your culture or is obviously different or alternatively, if you are unlucky, dysfunctional and uncomfortable. However your family is, there will be that connection and familiarity that does not come with any other relationship.

Your parents and their relationship towards you, whether beneficial or detrimental, will be formative. You may wholeheartedly accept your parents' views and behaviours or totally reject them but whichever you choose they will form part of who you become. If you have siblings they will, possibly, be the only people who truly understand what you have experienced as you grew up and why you are the way you are. Even a sibling cannot wholly understand your experience because, one, they are not you, two, they are experiencing a slightly different time zone (unless you are twins) and three, they will be in a different birth order to you. All of these elements impact on the experiences which go into forming who you become within the family you grow up in.

If your experiences with your family were better than they were worse, I would suggest that it is important to maintain those family ties, even if it is just in a superficial manner. The loss of a reasonable family and siblings and parents who did their best, even if it wasn't what you wanted or it didn't suit you, is hard to replicate or replace. I would also suggest that as you grow and mature and form your own family and maybe have children, that your perspective on how you grew up in your family, will change. As you parent your own children or form a relationship with your long-term partner you will become more aware of the pitfalls and difficulties of raising a family and may be able to forgive your own family for any perceived failings.

However if your experiences with your family were dysfunctional or abusive and have left you with long-term psychological consequences that impact your life, then I would suggest that you may want to divorce yourself from your original family. It is also entirely possible that you may not and that you may choose to work through your childhood experiences with some sort of supportive help and resolve issues far enough that you can maintain some sort of family connection. It is entirely up to each individual. If you do decide to "divorce" your original family you will need to recognise that in some way this will also be a rejection of how you were as you grew up and will have a far-reaching impact on how you are as an adult. It may be that this is the best choice you can make. Only you can decide and you may need some professional help to reach this decision.

Sometimes people whose situations have been abusive and damaging need to wholly reject what was done to them and in particular those who perpetrated this dysfunctional and damaging behaviour and the family in which this happened. You can then set about creating a better "family" with friends and colleagues who you choose for yourself, being aware not to recreate the past's damaging relationships. It can be extremely validating to have a sibling or relative who confirms your view of what happened to you and can support you in your bid to form different, healthy relationships. If you do not have a sibling or any other supportive relative, a good friend or partner can often help create a better and different future as can a good counsellor or therapist.

However your family is, it will have been formative as you grew up. Whether you choose to stay connected or to reject your original family, or whether you create new rules which suit you better and allow you to stay in contact, it is important to realise what the impact will be on you and to take steps to make sure that your current relationship with your family enhances who you are or who you wish to become. If it doesn't then you need to change the dynamics in order to get what you need or you must move away from this particular family set up and form a new and better one of your own based on your own established and emergent adult values.

Forgiveness

Learning to forgive, both yourself and others, is essential to a life that is to be lived in the present. If you are constantly holding on to past hurts they will overshadow who you are and stop you from fulfilling your potential; this is like walking around carrying a sack of boulders on your back.

The key is to address hurts as they occur. If someone upsets or offends you it is important to gently point this out. Saying nothing but remembering or holding it against them does nothing to alter their behaviour and a lot to influence yours. You will be holding a grudge or will subtly (or not so subtly) alter your behaviour around them. Worse still you could become a "tale teller" or moaner. Someone who never actually says what the problem is to the face of the perpetrator but who goes around bad mouthing them to others – pretty cowardly.

When you address a problem as it happens, you give the other person a chance to say what their thinking was and/or apologise. This dissolves any ill feeling or hurt instantly and wipes out any need for recriminations or forgiveness. Sometimes a fear of confrontation stops us from addressing a problem. Obviously with strangers in a difficult situation good judgement is needed and the best course of action may well be to say nothing. However if you then find yourself dwelling on the incident, forgive yourself and the protagonist. It is OK you didn't confront them; safety comes first. It is fine to have good boundaries and principles but they are not much good to you in hospital or the morgue. You don't know what made them act as they did – let it go or it will colour a part of your life at no cost whatsoever to them!

However, in social situations, gentle confrontation is all that is needed. Use humour if possible. Teasing the person is a good way to get them to see what they are doing. "Did you really make a sexist remark, surely not!" said with a laugh makes the other person seem Jurassic in their views whilst you appear entirely moderate and you've made your point!

If you have issues left over from childhood caused by poor or inadequate parenting, abuse or neglect these will need to be addressed. It may not be possible to entirely forgive some behaviour but with professional help you can lay most incidents to rest so that you are not the one carrying around the hurt and damage; you need to let this go in order to be able to move forward and live your life fully in the present. If offences were committed against you, then you are not the villain, forgive the perpetrator for their weaknesses and their damaged existence but, please, do not carry that damage on into your own life. Carrying boulders is exhausting and pointless, put them down by forgiving and letting go and start building something new and good.

Frame of Reference

Everyone has a frame of reference and each one will be unique. A frame of reference is the way we perceive the world to be, based on past experiences and the world view expressed to us by significant adults when we were children. It is our unique collection of opinions, norms, beliefs, expectations and criteria that form our own personal mental reference files. We then use these to judge, categorise and test all that we encounter.

If a friend and I went to the circus and were asked to describe the scene before us I might say "I can see many happy people with their children eating popcorn and enjoying the spectacle of clowns and acrobats as well as the animals and the exciting atmosphere". My friend's view could go like this "I see crowds of people jostling each other to gawp at an outdated form of entertainment which borders on the Roman arena and makes animals perform unnatural acts for human's pleasure." These are fairly opposing views but both are valid. Due to different past experiences, opinions and perceptions, we both feel completely differently about a single event.

If you can extrapolate this example out to every-day situations, the same results will occur. No two people will ever view the same situation in the same way. With society's many nuances there will be hundreds of thousands of differing views, maybe even millions. However if our upbringing and culture are similar we will have biggish overlaps and even if we are from virtually alien cultures there will be some small measure of overlap. It is these overlaps, however small, that are the key to understanding each other, establishing common ground and eliminating prejudices which stem from fear of differences.

It is in our nature to categorise and judge the world around us and consequently the people that we come into contact with. This is how we make sense of the word by labelling and cataloguing everything around us. However this is not always helpful when dealing with other people. If your own experiences have been fairly narrow – maybe you haven't travelled much, your education may have stopped after high school, your parents and relatives all live in the same town as you do and so do your spouse's family and friends, you may find it harder to place someone who is completely outside your experience or in other words does not fit into your frame of reference. However the reverse may also be true, people in very close-knit societies who feel very secure in their immediate environment may be more relaxed and laid back about someone very different. The trick, however you feel, is to find the overlap and as you are both humans with the same basic fundamental needs, be assured there will be an overlap, however small.

Abraham Maslow (Maslow 1987) came up with a hierarchy of needs and these needs express our very humanness. They start with basic physiological needs such as those for shelter, food and sleep, progressing through to needs for safety, needs for love and belonging, need for esteem and ending with need for self-actualisation. If you have no common ground in the more interpretable needs, such as what is love, then you will always have common ground in the basic needs of food, shelter, care for your children etc. and it is here that you can begin to build common ground with another who appears very different from you.

So if you find yourself at a loss as to how to build bridges with someone who is, on the surface, very different from you, think about the basic needs for shelter, food, safety etc. and you can begin by asking questions such as "Where are you living?" "Do you like the area?" Or if they have children "Have you found a good school?" If language is a barrier try sharing some sweets or snack foods and that will open up feelings of good will and the beginnings of common ground will be formed.

It is our differences which make us unique and interesting but it is our essential humanness and the needs that go with being human which bond us together across nations, religions and genders and it is these we can use as the building blocks for good communication, knowledge of others and the elimination of prejudice through ignorance and fear.

Maslow A H (1987) *Motivation and Personality*, 3rd : Harper and Row (first published 1954)

Fear

Fear is a very useful emotion; it lets us know when we are in danger and prompts us to act. However it can also be incapacitating in situations where the fear is imagined or anticipated without evidence.

We all still retain the amygdala which is a small walnut-shaped part of the brain which existed when we were reptilian. It is concerned with very black and white decisions e.g. "flee or die" "kill or die" and is not useful for considered judgements of whether we are in danger or not. The amygdala is the "rapid-response unit" of the brain and can be triggered by very primitive events such as loud noises or having to suddenly apply your brakes whilst driving. This causes a rush of adrenaline and if your belief is that you are still in danger, this is followed by the stomach shutting down, sometimes being sick in order to divert blood away from digestion to muscles that may need to be used to flee or fight. There can be a feeling of breathlessness or dizziness and an increase in heartbeat – all readiness for imminent action. There is also a loss of logical coherent thought and a switch to reaction rather than being proactive – we respond, rather than take the initiative. This is absolutely brilliant if a knifeman has just jumped out in front of us and rather less useful if a crowd of excited teenagers have burst out of a club laughing and shouting.

Where our fear response becomes a hindrance is when we respond to every day occurrences with alarm or overreaction causing hyperventilation or dizziness (panic attacks) or a freeze response (incapacitation) or a need to check things over and over in order to make sure we are safe (Obsessive Compulsive Disorder "OCD"). This is when our fear response has gone into overdrive and we have switched from rational, objective assessment of a situation and our danger in that situation to a rapid, unthinking, biological response. We need both responses available to us but in the twenty-first century we are unlikely to need our rapid response on an every-day basis. When we are experiencing panic attacks or OCD behaviours or find ourselves incapacitated by the fear of the unknown in ways that interfere with our pleasure in every-day life, then its time to get help. Fortunately an over-stimulated fear response is one of the easiest to treat with very high success rates.

Most anxiety or fear disorders respond very well to the talking therapies and Cognitive Behavioural Therapy has a high success rate in treating anxiety as does Mindfulness. It is possible to wean yourself off anxiety responses without help by gradually exposing yourself to small amounts of what you fear. For instance, if you were afraid of large crowds, you and a friend could start by visiting a relatively empty coffee shop. Then you could grade up to busier environments over time as your senses gradually register at each stage that there is no threat. You would know you were cured when you were able to sit in a crowded theatre and enjoy the performance without worry.

If however you have actually been in a terrorist attack, a war situation or have been attacked, robbed or mugged then any fear response is a reasonable one and you may have flashbacks or an overwhelming fear that the same will happen again. This is Post Traumatic Stress Disorder (PTSD) and is also able to be treated but needs specialist intervention. Many people have had very high success rates with counselling, CBT (Cognitive Behavioural Therapy) and EMDR (Eye Movement Desensitisation and Reprogramming). You need to see your GP to get a referral.

In conclusion, whilst it is reasonable to be aware of danger and take steps to avoid dangerous situations, if your life is being unreasonably spoilt by unsubstantiated fears it is time to get help. After all an over-active fear response acts like a jailer, curtailing our enjoyment and narrowing our lives and fortunately this is something relatively easy to address.

Generalisations

Generalisations are not helpful. They awaken our prejudices and stop us from viewing other people as individuals. When we find ourselves using terms such as "they" and maximising language such as "always" and "never" you can be sure there is a generalisation afoot. "They never clean up after themselves." "Young people are so selfish they always take the best…." We also make our world a more frightening place when we use these generalisations, as though we are inventing tabloid headlines with which to scare ourselves. Moderating words such as "some", can help us not to generalise. If we have had a bad experience with a youngster it is fine to say "Some young people are…." But even better to be specific "When I was at the bus stop last week, a young boy of about fifteen was so rude." In this way we are not generalising about all young people and are recognising that they come with all sorts of different behaviours both good and bad.

It is natural for humans to categorise people as "us" and "them" as in early history we were formed into tribes or groups who had to compete with each other for scarce resources. However this is no longer the case in most of the western world and yet we spend a lot of our time lumping people into groups. Try to recognise the uniqueness of the individuals you encounter and if possible avoid using labels to categorise people. The more relaxed and less judgemental you are around others the more they will be able to view you as an interesting individual, too.

Generations

When we encounter people of different generations it is understandable that they will have differing views and values. This is really the same point made in "Frame of Reference". Try to identify your similarities rather than differences and try not to judge other generations by your own criteria or standards as they may simply not apply.

If you are living and/or working with older or younger people you will need to take into account their different beliefs and expectations and find things you can value about them. Often another viewpoint regarding problems or unresolved situations can be very helpful and cast an entirely new light on circumstances. For instance when travelling with my teenaged son in America after I was recovering from a long-term illness he persuaded me to climb Yosemite Falls. These happen to be the sixth highest falls in the world! Half way up, I looked up the mountain and said "I shouldn't have tried this, I'm not fully recovered, look how far we've got left to climb." My son turned round to me and said "Look down the mountain, Mum, you can hardly see where we began – look how far you've come. Have a little rest; I think you can get to the top. Imagine how good the view is going to be." It was.

Generosity

I believe that this is one of the most underrated human behaviours. Generosity is almost always appreciated and recognised and a generous act enhances us as we give pleasure to others. My sister always recommends that if you can afford the slightly better bottle of wine, the bigger box of chocolates, the larger bouquet of flowers without crunching the budget, this will always be noticed and appreciated and I have found this to be true more often than not.

Generosity with your time will also be appreciated. Your children will always remember the days you played with them for hours at a time – they won't remember how much you spent on their eighth birthday present. Sitting with a friend who is bereaved is not time wasted, it's time well spent. Dropping off a child after a party so the mum doesn't have to come out herself will be appreciated and probably reciprocated.

Generosity of spirit is something harder to grasp. This is where we give people the benefit of the doubt and are less quick to judge negative behaviours. This is when we look kindly on other people believing that most people are generally good most of the time. This is where we hope to cultivate good behaviour in others through our own example rather than condemn others for their less-than-perfect behaviour. I realise, however, that this depends on our experiences and if life has been very tough in a dog-eat-dog world then generosity is hard to cultivate as you may be viewed as a "soft touch". Nevertheless I believe that generosity has a knock on effect and that those on the receiving end of generosity are then encouraged to be generous themselves. If you doubt me wait until the next time you are in a long stream of traffic. Now let someone from a side turning into the line of traffic. The chances are that in the next five minutes the person you let join the mainstream will let someone else from a side road join in too. Being good to others is good for us and sets up a positive cycle – try it and see.

Genetics

Genetic inheritance obviously plays some role in what traits we carry. However it is our environment, interaction with others and experiences which ultimately shape how these genes express themselves. Genes are not good or bad, they just are. However they can be shaped for good or not. If you are impulsive and seek excitement, the outcome in a neglected, feral childhood might be to become an arsonist or robber or be labelled with ADHD. Conversely those same genes may express themselves as a bomb-disposal expert or fire fighter when channelled and directed by wise adults and a nurturing environment. So if your behaviour is negatively labelled or you are tempted to label another negatively, try to see the flip side of that behaviour; a dogmatic person may be tenacious, a bigot may be a patriot. If you are instrumental in any aspect of rearing or teaching children, please remember, traits are not good or bad it is how they are shaped by those around us that determine the outcome. Remember, too, that you have some say in how you choose to employ the characteristics you have inherited and that we are not victims of our biological inheritance. Genes are just a set of tools that we have been given to work with, whether we choose to use them for demolition or construction is in some part down to us, especially when we become adults.

Groups

We are naturally group animals who like to "belong". A group will often replicate our original family and bring up many of the feelings we had as children. If we are not aware of this we can get easily "flipped" into Child or Parent behaviours. Perhaps we felt overlooked as the "third child" or the "youngest" and if we are not careful we can project those feelings when entering group situations. So when joining a new group (for pleasure or work), be aware that you may have long held beliefs about your own "position" within a group and try not to let that influence your behaviour.

When you enter a new group you are the "outsider". It is useful to keep a moderate profile and to reserve judgement on who to buddy up with until you understand who does what in your new situation. Don't "try too hard" to fit in. It is inevitable that you won't belong to start with and this is an uncomfortable position. However it is better to be uncomfortable and to take your time assessing how you fit in and what your role is before making alliances you may regret. Be friendly and open but be wary of revealing too much personal information until you understand how your new firm/group works. Giving away confidences is a quick way to make friends but it can be very costly if these are then bandied about and become common knowledge or alternatively colour someone's view of you out of context.

When a new person enters the group it alters the group's identity which can be very uncomfortable for some people. Be empathetic but keep your own boundaries and integrity and you will be fine. Inevitably there will be a period of adjustment for you and others but if you are honest in what you do and well-principled, you will come out unscathed. Remember fitting in takes time and it is normal to feel uncomfortable and slightly "out of it". Others will have to shift positions within the group in order to accommodate you and this may cause temporary discomfort. So when entering a group, take your time, be aware of projections you may carry over from past groups, be kind to yourselves and others and expect a bit of turbulence before you become truly integrated.

Being the leader of a group is entirely different to joining a group. It is a position of great responsibility. If you are to be the leader of an established group, go slowly. You are effectively the new "parent". Try not to make instant judgements about people (these are usually from Parent or Child) but take your time to see how people function and build up a picture of their strengths and weaknesses. Be careful to treat all the members of your group in the same way as they will be very quick to spot any inconsistencies and signs of favouritism.

You will need to establish very quickly what your expectations are and let people know your boundaries (see Boundaries). Being the leader can be an isolated position as you are not quite "in" the group nor entirely "out" of the group. As mentioned above, you cannot afford to be too chummy if you are going to be in a position of authority. Maintain an interested and empathetic distance and be careful not to reveal too much of your own personal information. As long as you are honest, direct and interested in the people who work for you and you recognise that establishing a leadership position takes time you should be very successful. (see Boundaries and Frames of Reference)

Happiness

"Happiness is a how, not a what; a talent not an object." – Herman Hesse

Getting what we want brings us happiness, right? Wrong! We believe this and go in search of happiness as if it were something that could be "found" or "obtained" but it is actually something that we can and do manufacture internally. "There is nothing good or bad but thinking makes it so." (*Hamlet*, William Shakespeare).

Dan Gilbert, a Harvard psychologist has run a series of workshops which explore the idea that whatever happens to us, we have the ability to synthesise (i.e. manufacture) happiness; it is not something we "find". A survey between lottery winners and paraplegics showed that a year after the event which either made them extremely rich or caused them to be wheelchair bound each group was as happy as the other. When people are asked to imagine which scenario would make them happier – winning the lottery or becoming a paraplegic – they obviously choose winning the lottery. This is wrong but it is the *expectation* of what winning the lottery will bring us that causes us to believe we will be happier if we win it and it is our *expectation* of what it means to be disabled that causes us to believe it would be a terrible fate. In fact humans appear to have a "psychological immune system" which enables us to make the most of any situation and believe that it is for the best.

Time and time again people in difficult situations will express how pleased they are that they went through (whatever) and how much they have learnt and how their lives have changed for the better. Equally there are others who seem quite simply unable to see the positive side of a situation. So are there things we can do in order that we become mostly happy?

Some psychologists believe they have come up with a happiness formula. Pleasure + engagement + meaning = happiness. Certainly these are recognisable ingredients for happiness but there are problems. If we become too engaged in anything we can become obsessive and overtired and lose our enjoyment. We can take great pleasure in the experience of gambling but this does not mean it will make us happy. So a formula for happiness does not seem to be foolproof, although there is some basis for happiness in this.

Certainly wealth does not bring happiness. In a BBC survey in 2008 they found that although we have become much wealthier in the last fifty years we have also become unhappier. Fame, also does not bring happiness. We only have to look at a selection of famous people to see many with marriage problems, drug addictions and the difficulties of living in the public eye. Pursuit of happiness is illusory. If we keep seeking "happiness" as though it were a thing instead of an experience we risk missing out on the experiences and everyday pleasures which go to make up our happiness.

Many psychologists believe that we have what is called a "set point" for happiness. This means that if two people face the same situation one may view it as a problem and the other as an opportunity. This point is probably set through experience and circumstance when we are growing up. However we can learn to challenge a negative set point by arguing with our own beliefs about certain situations and finding examples that disprove our assumptions. Professor Martin Seligman, suggests that we play to our strengths. By pursuing activities we are not good at or dislike, we set ourselves up for discontent and unhappiness. However by playing to our strengths we raise our chances of success and approval and in this way raise our happiness levels. The third aspect of increasing our happiness is to count our blessings. Many people focus on what they want rather than what they have. This is not productive and can cause envy and misery. Focussing on what we have and the pleasures this brings us, enhances our happiness.

In conclusion, happiness cannot be "obtained". It is rare to find happiness by the acquisition of wealth or "things". There is no foolproof happiness formula. We are all able to manufacture our own happiness to some extent and if we obsess too much about whether or not we are happy we may miss out on the experiences of living and relating to others that are likely to bring us pleasure and contentment. So don't look for the pot of gold at the end of the rainbow, enjoy the rainbow instead.

Hate

Hate is an exhausting and destructive emotion usually born out of extreme anger or sadness. If you are harbouring feelings of hate you are very likely to do yourself some form of damage. If you act on the feelings of hate you may find yourself on the wrong side of the law or at the very least losing friends and alienating people. Try to work out where your feelings come from and seek redress either through the law or through reconciliation of some sort. It will help to talk your feelings through with a trusted person and get another perspective.

Hate is corrosive and the person who holds onto these feeling is usually the one to end up damaged and bitter. If at all possible try to reconcile your feelings (maybe through therapy) and then let the feelings go and move on. Hate will stunt your life, exhaust and diminish you. Instead try to channel those feelings into being the most successful you that you can. Trite but true.

Heads Up

This is two fold, really. To get a "heads up" is to be aware of something before or as it is happening – not after the event. In order to achieve this you need to be aware and perceptive as well as being receptive to incoming information. With this goes the physical act of walking with your head up; in other words looking where you are going and being aware of situations and people around you.

You miss so much if you do not walk or travel with an awareness of your surroundings. Try not to be electronically distracted with your phone or MP3 player. Keep your head up, make brief eye contact with people; it is remarkable how many smiles and nods you will receive. If you are on your phone, listening to music or simply walking whilst looking at the ground you will be disconnected from your surroundings and fail to pick up any cues that may be in the environment. You will miss simple cues like the sky clouding over resulting in getting wet or you could miss more complex cues such as someone crossing over the street to follow you home or the speeding up of footsteps behind you. When you cut yourself off from your surroundings you disable your innate ability to pick up cues for danger as well as friendly cues for connection and human contact.

As for getting a "heads up" for situations the same approach applies. Pay attention. Notice when people or situations change and then check out why that may be. People often say after an event "I had absolutely no idea he was going to…" When questioned more closely it is often the case that there were many small clues which had they been noted and then followed up on may have averted disaster, personal unhappiness or simple misunderstandings. So keep your head up, pay attention and things will not "just happen" you will see them coming with time to spare.

Help

At some time in our lives we will all need help of some sort. Many people have been brought up to think that they must manage alone whatever the situation. This is plainly a limiting belief. If you never ask for help or give help to another then you will severely limit your human capacity for empathy, altruism and connection. These characteristics are like muscles and grow in strength when used. Would you help a friend who asked you if you were able? Most of us would answer yes – so why wouldn't you ask for help if you would so easily give it? The answer is that many of us fear rejection or have been taught not to show a vulnerable side.

When asking others for help we are bound to encounter rejection. This will not necessarily be because the person we have asked does not want to help us; it may simply be that they have commitments which mean that they can't. In order to be able to successfully ask others for help we must recognise that there will be a proportion of people who will refuse – for whatever reason – and we need to be able to take this in our stride. So if you ask one person can they pick up your child from school and they say that they are sorry they can't today then you need to accept their answer and move on and ask another person.

In asking another for a favour you must be careful to allow the other person to refuse with no blame attached. In other words you need to be able to accept a refusal without taking it personally. There will be all sorts of reasons why people cannot do things and most of them will have nothing to do with you! However if you make people feel guilty for refusing you they will tend to avoid you and be unwilling to offer favours in the future. As for appearing vulnerable, this is usually a side of others that allows us to warm towards them. It is hard to warm towards the "always-perfect" organised and controlled person. Most of us, however, can warm to the person who is on overload and just needs a helping hand. If you are someone who often helps others and gets pleasure from this then you can give your friends pleasure by occasionally allowing them to do something for you.

People living and working within a community where responsibilities are shared and members look out for each other, giving help where help is needed or asked for generally thrive much better than communities where each person is out for themselves. The recent financial collapse is a case in point – one of the companies that has survived and thrived is The John Lewis Partnership. This is a co-operative where each person working in the company has a financial share in it. This encourages cooperation between departments and divisions in the company and the company has thrived to give everyone (yes everyone!) a bonus of 15% in 2010. Helping others and asking for help is obviously not about financial wealth. However, it is about personal and community well-being. If you live in a community where people know each other and care about each other there will be less crime and people will feel much safer and happier. It is much harder to commit a crime against someone you know and even harder to abuse someone who has helped you.

Asking for help and giving help to others helps foster the admirable traits we all have and helps build a better community for all of us as well as giving a good example for the next generation. So when you next find yourself in a tricky situation where you could do with some help – ask!

Honesty

Honesty pays in the long run. In relationships it is absolutely vital as without revealing how we feel we cannot achieve true intimacy with another. However, being honest does not mean being blunt and rude or volunteering an opinion when you have not been asked.

It is absolutely fine to duck the question if asked personal questions such as "Do you like my hair/dress/new car? You can respond neutrally or redirect e.g. "That cut is very classic." "I saw that very same dress in Vogue this week." "What a wonderful colour your car is." It is not important to be wholly truthful in your opinions as they are precisely that – *your* opinions. Where it is important to be truthful is in matters concerning the cornerstones of a relationship.

It is not OK to go along with someone on fundamental issues such as where you will live, the upbringing of your children, what gives you sexual pleasure or how you wish to be spoken to or regarded. You need to make sure you let your views be known and that you listen to the other's point of view; you may need to compromise. If, when you are going out with someone, you mislead them by going along with them and not expressing your own views, then at some point you will come to grief. Your resentment at your own needs being subsumed will come out in some way. Maybe you'll be sarcastic, maybe you'll be unhappy, maybe you'll never reach your full potential and fulfil your hopes and ambitions and you'll become bitter. I can't tell how these squashed needs will reappear, all I can promise is that they will.

It is important when you meet others to gently let them know your values and expectations (see Expectations and Values) in order to avoid future misunderstandings. Then when they know who and what you are they can decide how much of a relationship they wish to have with you. If you build on firm foundations then you will be able to take the knocks and bumps that come with any relationship but if you have falsely represented who you are, others will be disappointed but more importantly, so will you. In relationships of any kind honesty really is the best policy.

Hurry Up

It is interesting that many of us, when we find ourselves under pressure, tend to speed up in order to successfully achieve more. Sadly there is a cost to this and quite often it involves our health, well-being and relationships. When we operate at full speed we send a physiological message to ourselves causing an adrenalin and cortisol surge which can make us impatient, anxious, irritable and nauseous. Operating quickly instead of taking our time leads to mistakes and causes us to forget and overlook items. By contrast if we take time to slow down, breathe properly and assess the situation we are then in a position to prioritise. We can then work through what needs to be done rationally and in an orderly fashion.

The types of people who possess a strong "hurry-up" driver will usually be perfectionists who like to be in control. These are people who have been brought up to believe there is a right and wrong way to go about situations and that alternative solutions are usually lesser or flawed. These people usually hate to deviate from their planned behaviour, whether they be travelling, working or cooking and therefore, seldom have another way to achieve all that needs to be done. People who are inclined to speed up have been taught that to ask for help or protest at being overloaded or overworked is a sign of weakness. The only solution remaining is to hurry.

If they have children, these children will usually mimic hurrying behaviour and start to become anxious and goal orientated or they will be on a deliberate "go slow" to counteract their parents' undue haste. Either scenario is not desirable. If we are goal-orientated then we often miss out on the pleasure of the process of what we are doing, rushing instead to complete tasks and "box-tick" our way through items. Alternatively a child that is deliberately slowing down may miss natural "milestones" and be wrongly labelled as slow or stubborn when all they are doing is reacting to a situation that is causing them anxiety or discomfort.

In order to counteract a "hurry up" driver one must first recognise it. If you are constantly late, always rushing, feel overworked and under-appreciated you are probably going too fast for your own well-being. If you also suffer from headaches, indigestion, insomnia, anxiety, irritability and are easily moved to anger or tears you are definitely doing yourself some physical damage and if this is prolonged you could develop serious conditions such as a cardiac problem or depression. We are not designed to go full tilt for prolonged periods. So if this is you, what can you do about it?

Firstly, sometimes we are going to have periods where we need to fit more in and it is OK to occasionally be operating at full tilt, such as at Christmas time or just after the birth of a child. However it is definitely not OK for these periods to stretch over months. If you have too much to do, ask for help or delegate. (see Help and/or Delegation) Secondly, prioritise. If you have a new baby giving dinner parties is not a priority. If you are entertaining sixteen for Christmas dinner, dusting skirting boards is not a priority. Taking some time out each day to sit and eat a properly-cooked meal or to read a favourite book or to do a little gardening is not time wasted – it could save your life! The things that counteract stress are hobbies that we can lose ourselves in, regular, moderate exercise, good nutrition and low reliance on stimulants e.g. caffeine, nicotine, sugar and alcohol also we need friends or family to support and nurture us as well as a good night's sleep. These need to be a priority. So if you hear the siren call inside yourself to "hurry up" ask yourself what you are hurrying for. Is it for your health? Is it for your contentment? Is it for your children's security? Remember to slow down, take stock, prioritise and deputise and soon you will be able to turn a deaf ear to your internal "hurry up" impulse and achieve a more balanced and comfortable life.

Hygiene

This is not meant to be patronising but I have noticed when standing in queues, taking public transport or sitting next to strangers in the theatre, some people smell bad. It is important from a health point of view, as well as socially, that we keep ourselves clean. From a very early age humans will ostracise contemporaries that smell. I have worked in some very deprived areas and in my experience it is children who smell who are much more likely to be left out socially than those who have behavioural issues. It is important to wash with soap and hot water often enough to avoid malodour. Once we hit puberty this means washing under arms and the groin area every day. Get a good friend to tell you if you need to use deodorant (most people do). Teeth also need to be brushed with a good all round toothpaste at least twice a day and after every meal when wearing a brace. Some people with particularly oily hair will need to wash it every day; this is particularly true around puberty.

If you do not have access to a bathroom, a kettle of hot water, soap and a flannel will suffice for a strip wash. Many public places have showers such as railway stations and swimming pools.

It is not just you that needs to be clean but also what you wear. So clean underwear every day (you can wash it out overnight) and no clothes with food or sweat stains. It is particularly important to be clean when turning up for an interview, first day at a new school or job and for a date. This may be very obvious to most people but given how many people I come into contact with have bad breath or just simply smell, I thought I would spell it out.

I did it my way

If you are constantly doing things "your" way what are you missing out on? A lot is the short answer. There is very rarely just one way to do things. If you are someone who likes things entirely "your way" you will be seen as very controlling. Being controlling is one of our safety mechanisms that we use to create an illusion that we are in "control".

If you feel that you have very little control over your life in general then you are more likely to be "socially" controlling. This may take the form of always dictating where you go out. Or it may be that you establish what "having a good time" constitutes. You may be the "group leader" in your social circle deciding who can join and who can't. Alternatively you could just be someone who always wants tasks done their way. Dishes must be washed in a certain way. You must always buy your meat from the local butcher. Only you know how your son likes his bedtime drink. This is an attempt to establish yourself as essential and usually stems from a lack of self esteem and the underlying belief that you are not essential. The fact is that we are not in control of everything and we are not entirely essential. Once we take this on board it can be very freeing.

Being in control all the time is exhausting, doubly so because it is a fear response and usually triggers large amounts of adrenaline as you need to be "on guard". Letting go of the responsibility for everything means that you can sit back now and again, that you can learn new ways of doing things and new ways of being. You can find out that a barbeque does not have to mean an event organised with military precision; you can just ring up a few friends one evening and get them to bring over whatever's in the fridge whilst you fire up the barbeque.

The release of control heralds in spontaneity and fun, learning new skills and finding new friends. In the past people will have been too scared to approach you for fear of getting things "wrong". Once you establish that there is no "one way" of doing things, people will feel freer around you. The issue of control is really a Parent ego-state that has got out of control at the expense of your spontaneous Child. When you let go of the "rules" (who made these, anyway?), ease up on yourself and others you create more room for enjoyment and relaxation. So by all means do things "your way" now and again but for a more relaxed and enjoyable life, learn to let others do it "their" way, too.

Illness

Everybody gets ill from time to time. Bodies are wonderful and will do their best to get back to a fully-functioning state if at all possible. You need, however, to take responsibility for your health and help yourself to get well again. If you have a short-term illness such as the 'flu or an upset stomach you need to be sensible. Take time to rest, drink plenty of water and give your body the space it needs to restore itself. Your body will heal much quicker in almost all circumstances if you resist caffeine, alcohol, tobacco, sugar, high-fat food and other stimulants that upset the balance and make your body work harder.

If you have a long-term or serious illness make sure that you get good advice and if you are not sure of your options ask for a second opinion. The internet is also a wonderful source of information but be careful not to take everything at face value and to do your own research. Living with a long-term problem is hard. You will need to allow yourself time to adapt to your new circumstances and maybe time to mourn the "healthy" you that, for the moment, no longer exists. Let people know what works for you. Would you like them to visit, help with the shopping or take the dog for a walk? Friends really want to rally round but often are at a loss what they should do and so they do nothing.

Don't forget to experience some of the things that you can still enjoy: a favourite DVD, a manicure or massage, reading or listening to books on tape. There will be many things you enjoy that are still possible, despite having a long-term or debilitating illness.

When I was twelve I got hit by a car and spent twenty-two weeks in hospital. I was able to read many of the classics which formed my love of English and writing. When I went home the hospital told my parents that I would not be able to partake in sport again. Luckily they didn't tell me! Three months later I climbed Snowden and was riding and swimming again. Believing I could do whatever I had done before certainly stood me in good stead and having something to do during those five months that I really enjoyed has left me feeling that my time in hospital was not wasted but just another, albeit different, part of my life.

I was lucky as I recovered and never thought I wouldn't but I think the lessons I learnt can apply whatever the situation. Do not see an illness as time out of your life – this is still your life! Believe that you can still do things that give you pleasure. Maintain a positive outlook and tell people when you need help and what sort of help you need. This will make life better for you and for those around you and hopefully go towards making an illness or accident bearable and possibly even productive.

Impasse

An impasse is best explained as a dichotomy; it is a belief that in following one idea or path you cannot also follow another. It is the belief that they are opposing desires. These self-limiting beliefs are usually acquired in childhood and transactional analysts believe that they are two parts of the personality in conflict with each other. For instance there are those that believe it is not possible to be both a successful professional and a good mother. This may be your Parent wanting you to be successful warring with your Child who wants you to be nurturing and nurtured. Equally there are people who believe you cannot be a "good mate" and "the boss" to the same person. Some would have us believe that you cannot be both virtuous and sexy. Certainly these positions may be delicate and require some finesse to manage but there are plenty of people who manage these examples very well. Impasses are positions where you believe you can be "either" one thing "or" another but not both. They are not facts.

In order to overcome an impasse, first of all you need to work out what you want. Then you need to ascertain your priorities and thirdly you need to work out a practical way to put these wants and needs into practice whilst not losing sight of your own values and beliefs.

As children we are often given what appear to be opposing messages during the period when we are growing up. Dress nicely but don't draw attention to yourself. Work hard but don't show off by being too successful. Be nice but win at everything. However, although the child may have ingested these messages as "either/or situations", as adults we can recognise that it is possible to be both nice and successful. We must recognise our self-limiting beliefs and challenge them. Then we need to find ways to hold on to our own core beliefs and to achieve the things we want for ourselves. Often we will need to examine and challenge our family messages. These are often outdated and will have been passed down generations as "What the Browns believe" or "How the Smiths behave". Well these are not carved in stone and may be very muddled and ancient family beliefs that are simply not valid in the twenty-first century or just do not apply to your life and beliefs.

Once you have identified these dichotomies you can set about challenging them. You can have your own rules of conduct and your own beliefs so that it is entirely possible for you to be both successful and nice or both virtuous and sexy. Whatever your dichotomy the important message here is that it is your beliefs and boundaries (see Boundaries) that are relevant to your life not some ancient family motto which has been handed down to you without examination of its veracity or use.

Once you recognise what beliefs are sabotaging your success you can set about changing them. Then you can adopt beliefs that suit who you are and what you want to become. Maybe you want to be a really good mother and you believe that the work you do inside the home is just as valid as paid work outside the home. Maybe you want to be a very successful sportsman and keep your friends – you adopt the practice of staying in touch with old friends on a regular basis no matter how successful you become. Only by examining and challenging self-limiting behaviours and accepted ways of being can we understand and get to the heart of what we believe in and the things we value. We can then set about achieving all of which we are capable.

Incentives

Every one needs incentives. It is not possible, however good and kind we are, to be constantly altruistic and self-sacrificing, there has to be a quid pro quo – or tit for tat. Most people are looking for some form of recognition – a "well done" or a "thank you". It is when we forget to acknowledge what others have done or do for us that resentment may build. The same is true if we ourselves are under-acknowledged or unappreciated. So remember to thank and acknowledge others. Specific language works best. "It was really kind of you to take out the rubbish." Rather than "You are such a helpful person." Or "Thank you for finishing the report for me. The wording was really good." When we are specific in our praise it is more authentic and much easier for the receiver to know which behaviours to repeat – this applies particularly to children (both big and small!).

If you are feeling under-appreciated or under-praised then let those around you know. Not in a "poor me" way but again by being specific. "I really thought that you would appreciate me coming out to collect you at midnight but you said nothing." Or "I felt hurt when you didn't thank me for…" Don't forget that you can also acknowledge and nurture yourself. You can give yourself small treats for jobs completed and a mental "pat on the back" when you have achieved something you are pleased with. This really is the same message as outlined in Expectations. So remember to nurture yourself, acknowledge those around you and to let others know that you expect to be appreciated, too.

Indicators

Indicators are signs of what is to come. They can be either physical signs such as worn tyres on your car, or signs from people such as curt replies or shrugging of shoulders. We ignore either of these at a cost. Firstly, this is about being aware of what is going on around you both in the environment and with the people you come in to contact with. Secondly it is about the consequences of ignoring these indicators and of taking responsibility for what then ensues.

Many people will claim that they cannot understand how something happened and that it was definitely not their fault. In a few cases this is true. However in many more there are signs and indications of what may occur and looking back we can see that had we attended to the small things, a larger event may have been avoided.

For instance if you know your car tyres are a bit worn and a weather warning of snow goes out and you do not act upon this knowledge then later, when you skid in your car, causing several thousand pounds' worth of damage, it will not be true to say it was not your fault. You can claim that there were unusual circumstances: "the snow". You can claim that the tyres were going to be replaced at the next service just a few weeks away and that it was bad luck. However you word it, had you paid attention to the small indicators – your knowledge of the state of your tyres and the weather report, it is just possible you may have avoided the accident. In some instances avoiding an accident is not possible and it IS simply bad luck but when we have prior information which we choose not to act on, we must take responsibility for the consequences. We do ourselves a disservice when we do not recognise our own part in events – we discount our own abilities and power to act and become helpless instead of proactive (see Discounting).

The same is true with people. Usually, they will give off many signs that they are unhappy or dissatisfied with a situation. People, generally, do not blow up out of the blue. A change in behaviour such as long silences and shrugs instead of conversation, body language such as crossed arms or the head turning slightly away when you are talking to someone are all indications that the person is unhappy about something. As humans we are designed to notice these things and it is well worth our while to bother. Many a relationship or friendship could be saved if the early-warning signs were heeded. If you notice your friend being colder towards you than usual, if you value the friendship, ask if they are OK. If a colleague cuts you off and ignores your suggestions, if you need to work with them it will be worth your while to pursue what is going on. It is not OK as a functioning adult to claim that you had no idea what was going on. This leaves you vulnerable to loss of job or friends and open to situations where things "appear" to go wrong for you. If you are someone to whom a lot of "unexplained" things "happen", start asking yourself "Were there any warning signs?" "Did other people know what was going on?" Often you will find out that there were signs. You then need to make it a priority in the future to pay attention to early indicators.

If you are not generally aware you will need to practice noticing small signs or get a friend to help you. This will not be a wasted process as things will stop "happening" to you. As you start taking responsibility for what occurs, you can make sure that it is the good and not the bad events which happen to you. Lucky people usually turn out to be those that are vigilant and proactive. This does not mean you need to be a "control freak" and monitor every single situation, It just means being aware, acknowledging the obvious things you can do and taking responsibility for the care and safety of yourself and your nearest and dearest.

It is what it is

This is about accepting how things really are. There are certain events, situations and people that you can change and there are those that you can't. Identifying the difference between the two can save a lot of time and trouble. A lot of the skill in identifying what it is possible to change and what needs to be accepted lies in a good assessment of a situation and a thorough examination of projects before you commit to them.

If for instance something appears "too good to be true" it generally will be. A cheap holiday off the internet is exactly that. If you are then disappointed because the transport is ropey and the hotel is cramped, one, you should have checked just what it was you were buying and two, once you find yourself in this situation you need to accept "it is what it is". Trying to get money back or to complain when you have signed up "blind" for something without checking it out and knowing it was really "too good to be true" is futile and simply a waste of your time and energy. However when you have checked out a situation and have been promised certain standards or conditions then you have every right to try to seek what you were offered and look for redress if this is not forthcoming.

Sometimes situations will be not of your making just simply out of your control. If you can recognise this during the event and adopt a philosophical view you will expend a lot less futile energy and have plenty left for things that you are able to influence. If you are on the underground and it grinds to a halt in the tunnel, huffing and puffing to other commuters will achieve precisely nothing. If you have brought a book with you, you can employ your time more productively. However, whatever you end up doing to pass the time you can be assured that you couldn't have seen this coming and unfortunately, there is nothing you can do to alleviate your situation. Knowing this and acting accordingly will save a lot of hassle. Assessing the difference between what you can and can't change and what you should and should not accept takes maturity and skill but these skills can be learnt early on in life freeing up the rest of your time on the planet for more productive endeavours than banging your head against a brick wall!

Jealousy

Jealousy is mainly an expression of insecurity and lack of trust. Jealously is an externalisation of an internal doubt or fear about ourselves. Rather than addressing our own insecurities we project our fear and misery outwards and on to another. If you are jealous of another person it is probably due to a belief that they have something you want. Underlying that belief is either that you should have got what they have, or that you will never be able to have what they have. If you believe you should have what they have, then you need to look around and see why you haven't got it. In a job situation they probably have different qualities to you, ones you admire but fear you don't have. Or else they may have a different background or upbringing – do these make you feel insecure? In a personal situation you may fear they are better liked than you, more socially at ease and polished. As long as you are dwelling on the person of whom you are jealous then you are not addressing the real problems, such as retraining to a higher level or honing your interpersonal skills.

If you are possessively jealous of another person then this will be because you either don't trust them and/or believe they don't value you enough to stay faithful in the relationship. In a friendship there is no exclusivity and you cannot rule out other friendships or choose whether your friend sees or goes out with other people. You need to be self-assured enough to know that you are also a good friend and that your friendship is valuable to both of you. If this is an issue that crops up a lot and you still like to have exclusive best-friend relationships as an adult, you may need to have some sort of counselling to address this.

In a sexual relationship or partnership you need to set

boundaries as to what is and what is not acceptable to you both. If your partner behaves deliberately outside these boundaries or intends to make you jealous then you need to address their insecurities and discuss why they feel the need for others' attention. If you are overly jealous, yourself, don't like your partner having other friends and are looking for an exclusive relationship, this is unlikely to be realistic.

Most people have a variety of friends even when they are married or in a long-term partnership. Someone with several friends for different activities and pastimes is likely to be a popular and well-balanced person with several interests. If this is your partner and you are jealous you may need to develop other friendships and interests of your own. If you are consumed by unreasonable jealously then you will need to see a professional to help you deal with your insecurities. Jealously holds the person who exhibits this behaviour to ransom. It encourages you to be paranoid, feeds on your insecurities and eats away at you. Letting go of jealous feelings and concentrating on your own personality and attributes will free you and your loved ones from a pointless, corrosive mind set and that can only be good.

Job

Your job is fundamental to who and what you are and will be one of the biggest factors affecting your work/life balance. Some people will opt for vocations such as doctors, nurses, rectors or teachers and some of us will simply want a job that pays the bills and leaves us to enjoy our leisure time. In between these two is the possibility of a job interesting enough for us to become engaged with, without it taking over our lives.

Working takes up a huge proportion of our adult life so we need to think carefully about what skills we have and to what we are best suited. Try, if possible, to get good careers advice and to shadow someone who is doing the job you think you want. This is a very good way to see what the day-to-day life is like in a particular career. If however, you find yourself having trained for a job that you then loathe, it is never too late to change. I started life as a secretary aged seventeen, retrained as a nursery-school teacher at twenty-four and then studied for my degree in my late thirties and went on to do my four years post-grad diploma in my early forties. I was working part-time and bringing up two children by myself but I had worked out that this was important enough to me to make sacrifices along the way. It is not easy to change careers halfway through your working life but it is possible and many people have successfully achieved this.

There is a work/life sum that you can do to see if your job is one that is relatively well balanced. There are three elements to the work/life sum. They are payment, time and satisfaction. If you are doing a job that is hugely satisfying you may not mind if the hours are long and the pay is modest. If you are doing a job that is enormously well-paid you may not mind if the hours are long and the job is dull. If you are doing a job that leaves you lots of spare time you may not mind if it's not that well paid and it's quite boring. However only you can do the sums and see which equation suits you.

However there is no doubt that if you are doing a boring job, with long hours and poor pay sooner or later you will want to give it up. The equation is simple; you need to have one element very strongly in your favour before you can consider whether the job will suit you. If, before you go for interview or choose a career, you can work out which element is most important to you, you will be able to work out what sort of job you want and what sort of job you can tolerate.

It is not always possible to be working at something we enjoy. If you find yourself in this position try to be as good as you can at your job. Somebody cheerful and willing is much more likely to be promoted or helped to move departments than someone going through the motions until pay day. There have been several studies that show that the lower the control you have in the job the more likely you are to develop coronary heart disease. (Bosma, H 1997)*. Low job control has a negative effect on health even allowing for other factors such as low pay or poor housing. Try, therefore, however mundane your job appears, to become engaged with it. Try to work out different ways to improve the job or to give a better service. In this way you are not only protecting your health but you are more likely to be noticed and moved to a more interesting position.

Remember you are going to spend up to a third of your life working so it is worth investing some time and effort into your chosen career or job. Even if you didn't actually choose what you end up doing, given that you have to spend such a lot of time doing it, you might as well be as good as you can!

*Bosma, H, Marmot, MG, Hemingway, H Nicholson, AG, Bunner E, Stansfield A, Low job control and risk of coronary heart disease in Whitehall II Study, *BMJ* 1997; Vol. 314; 558-65

Joy

Try to build small moments of joy into your life. Acquisitive behaviour in Western societies seems to have developed at the expense of pleasure in the small and joyous things of life, which are often free. Even in the most straightened of circumstances it is possible, if we focus on it, to take pleasure in a friendly smile, a hot cup of tea, a cheery bus driver. However we must be attuned to the small, good things in order to recognise them. (see Heads Up).

Many of us have been taught from an early age to override our own senses. For instance when we get a headache instead of looking for the cause we treat the symptom and carry on. Many of us do not pay attention to our bodily sensations and tend to learn to ignore them. If you live in a big city you may "screen out" pneumatic drills, underground trains, mobile phone calls, litter and beggars. We shut down our senses in order to continue with our daily tasks. These are our pathways to pleasure, touch, feel, smell, sight, hearing, and if we focus on these we can take great pleasure in ourselves and our environment. Pleasures such as walking along the beach barefoot, smelling the new mown grass and hearing the dawn chorus in spring are all free. I am not suggesting you don't screen out things when you need to just that you make sure it doesn't become a habit which stops you enjoying everyday pleasures when you can.

It is these small, everyday pleasures which are sustainable, at no great cost to ourselves, which will enhance our lives. The big, expensive objects that we may desire are not necessary to our happiness. In fact acquisitiveness can be detrimental to our health. Acquiring objects will bring a temporary pleasure but this is very short-lived and not sustainable; so that we find ourselves seeking the next goal. There is a tendency not to focus on and enjoy our achievements once we have attained them.

Try to really relish personal milestones, such as passing exams, getting your first car or your first job and recognise your achievements. In this way you focus on the immediate, instead of always looking over the horizon for the next "best thing". This is how we become satisfied and take pleasure in what we have rather than what we want. This does not mean existing without goals and ambitions, just remembering to focus on what you already have and to tune in to all the wonderful things that are already available for you to enjoy. So by all means work towards fulfilling personal ambitions but also remember "to smell the roses" along the way. In this way you add a measure of joy to your life, wholly unconnected to wealth or position but very much connected to your humanity and your capacity for simple enjoyment which comes with that.

Judgement

One of the things humans do naturally is to assess, grade and categorise what they see around them. This is normal so that we can judge situations and events as they arise and starts when we are babies trying to distinguish one object from another. Our parents will pass on their opinions, beliefs and judgements and we will also gain other perspectives from the culture and environment in which we grow up. Therefore, there will be many different views of what is and isn't acceptable according to how we have been brought up (see Frames of Reference).

What I would suggest, in order to embrace as many others' ideas as possible, is that you decide for yourself what is and isn't tolerable for you based on your own judgement and experiences. This is how we set our own boundaries and let others know what our limits are and how we expect to be treated (see Boundaries).

However, when we add a "value" to that judgement we can run into difficulties and alienate others. Just because certain behaviours are the "norm" for you does not mean they are the only ones that are valid. When we set up "rules" by which we judge others we are also setting ourselves up; if we fall short, or our friends and family do not measure up – are we lesser people? This is why the law allows for "mitigating circumstances" because many situations are not clear cut. Value judgements are the beginnings of bigoted behaviour and segregation of groups. Additionally, this is how we separate and segregate ourselves from those who are different. I would suggest that the measure of a civilised society is its capacity for tolerance and its ability to embrace other cultures whilst maintaining its own identity. I would say the same is true of civilised humans.

It is very difficult to take a set of rules by which we live and start applying them to another person's life. We know nothing or very little of how this other person was raised, educated or nurtured. It is one of the reasons why different countries have different laws. We start very young judging and excluding others. We want to play with the slim child, or the pretty child, not necessarily the kind or the good child. We value certain looks and behaviours above others. Parents encourage their children to behave in certain ways, rewarding them when they comply. This, unsurprisingly, can lead us to believe that some people are more valuable than others. I would refute this and say that it is merely a construction based on how we have been brought up.

When we stick rigidly to our judgements we are in danger of excluding whole sectors of the population from our sphere and reducing our capacity for friendships where we can embrace differences. We also cut down on our ability to grow and learn from experiences and lives different from our own; we are in danger of remaining "small people" with a limited understanding of anything "foreign" to our lives. When we judge before we have met someone on the basis of who or what they are, we become prejudiced. We need to make sure that we use our ability to judge based on the facts available to us and on a set of morals and ethics that we believe are true and fair, not out-of-date beliefs which have been passed down to us through our culture. For example if we see someone stealing we can be pretty sure that a judgement that this is "wrong" is a pretty fair one. When we use our ability to judge in order to enhance our society and culture, whilst remaining open and embracing differences which may enrich and inform our lives, then we are behaving at our best as humans.

Karma

This is the Buddhist belief that everything you do is measured and that this then influences the luck and life chances you receive either in this life or the next. I do not believe that there is some deity judging whether we have been good or bad and then handing out favours. However, I do believe that every good and kind act we do has an influence on how we perceive ourselves, on our well-being and on our future decisions. Each good act we do stacks up to emphasise our personality and in this way begins to inform who we are (good) and how we will behave in the future.

There has been research to show that babies who do not get empathetic care from their caregivers will fail to develop empathetic abilities themselves. Whilst there is no proof that good acts "exercise" our capacity for goodness and make us kinder people, there is a lot of proof that altruistic acts and voluntary service enhance both our physical and mental well-being.

I also believe that many people, once they have taken a wrong turn or committed an offence, start to believe that they are set on that path. They believe that this is who they are. So that every unkind or bad act weighs on their conscience (either overtly or subliminally) so that they begin to believe that they are bad people. Being bad they have little to lose and so behaving well assumes less importance.

There is certainly proof that children live up to the expectations of adults, either good or bad. In 1968 Rosenthal and Jacobson gave an intelligence test, to children aged between six and twelve, in one school in San Francisco. They then created two groups, both of similar intelligence. They told one teacher they had "exceptional children" who were expected to perform well and the other teacher was told nothing, her group acting as a control. At the end of the experiment the "exceptional children" showed significant gains in IQ when tested after a year. There is also plenty of proof that believing oneself to be hopeless at something is self-fulfilling – if you believe you will fail you almost certainly will.

I suggest that adopting a belief in Karma will enhance your life. Every good act you do will enhance who you are and every unkind or deliberately bad act will detract from who you are. Think about it.

Rosenthal R and Jacobson L (1968) *Pygmalion in the Classroom*, , Holt, Reinhart and Winston

Kindness

Kindness, like generosity, is never wasted. As mentioned above, it is something that can enhance you as a person and is almost always appreciated by others. Little acts of kindness remind us of our humanity and also allow us to influence other people's lives for the better. For instance making a cup of tea or a drink for a tired spouse lets them know that you notice how they are. Helping a child find his i-Pod charger lets them know that you understand their music is important. Helping a colleague at work lets them know that they are part of the team and important. Helping strangers, with bags, on and off transport or with directions is a good way of signalling to other humans, ways of enhancing the world at very little cost to ourselves. These little acts of kindness will almost always be noticed, will build our empathy and social interaction muscles and gives us a chance to be thanked and appreciated. Win, win.

Try also to remember to be kind on yourself. The chances are if you are hard on yourself you will also be hard on others. Remember there are often mitigating circumstances to events and that not all situations are black and white. It is good to want to do one's best and to get things right but as humans we must learn that this is not always possible and that sometimes there are several ways that are "right". A flexible approach with a dash of kindness to oneself and others makes a very good recipe for success.

Knowing

This is in two parts; knowing what you want and knowing what you know.

Surprisingly many people set out to achieve certain goals, a job, a degree, a relationship without having first established what it is they really want. You cannot achieve success if you don't know what your goal is. For instance, when going for a job interview it will be important to know what job you will take. Will you take a lesser job if it's offered? What salary are you looking for? Would you take a 10% drop, 20% drop? What's your limit? Establishing in advance and being clear what you do and don't want and which points you might negotiate on, are fundamental to achieving a successful outcome. When negotiating with others, people will be able to sense if you are wavering over an issue. If you have worked out in advance where you limits lie and what you will and won't alter, then you have a good chance of getting most of what you want. (see Job) Work out what are your "deal breakers", work out where you are flexible; if you fail to plan you are planning to fail.

Knowing what you know. Many of us have a wealth of knowledge, common sense, practical knowledge, parenting skills, academic information and much more besides. However this is really about self-knowledge. You need to work out your strengths and weaknesses, your high points of knowledge and your low points. We need to have confidence in what it is that we know. This is useful for everyday life but it is also particularly useful when situations are uncomfortable or tricky. This can be when we are being challenged by others and also when other people may try to "de-skill" us by trying to get us to falter when we have declared something. For instance, if you think you might have been bullied, then you probably have. Check it out with someone you trust. Try and relate what happened without too much emotional information. Remember "you know what you know" about your own emotions, responses and feelings.

If you are stating something that you know, from past experience or because you were at an event and witnessed it, then this knowledge is part of your "knowing". We must all recognise, however, there is room for error when recalling events or facts and we must be careful not to be too dogmatic. There is no shame in admitting you don't know something or that you need help.

Knowing what you know is more about an emotional knowledge. You know how you are affected by events. You know if you like certain people and not others. So you may be a bit hazy about the exact dates of a party or whether it was a barbeque or a buffet but you will be certain beyond doubt to know if you enjoyed yourself or not. Having other people say it was marvellous or that you enjoyed yourself when you did not, is treading on your self-knowledge. This is where you need to establish with self-confidence and good humour, that, yes, maybe they did have a wonderful time and yes, many people did seem to enjoy the party but actually you did not. Your experiences are yours and establishing them and owning them without letting others hijack them is part of setting good boundaries and limits for yourself and others.

Kudos

Everyone wants a little bit of Kudos but be sure to ask the price. Kudos means honour or praise and is something we often want from other people. Kudos, however, can mean living up to others' values and goals and not paying attention to our own. I would suggest that you do not aim for Kudos in itself but view it as the icing on the cake.

The most important aspect of doing anything is to make sure that you are happy with how you are performing, that you know that you are giving the best you can give. This does not always mean 100%. If you are a parent, a carer and have a job as well as friends and interests, it will not be possible for you to give most things 100%. However you will be able to give them your best shot and that is good enough. Sometimes that may mean muddling through. I would suggest that you have your own Kudos-ometer which measures how you are doing by your own criteria. These may be criteria that are completely different from other peoples, such as "am I earning enough to give my mother a bit of extra care?" or "did I spend enough time with my best friend when she needed help?" These may be your personal priorities and I would suggest that you measure yourself by how much you have let your own standards slip, or not. If you are doing well I suggest you award yourself a bit of Kudos.

Don't wait for other people's judgement to let you know if you are doing well. You know yourself what your limits and priorities are – judge for yourself, how are you doing? When you are doing well, give yourself a pat on the back and a reward – a favourite telly programme, a cup of freshly-ground coffee, a long soak in the bath. When you are doing poorly, remember you are human, life is sometimes hard, you may need to ask for help… and you still deserve a reward because recognising when you are not doing so well is an achievement in itself. So by all means enjoy Kudos when it comes your way but remember not to make it the goal, just the by-product.

Loneliness

Loneliness is not the same as being alone. Many people enjoy the solitude that being alone brings. Loneliness is a subjective state of isolation, where the person feels denied the company of other people. As more and more households become one person and we communicate by electronics rather than face to face, there is a much higher risk of someone being badly affected by loneliness.

Culturally we are now set up for individuality rather than community but there are things we can do to improve this. Although loneliness can still carry a stigma, more and more people are recognising that it is a symptom of twenty-first century Western life. Therefore I would encourage you to confide in someone – your GP, a family friend, a teacher. If there really is no one to tell, it is worth joining a group, or if you are housebound or disabled doing this on line, and start to get connected to other people. If you are not on the internet try contacting a charity or group that covers your particular circumstances. If you are elderly and alone, Help the Aged can help. If you are a young mother at home, then the NCT or Mumsnet may be a way of contacting others. If you have a disability there will be a group supporting your particular cause – make contact.

Also, importantly, make contact yourself. Talk to the lady who comes to help around the house, wave to your postman, smile at your neighbours. At one point in my life, as a single parent with two small toddlers, apart from the radio, my main source of contact and information was my window cleaner. Twelve years later he is still my window cleaner and I know all about his family and he about mine. No, he is not my best friend but he is a good, kind, friendly member of my community who I know would lend a helping hand if I asked.

Making friends and human connections are about seizing opportunities. It is also about expecting other humans to be (mostly) friendly and interactive and not taking any rebuffs personally. You have to be up for contact to attract it. If you walk around with a scowl on your face or you are permanently looking at your feet then you will not make contact with others and you will miss opportunities for engagement. I would also add here that people who are not alone could try to be more aware of people who are. Some people are very insular and (rather unkindly, I think) ignore their waving neighbour or the old man at the newsagent as they are secure in their world. Remember, you too will get old and circumstances can change; a few minutes' chat will cost you nothing.

If you are able and can afford it, think about acquiring a pet. A small animal such as a budgie or hamster takes very little looking after and can be a source of great pleasure. Most cats just need feeding and somewhere warm to sleep. If that doesn't appeal maybe learn something new. The library will often have a list of free activities and groups, as well as classes for Bridge, Yoga, Reading groups etc.

Loneliness is something that is very hard to endure. It is bad for your health and can lead to depression and early onset of heart problems as well as a general lowering of immunity. So, please, let someone know. There are many people and organisations who would like to make contact but if they don't know you need them they cannot help. If you are lonely you will have to make the first move. Be brave and do it and don't let life pass you by.

Looks

There is no doubt that human beings are affected by the good looks or otherwise of other humans. We are designed to be attracted by certain body shapes and by symmetrical facial features. Biologically these are the appearances most likely to be apparent in people with high fertility levels which is why the attraction may be very strong and purely chemical. However we are not tuned into others' looks purely on a biological basis. We live in a culture in the West that places a very high value on looking good and on good looks. It is something that almost everybody is susceptible to on some level. We need to be careful, however, as trite though it is "looks are only skin deep". Looks do not translate into anything else other than looks. You can be a good looking murderer, con-artist, rapist or idiot just as easily as you can be all of those things if you are very plain.

We can be easily conned by our society which does indeed reward people merely for how they look. We can end up believing that somehow if you are good looking you must be something else as well; maybe clever, or charming, or funny, or talented. You may well be but you may just as easily not be. It is a hard fact of life that if two equally talented people go for a job then the better looking one is much more likely to be given it. If we are aware of our susceptibility towards good looks then hopefully we can catch ourselves before we operate with that bias.

If you are one of life's ordinary people then you can make sure that you make the best of what you have. Cleanliness, being the right weight for your height, wearing what suits you and what is appropriate as well as being polite, funny, kind and charming will go a long way to making sure that the first thing people notice is you and not necessarily what you look like. If you like who you are and enjoy what you do you will exude confidence. Confidence can be spotted a mile off and is very attractive.

So be careful not to exhibit a bias towards people merely for how they look; this can be an imposition and is also very patronising. It suggests that how they look is more important to you than who they are. If this is the case maybe think about your values and what those values will bring you. If you exhibit shallow tendencies you will more than likely attract shallow people. If you are on the receiving end of being pursued solely for your looks you will need to let people know how you feel about this and demonstrate good personal boundaries (see Boundaries). Remember it is normal for us to be attracted to good looking people but we must be careful not to exploit our looks if we have them or forget that what makes a person good, funny, interesting or kind has nothing to do with how they are packaged.

Loss

Learning to dealing with loss is about accepting the changes that the loss will bring. There are many types of loss, the obvious one being the death of someone close to you. Other losses include loss of job and/or income, loss of a relationship through any cause, loss of your home or security. Loss can be defined as losing something you had or something you expected to have, such as in the circumstances of a miscarriage, when you expected to have a baby.

People deal with losses differently. The first step is recognising that you are experiencing or have experienced a loss. Many people discount their loss (see Discounting) and override their feelings by "getting on with it". Getting on with it may, indeed, be part of coping for some people but many therapists believe that what is ignored will multiply. It is important to deal with feelings of loss when they arise and the implications of that loss. If you have lost a job, you may have not only lost your income, but your status and your colleagues and your career's future, as well as something that occupied you for a large percentage of your week. You may be suffering from a loss of purpose as well as the other losses mentioned above.

Generally, until other things have filled the void left by the loss and until you have become used to the changes wrought by that loss, you will be aware of what it is you now don't have rather than what you do have. It is important to find someone you can confide in how you really feel. Try to acknowledge that this is a painful experience and treat yourself kindly. Taking some form of action is usually beneficial. If you have lost a relationship it may be time to take up a new sport or hobby. If you have lost a job you may benefit from revising your CV or polishing up your computer skills. If you have lost a baby through miscarriage or a friend or relation has died there are many support groups and bereavement counsellors who can help and can be accessed through your GP.

Don't suffer alone but get help. Once you have come to terms with your loss you may be able to find a new or different direction that will bring you different rewards and pleasures. It may be that you do not end up where you thought you might but that you arrive somewhere equally rewarding, just different. It is not what happens to us that matters but how we deal with what happens.

Love

What is love? Being "in love" is mainly the huge attraction we feel for another human which multiplies when reciprocated. However I would suggest that after the initial heady rush of attraction has abated that "loving" comes when you work at building a life together and sustaining each other. This is much harder work and not nearly as glamorous as the initial whirlwind attraction.

It is important to be wary of instant attractions as these can often be based on unfulfilled Child needs that we developed when we were children in relation to our own parents. The way we were brought up, our family situation and what we were and were not given when we were children will set the "love barometer" for us. We will be attracted to people who can either, fulfil the role that was occupied by a very loving parent or, to a person who can fulfil the needs that were left unmet. Neither of the situations is the basis for an Adult to Adult relationship and may be the reason why so many relationships eventually founder.

111

If we have needs that were not fulfilled as a child then we must first address these ourselves. If we do not come to terms with what our parents could not give us, then we will be looking for our partner to supply this missing emotional fulfilment. This will place an unbearable and unreasonable demand on our partner and unless we take steps to address our childhood experiences our adult relationships will continually flounder or be unhappy.

Equally if we had a very loving parent who appeared to meet our every need, we may be unable to operate as a fully functional Adult without this "other" who adores us. If the prospective partner does not replicate the role occupied until that point by the parent then the relationship may founder or else a co-dependent relationship will form. This is where the behaviour of one partner, although dysfunctional and not Adult is wholly supported by the actions and behaviour of the other partner. If both partners stay in their allocated roles, these relationships can flourish. However one partner usually becomes tired of being the "carer" or the Adult to the other's Child and it is then that the relationship collapses.

If there has been an overly protective relationship with the natural parents then it may be that no partner will ever "measure up" and so no long term relationship can be established until these leftover Child issues are dealt with.

If we find we have an initial attraction based on a physical, mainly chemical reaction unless we make an attempt to find common interests and pursuits and to find out who the other person is and how they function, then this type of relationship is also unlikely to last.

Loving another human being is hard work. It requires honesty and emotional intimacy. As a couple supporting each other through difficult times and happy times, ideally you will help establish a mutual bond. You will become aware of each other's strengths and weaknesses. You will forgive your partner their mistakes and they will forgive you yours. You will be a strong partnership together but will still function as individuals when apart. Of course there will be difficult times when you want to walk out and forget them but what you have built together will be worth more than the satisfaction of having the moral high ground, or of being "right". Hopefully you will have someone watching your back, standing by your side and holding your hand through thick and thin. Loving requires self-sacrifice, tenacity, honour and guts. You know that you have "loving" if despite all the awful things that have happened, your relationship stills seems worth it and you can still "have a laugh" and recognise what a truly amazing couple you make.

A good relationship is like a garden; it constantly needs attention, pruning, watering, weeding etc. If it gets the right attention the results can be spectacular and there are moments when you can sit back and enjoy what you have created. If you neglect it the flowers will become choked by weeds and the lettuces will "bolt". However like a garden it is never too late to turn it around should you be willing to put in the time and effort required to get things flourishing again. One of the keys to a good relationship is to think the best of the other person. If your partner has behaved in an unacceptable way, then ask them what was their thinking behind their action before you rush to judge; hopefully, they will accord you the same behaviour. Benefit of the doubt is a good partnership rule until you have irrefutable evidence that it is not (even then it is still a pretty good rule!).

If things have gone awry you may need help to start to put things right. Good listening skills and empathy will go a long way to supporting any relationship and remembering why you agreed to partner this person in the first place will remind you of all the traits that attracted you to them and why your relationship is worth saving. If it is too late to save the relationship try to behave with grace and diplomacy when you leave, particularly if you have children (see Divorce). Even though you may feel betrayed and hurt, creating bitterness and ill-feeling will not serve you well; in the long run as it is you who will be unable to move on.

If a relationship has run its course, sadly, this only needs a consensus of one, then try to be grateful for all the good experiences you have shared and to part well. You will get other chances at love.

I do not believe that "real love" can only be found with your "true love" or your "soul mate". If the circumstances are right and the participants are willing then love can be created with hard work, attention to detail, optimism and hope. As with the garden analogy all you really need is some fertile soil and a bit of water – nature will take care of the rest. Once your love is blossoming then you need to make sure you tend it regularly and it will flourish. Remember, you cannot afford to be complacent or neglectful or before you know it you will be overrun with weeds and a lot of work will be needed to put things right. All love, not just romantic love is valuable and necessary to humans; it needs constant, gentle attention and appreciation. After all you are very lucky if you have someone to love and someone loves you.

Lying

We all lie at some time. A study by Dr Kang Lee, Director of Toronto University's , has revealed that children who learn to lie effectively from an early age are more successful than those who don't. Lying requires the brain to manipulate facts and then keep track of the manipulation. As adults, I would suggest that rather than actively lying, it is not always necessary to tell the truth or in any case, the whole truth. Certainly if you are asked to relate an event that you have witnessed you can do that as accurately and truthfully as possible. However, it is well known when comparing witness statements that very few actually tally completely. After all what is truth? Is it your opinion, is it a fact, is it a cultural belief? A statement such as "That person is unhealthily fat" could be all three. It could be none of those – fat in whose culture? Unhealthy? Not necessarily until blood pressure and cholesterol have been measured. In your opinion? Well who asked you?

Unsolicited opinions on other people's dress, style or life choices are totally unnecessary. Your opinion is exactly that and should not be volunteered unless asked for. Whether or not you think someone's dress or hair is awful, they don't need to know unless they ask you. Even then you can temper your answer. If someone close to you asks for the truth be very sure that they are able to hear it. So if your friend looks ridiculous with a beard (and after all that's just an opinion), then if he asks you for your opinion, be gentle. "I'm not sure it suits you", or, "I thought you looked better before." are not lies they're truthful but kind answers.

Another frequent reason for lying, particularly by children, is to get out of trouble. This is understandable if you are five or six and are worried about the consequences of what you have done. After all adults in your world have a lot of power. If however, as an adult, you find yourself lying in order to avoid taking responsibility for your actions, you probably need to address this. In some particular environments we can be made to feel very guilty or stupid if we have made a mistake; it is this fear that leads us to lie about mistakes and accidents. However this is not appropriate if you are an adult.

Everyone makes mistakes and circumstances will be much more straightforward if you relate what happened and how and why it occurred. Stick to facts and a brief apology. "Yes, I do seem to have made a mistake here. My intention was to... (whatever it was)... and I miscalculated and (broke it, lost it... whatever). I am sorry that I (broke it, lost us the customer, ruined the whatever)." Offer to put the mistake right if at all possible. If the other person wants to make a meal of your mistake, even in a subordinate position at work, you are entitled to point this out. "I have apologised... what would you like me to do now?" "Yes, you've already pointed out it was stupid, how can I get back on track." There are people who like to blame (see Blame) so put in your boundaries about how you want to be treated (see Boundaries). It is perfectly OK for someone to point out your mistakes but once you have admitted them and apologised it is not OK for them to capitalise on this.

Remember if you go in for lies about yourself, your life, your abilities, your background, then it is you who will come off worse.

Lying about yourself creates a false self, someone you may rather be but are not. Dorothy Rowe★ states that when we lie to ourselves we get muddled and don't know the truth from lies, as we believe ourselves to be truthful. Others then start to distrust us. It is then that we lose track of our own life story and "When we do this we lose track of who we really are." Lying to yourself is a really bad idea and distorts your sense of self and gains nothing, as who you believe you are is built on false beliefs. It is far better to admit that you may have made mistakes and are not where you want to be at the moment. You will then have a platform from which to launch a better way of being and a very useful personal file on "what not to do". As above, admit the mistake, apologise, try to make amends and then set yourself free. You are allowed to change how and who you are at any stage of your life; just make sure that you do this without the ultimate lie – the one to yourself.

★ *Why we Lie*, Dorothy Rowe 2010, Fourth Estate

Magical thinking

Magical thinking is something we learn in childhood, when we have little control, in order to keep ourselves safe and to make life more palatable. Magical thinking in adulthood is restrictive and a hindrance it stops us getting what we want and living in the present.

One sort of magical thinking enables us to put off living our life in the present and to hold out for a future when everything will be "just right". For instance if we are overweight, we might tell ourselves "When I have lost these twenty pounds then I will get a lovely partner and a fabulous job." This kind of magical thinking "If only I" (whatever it is, lose twenty pounds, move house, learn Italian) then all good things will abound, is a way of not having to work towards our goals whilst remaining just as we are. It allows us to put off becoming what we want by holding on to a reason why we don't have all that is wonderful, now. Much harder to have the self-belief that despite being overweight you are attractive and clever and deserve a great relationship and wonderful career.

Another sort of magical thinking is denial. This can happen after someone has died when we believe that they will turn up at any moment, or that they are on holiday or that we have dreamt their death and that we will wake up any moment. Be kind to yourself if you are experiencing magical thinking after a relationship betrayal or death. You will need to take time to readjust and face the reality of your new situation.

Other sorts of magical thinking involve promises to a higher power. "If I never swear again let this deal work out/let this girl fall in love with me." "I'll never drink again if only I keep my job this time." These kinds of belief mean that we hand over our fate to someone else not really believing that we are the one in control. It is a way of abdicating our responsibilities and also a way in which we do not have to acknowledge reality.

When we are children it is comforting to believe in Santa Claus and the Tooth Fairy. These stories help make life more palatable and exciting but carried over into adulthood they lead people away from realising their goals and encourage us to remain in a childlike state where we do not take responsibility for our own fate.

There are adults that still believe in fantasy figures who will look out for them. These figures are supposed to intervene on their behalf but not many believers would cross a busy motorway with their eyes closed! Humans have a very good reality radar, we have utilised and refined our ability to check out reality as we have evolved through the ages. We needed to assess the likelihood of a sabre-toothed tiger leaping out from a rock and to have a plan to deal with it should it occur. To abandon that finely-honed ability in order to hold fantastical beliefs is a mistake; it makes us vulnerable to the manipulative, and to misfortune and allows us to put our goals "on ice" by stopping us acting on our own behalf.

Acknowledging that sometimes bad things happen to good people and vice versa is a way of embedding yourself in reality. It leaves you ready to cope when life is not all that you want it to be but also allows us not to take bad luck as a personal misfortune. Investing in your own worth and abilities will make sure that you are able to take action to improve your life and that you are living your life in the present. Living on a wing and a prayer is not a great option. Yesterday is gone, the future isn't here. The present is all that we have; make the most of it.

Manipulation

Manipulation is what we do to get our own way when we are unable to achieve this in a straightforward manner. This can be because we are afraid to ask for what we want, we don't know how to ask for what we want or we enjoy the power that manipulating someone brings.

Manipulation is usually a bad idea. It is something we do overtly as young children to get our own way but soon learn that it is not regarded as an appropriate behaviour. Manipulation is a subliminal way of making sure we push through our own agenda but can get us in to trouble when we do it, as adults, at the expense of human relationships. Most of us give it up to a large extent although, of course, it is always in the repertoire of human behaviours and none of us are immune from occasionally using it.

However in some families there is an undercurrent of approval when manipulation is attempted. "The little devil, he tried to play us off against each other." These children learn that manipulation with a smile or a giggle is regarded as "funny" or "charming" and that they will often get their own way. This is a way to wield power, albeit charmingly. No reason, then, to be straightforward. These are life's charmers and are the ones we least mind being "conned" by. These are also the people who most hate being found out as they have bought in to their own limitless charm.

Other children may rarely be given anything by parents or carers unless they give something in exchange. "Give mummy a kiss, then." "Well, what have you done to deserve a trip to the park/zoo/shops?" They learn that in order to get things they want and need they have to have a bargaining chip. This is how they learn early on to manipulate. "If I take the rubbish out, then can I have a biscuit?" They have learnt that asking straight out for something results in them having to justify what they want or need. These are the people who as adults are very difficult to detect. We can often be manipulated by these people for quite some time before we realise it. They will appear to be reasonable negotiators but they are easy to spot once you realise that they never ask for something without offering something else in return.

The third group have learnt in childhood that they are very unlikely to get what they want by being straightforward and may have been shouted at or abused for asking for what they need. These people will continue to be afraid to ask outright for what they want or need and manipulation, for them, has become a survival technique which they have not outgrown or learnt is no longer necessary. They see manipulation as slipping under your defences to achieve what they want or need.

Most adult humans do not like being manipulated. If any of the behavioural styles above rings bells for you, it would be good to recognise this and start to drop the behaviour. If it has become second nature for you to be manipulative then you will need to start slowly trying new, straightforward behaviour on close friends and family. If you think that there is no need to change, after all you often get what you want, think again. Being manipulated is not a good feeling and most adults will know that they are being manipulated even if it's after the event. They will resent you for this and talk about your behaviour amongst themselves even if they don't confront you. Being manipulative stops you from having real, intimate friendships because everything is based on an exchange or getting something you want without being honest or straightforward about it. Relationships are reduced to a commodity-based bargaining exchange or the ability to get what you want in an underhand manner.

If you are on the receipt of manipulative behaviour you need to confront this. "You are very charming but nevertheless, I am not going to agree to… (whatever)". Or "It's very good of you to offer to host the book club party but I am afraid that this doesn't mean that I can lend you my… (whatever) as I don't feel comfortable doing this. Do you still want to host the party?" Or "I know you would like this job but I am sorry I cannot interview you unless you go through the correct office procedure." If the manipulator continues to try this behaviour you may have to confront them in a more obvious manner. "I get the feeling you are trying to manipulate me. I feel uncomfortable about that. Can you tell me what it is you want?" This is the same three-step procedure used in the Boundary section (see Boundaries), and is usually very effective.

Maslow's hierarchy of needs

Abraham Maslow was a key figure in humanistic psychology in the 1950s. So how is this relevant today? Maslow believed that you could not reach a state of "self-actualisation" until you had satisfied what he termed as "deficiency needs". Why would anyone care about this? Well, almost all humans, given the right circumstances have the potential for self actualisation. This is the pursuit of self-fulfilment for its own sake; not for riches, success, kudos or fame. There is no drive to attain a result, or an end product, the expression of the need is an end in itself. Maslow referred to this as a "being" need. After all that is what we are, human beings but instead we spend a lot of our time on the planet as human "doings". Maslow believed that self actualisation brings the ultimate in human satisfaction and contentment. He believed that people who attain this are "working at something which fate has called them to somehow and which they work at and which they love, so that the work-joy dichotomy in them disappears." (Maslow, AH, 1973 *The farther reaches of human nature* p.45, Harmondsworth: Penguin). This is not necessarily the case but I have included it here in case it is something you have recognised and want for yourself.

However, Maslow believed that it is not possible to attain this state until the "deficiency needs" are met. So before you can fulfil your potential as a human being you will need to meet the following. Firstly, physiological needs which are related to survival such as food, drink, sleep. Secondly, needs for safety including physical, economic and psychological. Thirdly, needs for love and belonging (see Robert Weiss provisions of social relationships, Depression) including affection, intimacy and roots in a family or group. Fourthly, the need for esteem which manifests in competence, adequacy, self-respect and respect from others. Once these four needs have been met then we can aim for the need for self-actualisation which Maslow defined as "becoming what one is capable of".

Maslow believed that self actualisation is the ultimate goal for humans. Whether or not that is the case can only be judged by the individual. Maslow did observe, however, that those he regarded as self actualisers made full use of their talents and capacities, they had no evidence of neurosis and had satisfied the deficiency needs outlined above. I would also mention that most of the self actualisers that Maslow identified were over sixty, so this is something that probably comes with maturity. The other point worth mentioning is that not everyone wants to achieve self-actualisation; some people are entirely content with three or four of the deficiency needs met or maybe a selection of them satisfied.

I include this in the book because it emphasises some of the satisfaction and joy of being a self-fulfilled human being and also to remind ourselves and others that being a good, altruistic, intellectual human also relies on being very fortunate. You would be a very fortunate person indeed if for the majority of your life all your deficiency needs were met. So aim high but remember that you need to balance your life first and attend to the physical and mental needs Maslow outlined if you want to reach total fulfilment. Also worth remembering is that self-actualisation is not about the pursuit of an end goal and in making it your goal you could be doing exactly that, which, after all, would completely defeat the object.

Mental health disorders

Mental health disorders have unfortunately become more common but luckily the stigma surrounding them has lessened. Mental health disorders can range from anxiety, through self-harm to full blown schizophrenia or bi-polar disorder. If you know that you have a life-long disorder make sure that you have regular check ups, that you take your medication and that you ask for help when you need it. Schools and employers are not allowed to discriminate against people with a mental health disorder and in many instances they are required to enable the person in order that they can continue their studies or perform their job.

So how do you recognise if you or someone else has a mental disorder or that you are developing one. A mental disorder is defined as some form of disordered thinking, behaviour or belief that handicaps or interferes with your normal life. I have listed the criteria for spotting depression in the Depression section but I will list here the main criteria for spotting the development or presence of a mental health disorder.

- A deterioration in academic or work performance or ability to complete usual every day tasks that previously caused no problems.
- Keeping erratic hours, waking up late or early, going to bed very late or early.
- Poor time keeping and irregular habits such as missing meals or appointments.
- Insomnia
- Obsessional attitudes to work, cleaning or exercise.
- Mood swings including erratic behaviour, anxiety, tearfulness and irritability, wild spending sprees or manic enjoyment.
- Feelings of being overwhelmed, hopelessness or worthlessness. What's the point of anything?
- Excessive drinking, smoking or drug use. Over or under eating.
- Change in appearance, unkempt, loss or gains in weight, lack of personal hygiene.
- Lack of interest in things that previously brought pleasure.

If it interferes with your daily functioning then it is a problem.

Seek help as soon as possible. First go and see your G.P. and if things are not resolved fairly quickly then ask for a referral to a psychiatrist or psychotherapist. There is a lot of help out there and with correct diagnosis and treatment, either therapeutic, pharmaceutical or both, the situation can be resolved relatively quickly so that a happy and fulfilling life can be pursued.

There are certain personality traits which have been found to be more likely to lead to mental health problems. You put a lot of strain on yourself by being a perfectionist. Having high standards is not in itself a problem but not knowing when to ease up or how to prioritise can lead to overload. Being a realist is important. If you want to party hard and get a first at university, then something's got to give; if you try to do both you will suffer, so an ability to see the bigger picture is important. You can work out just how many nights you can party and still maintain your grades without too much strain; it's all about realistic goals and balance in obtaining them.

Obsessive behaviours work in the same way in that if you feel there are certain tasks you *must* do you are in danger of overloading yourself. Insular people with few friends who find it difficult to confide in anyone are more likely to suffer when there are problems. Try to discuss your problems with someone as this is how they become normalised and shrink in proportion which allows us to put our worries into perspective. A pessimistic personality, someone who expects the worst is also more susceptible than an optimist. Someone who can see the good side of most things and who views problems as a challenge will be much more mentally robust.

Lastly if you take things too personally you will find most situations harder. It is important to remember that most things are not about you. If you go for a job interview and don't get it, a pessimist who takes things personally will think it is because they were rubbish. However an optimist will tell themselves that they didn't have much experience in that field and that maybe they need to try a different, less prestigious company. This ability to distance oneself from arbitrary decisions where you have no information to the contrary is one that can protect you. These personality traits in no way mean you will become mentally ill but they are ones that put additional strain on your system and in times of pressure can cause problems.

However, there are certain steps you can take to make it less likely that you will develop mental health problems even though there may be genetic and environmental factors that are outside your control. You can, however, control the following.

-   be social and keep up with your friends. Confide in them if things become overwhelming and ask for help.
-   Ease up, you cannot go full tilt at anything for long periods of time without some strain on your system showing up. Try for a balanced approach to life "All things in moderation" – Pythagorus
-   Keep regular hours. Sleep at the same time, more or less, eat well and exercise. It has been shown that regular exercise can keep depression at bay and alleviate anxiety. Thirty to forty minutes a day is optimal but anything will help.
-   Avoid depressants or excessive stimulants. These include alcohol, cigarettes, drugs – many of which can induce psychosis in those who are susceptible – and negative acquaintances. Avoid demanding or very needy people if you are not feeling robust yourself.
-   If things feel daunting, seek help early. Early intervention has a higher success rate and of course you will get back to feeling better much more quickly.

Many people have a fear of developing a mental disorder. However there is much help available now and there is plenty of reason for optimism. Many disorders are curable and almost all are treatable. A very kind doctor once told me that if you apply enough stress to anyone, eventually they will crack. Some people succumb physically and for others it is too much mentally. Whichever category you fall into (if at all) remember there is lots of help available but you will need to ask for it. If people don't know you are suffering they can't help and that would be an opportunity missed. A delay in seeking treatment is a delay in getting on with a potentially wonderful life. So act soonest.

Money

In the society that we have created for ourselves, it is very rare that we view money for the simple tool that it is. Money is simply a means of exchanging one thing for another: work for payment, objects for payment, services for payment. However, we often confuse money with status, the value of a person (rather than their abilities) with power and with freedom. Money will not make you cleverer, funnier, kinder, prettier or nicer. However, an understanding of your finances will mean that you take any mystery out of financial dealings and the more balanced approach that you have towards your income and its uses, the easier your life will be. You will have created a better power relationship with money and consequently will experience more freedom. I think it is fair to say that consumerism has created in us the ability to put a price on almost anything but not necessarily the ability to be able to rate its value.

In order to take some of the mystery out of money and its functions and understand and manage your own finances, it is important to be numerate or get the help of someone who is. The basic mathematical functions of addition, subtraction, multiplication and division as well as an understanding of percentages and a grasp of times tables are all that you need to understand monetary function. This is really important. As an adult you need to be able to measure outgoings against incomings, to understand any work contract you are offered, whether the promised perks really are perks and to be able to work out effective bulk buys and bargains when you are shopping. If you do not understand what it is you are being offered get someone numerate, who you trust, to help explain things. There is no shame in not understanding how the use and investment of money functions. After all, a whole lot of bankers, who are usually considered to be fairly numerate and knowledgeable about money managed to bring the world's economy crashing to its knees. So if in doubt, ask and always remember – there really is no such thing as a free lunch!

In relationships money often has a power base. Unless you are entirely happy with the concept, I would suggest that to allow yourself to be valued in monetary terms or to view another this way, is usually detrimental to almost any relationship I can think of. It is important in your relationships, whether friendships, employer/employee based or life partners to be frank early on about your income, expectations and money history. If you are not good with money, be honest and ask for help. If you owe a whole lot and cannot see a way to repay it, then own up and get help to work out a repayment plan. If the office pension plan is an enigma to you, ask someone to explain it.

In *Hamlet*, Polonius advises his son Laertes "Neither a borrower nor a lender be." This is not realistic in today's world but I would say that within your valued relationships lend and borrow as little as you possibly can. If you borrow money make sure you always pay it back – you have no idea how much that sum means to the other person. If you lend money be clear about a pay-back time frame and if you are let down, do not lend to the same person again. Obvious, you may think? Time and time again I have had friends and clients tell me tales of woe about the same person who does not pay them back. Yes, I am astonished that they continue to lend to a serial debtor but also I see the tangled emotional involvement that tempts them to do it "just one more time".

Depending on your emotional relationship with money it can be extremely difficult to refuse to lend to someone close to you when you have the money and you know that they don't. There is often a good reason for this imbalance and the "borrower" will never alter their behaviour until you stop bailing them out. Continually lending money to someone who fails to pay you back does not make you a "good mummy" or "good friend" or "good neighbour" it makes you slightly foolish and you become the debtor's enabler.

If you have had parents who neglected to teach you budgeting, or show you how savings worked then you will have a very different view of money compared to someone who was taught these things. You may have been brought up in a very deprived or alternatively, very wealthy family – neither of these experiences provides a balanced view. You need to work out how you view money, how your past impacts on this view, and whether it is still valid. Then you can work out how you can make money function well in your life; money makes a good servant but a very poor master. So, for instance, if you had a parent who counted every penny and budgeted like crazy who then died and left you a fortune or who had a secret gambling habit then you may have anxieties about "having enough" that are entirely understandable. Alternatively this experience could make you careless about budgeting because you have been lied to in the past about the supply and demand issues in your household. This does not encourage an Adult attitude to money. Instead you may have Child fears or insecurities or Parent beliefs and behaviours about money that keep you stuck and stop you getting to grips with your finances.

I am very careful about money having had a father who acted like we had a lot of money when we didn't and a husband who acted like we had hardly any money when the opposite was true. These false assessments of my financial stability have made me very careful about whom I trust and have made me sure to double check information I am given from banks or investors or even friends with regard to finances. It is me and only me who takes care of my finances as then I know exactly what my outgoings and incomings are. This works well for me. However, I realise that I must not be too distrustful otherwise I may miss something in the present that could benefit me because I am still going on past (and obsolete) experiences which make me respond in Child as overly cautious or paranoid. This is what you need to work out for yourself – what past beliefs you have about money, are they still useful today – maybe in part or not at all and then last of all what you believe now and how that will affect how you handle your finances. It doesn't matter what you choose as long as it works well for you and past experiences don't sabotage your present behaviours.

If you have not had much money you can make the mistake of believing it will "solve" everything. This is very rarely the case. In studies it has been found that money rarely makes us happy but if we understand it and its functions well it can bring satisfaction and security.

"It's easy to forget that things aren't 'loud' or 'bright' they are just 'louder' or 'brighter' than something else. Money is one more thing that our minds treat in this relativistic fashion." Jeremy Dean (Psyblog – UCL student)

If we can understand that how much money we have is relative, with regard to whom we find ourselves mixing with, with regard to our perceived needs, with regard to our beliefs and wants, then we can begin to be more at ease with it.

There is a neat money/time/enjoyment ratio model which is worth explaining as it helps most people work out whether a job or pursuit is value for money and/or worth doing.

1) If you enjoy what you are doing you will care less how much it costs/how much you are paid to do it or if it takes up a lot of your time.
2) If you find yourself with a lot of free time then you won't care so much if you don't get paid a lot or if the task you are doing isn't that enjoyable.
3) If you are given/have lots of money you may not care so much about enjoying yourself or whether you get much free time.

However if you have little money, little time and are not enjoying yourself then something needs to change as you will become very disenchanted with this ratio in a relatively short time frame. Ask yourself what you would do that you can't do now, with more money. Sometimes this exercise helps people to focus on what it is that they want or alternatively realise they have a great deal that they value already or that actually, with a bit of budgetry tweaking and some cutting back, they could afford many of the things that they currently believe are out of reach.

When you have reached the state where money is just money and you are in control of it, rather than the reverse, then you will be in the happy position of having money as your servant. If you can maintain this "mastery" and lose any mythical beliefs about what money can or cannot do for you, then you will have reached an Adult harmonious state in relation to money which should stand you in good stead for life.

Moods

We all have moods. Good, bad and indifferent. You are entitled to have whatever mood it is that you are experiencing. However, as an adult human being, it is not OK for you to visit your mood on others in such a way that you encroach on what is going on for them. For example if you have had some fantastic news and are on top of the world (hooray for you!), it does not mean that when you are meeting a friend for a drink you can dismiss their concerns about what is going on for them for fear they may ruin your good day. "Oh, don't worry about that, listen to what happened to me." Conversely, if you are feeling awful and can't wait to meet your friend it is not OK to go on an on about how awful your situation is as you may be encroaching on their wonderful day!

This is not about ignoring our friends when they need us. Nor is it about putting aside our own feelings on occasion to deal with others' more pressing problems. It is however about being reasonable and contained about your own feelings. It is not OK to put a damper on someone's party – not so long ago this would have been considered plain bad manners. Many of us have got so used to discussing how we feel that we forget sometimes the appropriateness of when and where we discuss our feelings. Some believe if they are not feeling good then no one else should be. This is very obvious with some parents who think it is fine for their child's tantrum to deafen everyone else sharing the space with them. Not so long ago parents removed these small people (who actually cannot contain how they are feeling and need an adult to show them how) and calmed them down whilst not inflicting their behaviour on everyone else. It is about being courteous to others.

If you are having a bad day, go ahead and have it, even share what's going on and elicit some much-deserved sympathy but do not let your mood be the order of the day, permeating what everyone else is doing and expect others to join in. After all it's your mood, not theirs and part of growing up is learning how to both contain and subsequently deal with how you are feeling.

Mothering/Fathering

If you had a poor experience of being mothered or fathered this can leave lingering "needs" that remain been unfulfilled. You may be looking for someone to take care of you or "mother" you in a way that didn't happen when you needed it. If this is the case you need to develop your own inner "nurturing mother/father". Many people who have been harshly parented will have developed a critical inner voice. This is the voice which causes you to mutter "idiot" under your breath if you make a mistake. This is also the voice which will ruminate over your mistakes, when you go over and over what you should have/could have/would have done but didn't. If this voice is very loud and persistent you will need to develop a larger but much kinder "nurturing parent" voice in order to counteract this.

This nurturing voice will be one that still recognises your mistakes but instead of saying "idiot" to yourself you will be able to say "I could have done better there" or "I need to apologise for that". This voice recognises that as humans we make mistakes and that this is inevitable. The kind voice of the nurturing parent, however, allows us room to correct these mistakes and learn from them without labelling the actions as "wrong" in some way. I believe that it is only possible to blossom if we are kind to ourselves and others.

Alternatively your parenting experience could have been that you had such vigilant parenting that you are not looking for any needs to be fulfilled; you simply want someone to continue the nurturing role. If you have experienced s(mothering) then you will not have been allowed to grow up and exercise your own abilities at taking care of yourself or containing your emotions and desires. Autocratic demanding people fall into this category as do narcissists, who have been so "loved" that they have become totally egocentric. There are also the "helpless" who cry out to be "looked after".

These people are "stuck" developmentally around three to six years. If you encounter someone like this you need to make sure your boundaries are very firm and this will encourage them to "grow up" and start to take responsibility for themselves, their own happiness and their actions. If you recognise this behaviour as your own then start to reclaim your own "power" by gradually assuming responsibility for yourself and allowing yourself to be a fully-functioning adult. Relationships with obvious power differences between the participants (except in legitimate parent/child roles) cannot be expected to reach an intimate and loving accord. It is not an easy task to reclaim your adulthood but definitely worth it. "I am the master of my fate: I am the captain of my soul." (W , *Invictus*). If we don't address the issues surrounding our parenting we pass them down the generations to be repeated ad infinitum. Don't let left-over parenting issues, which are way out of date, control who you are now or dictate how your children develop.

Neediness

If you have not had your needs adequately met as a child this will show up in later life as "neediness". All humans are needy; we need love, attention, social interaction, approval and many things besides but not to the exclusion of all else and not at the expense of anyone else. An overwhelming need to be the centre of attention is absolutely normal if you are three or four but is misplaced in an adult. If we are not parented in a way that helps us self-soothe when things go wrong then we will look externally for others to meet our needs. Also if we are not taught that although we are important and valuable it is not at the expense of others then we will fail to understand when we are not the centre of attention.

When we have needs that we do not meet ourselves they grow until they become a disproportionate and unsatisfied requirement. It is then that our behaviour will tend to alter as the need grows. We may become whiney or irritable or depressed if we have a need for company and social interaction that we leave unfulfilled. If we go too long with such a need unmet then we may withdraw from any intimate interaction altogether. Both Maslow (see Maslow's hierarchy) and Robert Weiss (see Depression) emphasise certain social needs and esteem needs that we as humans require to be met in order that we can function at our best.

A need for recognition and appreciation exists in all humans. If we lack good boundaries (see Boundaries) and do not see appreciation and recognition as our due for tasks and favours done, then we will continue to lack recognition and this need may leak into other interactions. We may constantly strive to be noticed at work, we may dress inappropriately to attract attention or get drunk at parties. If we have been under appreciated and under feted as children this need may become very exaggerated – think of the celebrities that are caught on camera over and over again exhibiting the same "over-the-top", inappropriate, behaviour. Ponder why they want to become "celebrities" at all?

If we have not been taught through our upbringing how to meet these needs for ourselves we may encounter social difficulties as adults, although everyone will have these needs in some measure as part of being human. However, once we recognise what our needs are and how to fulfil them then they will no longer leak inappropriately into interactions with others. When we feel sad or lonely or down we need to take time to think what it is we are lacking (if anything). All humans have periods of negative emotions and these are normal but if they impact on your behaviour causing you to feel negatively about yourself for long periods or causing you to change your behaviour in self-limiting ways, for example being incredibly rude to your friends or family or indulging in drink or drugs then you need to take action in order to fulfil your own needs so that your behaviour starts to support you rather than let you down.

It may help you to do the balance pie-chart (see Balance) to see where you put most of your energy. It may not seem obvious but if you are working incredibly hard and see little of your friends and family then although you may be appreciated at work some of your social and relaxation needs will be being neglected. You will know if your needs are unmet as you will become irritable, out of balance, stressed and this may affect your eating and sleeping habits. Tending to your needs is common sense. If you are lonely or stressed you will not be able to enjoy yourself and may, because of how you are feeling, reject the very thing you need. If you are feeling stressed and miserable you may not be able to accept an invitation when it comes your way. You may react in an overly paranoid manner when asked to join in some activity, wondering why you have been asked instead of expressing enthusiasm and accepting. Unmet needs distort our behaviour and our expectations so it is important to take some time for self reflection in order that we can recognise what we need and take appropriate steps to make sure that we get it. It is only then that we can concentrate on enjoying our lives and who we are in an authentic and adult way.

Negotiation

Everyone needs good negotiation skills. If you come from a big family you are probably quite used to negotiating for what you need, however not everyone picks up these skills in childhood and with autocratic parents who expect obedience, developing negotiation skills is risky and not always an option.

Negotiation is all about give and take. A relaxed tolerant attitude and a sense of humour will help. Be reasonable in your requests and if you meet with a point blank no then start to fish around by asking what might be permitted. For instance if you are a child asking to go to a party and you meet with a no you could start negotiating by asking. "What if I come home by eleven?" "How about if we all club together for a taxi and I phone when we get there and when I leave?" A mature attitude will be far more likely to result in some sort of agreement than a meltdown at being told no. Sometimes, however, you have to be able to accept no for an answer and back off gracefully. This will also stand you in good stead as you can point out your lack of temper and fuss when another request is due.

Hopefully by the time you are an adult you will have acquired some good negotiating tactics. If not here are some pointers.

Be reasonable.
Never shout.
Try to see the other's point of view.
Try not to use words such as never/always (see below)
Work out in advance what you want and what you might give up or offer in order to get it.

Make enquiries about what the deal-breaker might be and how you
could modify the request so you get a yes.

Show that you are willing to forgo some of your request and to
modify what you want.

Say thank you when you get what you want.

Be gracious when you don't get what you want.

Remember if negotiating with a bank or a company, there are other
banks and companies out there who may have different
requirements.

If negotiating with your boss, remember you need a fairly good track
record or a reasonable length of service with the company before
you can expect individual treatment.

Stay calm and remember no one gets 100% of what they want all
the time.

Negotiating is a life-long skill, so don't give up just keep modifying
your technique until you're getting some of what you want some of
time. That, for most people, is a good result.

Never/Always

By now, if you have read a fair chunk of this book or even a few
sections you will have realised that I am not that keen on extreme
words such as always, never, terrible, wonderful, monstrous, angelic,
nightmare etc. These words do not show the shades of grey in any
situation and are usually used to dramatic effect or to gain the moral
high ground.

For the most part these extreme words do not reflect what is
really happening. Exclaiming "You never take out the rubbish.",will
generally be an untrue statement. If you say "I thought we'd agreed
it was your turn to take out the rubbish. I get really annoyed when
you say you'll do something and then you don't." You are more

likely to get a reasonable response back. You are also allowing the other person to have a say without immediately putting them on the defensive. People on the attack or on the defensive are much more likely to use maximising or minimising terms and the results are a lack of space in which to negotiate or put your point of view reasonably. So, in an argument, try not to start off with these words which will escalate the situation.

Other reasons not to minimise or maximise are that people will not know when there really is something serious happening. If you describe bus journeys to work as a nightmare you will not be taken seriously if there is a genuinely awful morning's traffic when you cannot get into work on time. Try to be specific when describing events and avoid too much exaggeration.

The same is true of minimisation. If you are asked how you are and you reply fine whilst feeling truly awful then people will not be able to gauge how you really are. It also shows a lack of connection with yourself and an inability to communicate properly. You need to know how you are and how to express this to others. It is important, too, that you take care of yourself and let people know (to some extent) how you are feeling.

This does not mean that when socialising or telling a funny story you cannot be yourself and exaggerate for effect. Lots of people enjoy hamming up a story and others will enjoy your performance, knowing it is only put on for effect. But by using appropriate descriptions in everyday life we let others know that we are reliable and trustworthy and they can, in turn, respond accordingly.

Being OK

There is a wonderful book called *I'm OK/You're OK* by Thomas A. Harris. It is quite a long read – worth it in my opinion – and somewhat out of date now but the essence of it is that what we get in life is based on which life position we adopt out of the four OK/not OK ("NOK") positions. The ideal position is in the title of his book *I'm OK/You're OK*. This is a position we adopt when we feel secure in our own selves and content not to judge others but let them be who they are. This is what I, as a Transactional Analyst (TA) would call the Adult position; balanced, positive and non-judgemental. This is a position either reached through reflection, self awareness and maturity or for a lucky few, a position reached after a pretty balanced upbringing by IMOK/YOK parents.

The other three positions are less ideal but are positions that all of us occupy from time to time. The idea is that we do not spend any great amount of time in any of the other three positions but endeavour to spend most of our existence in the IMOK/YOK position. However, depending on your life experiences, some of the other positions may be more comfortable and familiar to you but they all have serious downsides, one of them being the vigilance required to maintain any of the other three positions.

The I'm OK/You're not OK ("IMOK/YNOK") position is usually adopted by someone who likes to be in control and is heavily invested in being right or having their opinion acknowledged as the "right" one. It is a one up position. This is where the OK person takes the Critical Parent position in TA and where the not OK person is relegated to the Child position. The up side of this position is the ability to convince yourself that you are good, hard working and righteous and others who oppose you are "bad", have poor values and are against you.

This is, however, an exhausting position to maintain; all the time needing to shore yourself up with your righteousness. It usually comes from having been coerced, ignored or dominated as a child. It puts the Parent and Child parts of yourself in conflict with each other. The Parent part of you frightens and cajoles the Child to do as it suggests and the Child part of you responds with fear or resentment. If your inner voice calls you "stupid" and is always exhorting you to do better you probably adopt the IMOK/YNOK position more than is healthy. If, when you get into conflict with others, you find yourself rubbishing them or their opinions this will be your favourite position. Maintaining these beliefs requires constant vigilance of yourself and others to make sure they and you come up to scratch. It carries a high internal cost of feeling worthless when you fail to measure up or alternatively, you will feel angry with others when they fail to meet your expectations. When it all gets too much you will probably flip back into the position you are trying to hide from and were made to adopt by oppressive parents when you were a child which is I'm not OK/You're OK ("IMNOK/YOK").

The IMNOK/YOK position is a one down position brought about by feelings of inadequacy or not measuring up. This position is adopted by children who are made to feel that their feelings are invalid and that they don't measure up in some way. This may not have been the intention of the parents but it is the result of parenting which does not listen to the needs of the child and expects the child to fall in with the expectations and demands of the parent regardless of their own wishes and requirements. This is the position adopted by the less-robust child. The more robust child will, as an adult, try to occupy the IMOK/YNOK position to escape from the feelings engendered as a child when they were in the IMNOK/YOK position.

Not feeling OK is not a good place to be and comes from having been disregarded as a child. The core belief is that all around you are fine but there is something wrong with you. If you do not get your needs met as a child you begin to think there is something wrong with you for having those needs. This is not true but it is the result of having parents who either could not or would not meet your needs. If you are the child of an addict or an alcoholic or a particularly self-obsessed parent, you may find yourself occupying this life position more than is healthy. If you can start to check out your own beliefs and values and move away from being dominated by the values your parents pressed on you, then you will start to feel more OK. You might gravitate to the IMOK/YNOK position above, which is more healthy but really a position that comes from Child anger at having been overlooked when little. It is natural (and good in these circumstances) to feel that anger that takes you away from occupying the NOK position. It takes time and self-awareness to reach the position of IMOK/YOK and virtually no one feels this 100% of the time but vacillates between the three positions so far outlined. The fourth position is one of despair and fright.

I'm not OK/You're not OK ("IMNOK/YNOK") is the scariest position to be in. We will all probably visit this position and hold this belief at some time, even if it is just for a moment or two. However if you feel like this a lot of the time you will probably need to have some counselling or therapy to help you towards one of the other less damaging positions. This is the position occupied by someone with depression, schizophrenia, paranoia or bi-polar disorder (in the depressive phase) or, indeed, someone who has been continually disregarded, frightened, abandoned and/or oppressed as a child. Although this position is indicative of a mental health disorder there are people invested in this position who hold down jobs and relationships and "manage" their lives as best they can whilst feeling constantly insecure and anxious. However being in this position IMNOK/YNOK will expose you to the likelihood of developing a mental health disorder more than any of the other positions.

The IMNOK/YNOK position is a no-win place to be and hard to shift from. The main reason for remaining in this position is the fear of occupying any other position. The position of trusting no one feels like the least risky place to be. This is a false premise. This position, in reality, is a position where you can expect to experience minimal enjoyment of what it means to be a happy, healthy human. If you occupy this position for more than 10% of the time you will be living a very restricted life. The only way free of this position is to start to challenge some of your beliefs about yourself and the world. You may need help to do this and will need to find someone you trust to work with. You can ask your GP for recommendations.

It is advisable when challenging long-term views held out of fear, to take very small steps towards relinquishing those views. After all your belief is that these views have kept you safe and dismantling them can leave you feeling exposed and vulnerable. For instance if you believe all people to be untrustworthy, you may be able to think of one or two people who deserve your trust, who are unfailing in their attempts to help you and who love you. If this seems an impossible task you could look at one or two people in history who have sacrificed themselves for others. These examples, such as Mother Teresa, show us that there are humans who are good, kind and trustworthy. It is also important that you acknowledge that all humans are fallible and make mistakes so that any expectations that a person is 100% trustworthy are seen to be unrealistic. The IMNOK/YNOK position is one that needs to be left behind quickly. If you favour this position I urge you to seek help as soon as possible.

IMOK/YOK is the position we occupy when we are at our best and the one the gives us the capacity for self-actualisation (see Maslow) and the most fulfilled life we can have. It is not easy to occupy this position 24/7, however, it is possible to occupy it more than any other position. The more aware we are of our own behaviours and past hurts the more we will be able to let go of our prejudices and out-of-date beliefs and focus on our own progress as humans and less on other people's effect on us. The more we take responsibility for our own actions the less interested we will be in interfering with or judging others. Once we have started aiming for the IMOK/YOK position for the majority of our lives then we are truly on the road to personal freedom and a balanced, happy, productive life.

Ostrich behaviour

The Ostrich's defence is to stick its head in the sand. I am not sure this is particularly effective for ostriches but I know it is a very poor defence mechanism in humans. There are times when we all want to bury our heads in the sand and not believe what is going on. Maybe we owe money to credit card companies and we begin to leave their letters unopened. Maybe our weight has been creeping up and up so we don't get on the scales and we avoid the mirror. Maybe our child has gotten ruder and more difficult and we turn a blind eye. Whatever the situation it cannot be improved or changed by ignoring it or pretending it isn't happening.

Some of life is very uncomfortable and facing up to problems that have escalated due to our neglect or lack of awareness is very uncomfortable indeed. However, the first step in rectifying a problem that has got out of hand is to acknowledge that it is a problem and then the next step is to confront the true size of it. Then you can begin to tackle your problem. It is important that if you need help, you ask for it (see Help). Once your problem is acknowledged and out in the open the threat to you will diminish (and with it any stress responses such as insomnia or indigestion). Then your task of putting things right will start to seem more manageable.

Sometimes when we have committed truly awful mistakes or our task to change things seems insurmountable, it seems as though there may be no way back. This is just something we tell ourselves to avoid confronting what we have done; it also means we never have to begin the work of making amends and changing things for the better.

Don't buy into the belief that you cannot change your situation.

It may be extremely hard, painful and humiliating but you can always, at any time, choose a different way to tackle your issues. Once you have made a decision to alter your behaviour, stick with it. Most things that are worth having take considerable effort on our part – it's worth bearing this in mind. Give yourself a pat on the back for being willing to admit you're not getting certain things right and that you want to start changing your behaviour. After all an ostrich is not a great role model!

Opinions

Everyone has their own opinions. This is normal. However what is unhelpful is when you want other people to buy into your opinions and agree with you. We are very diverse, we humans, and it is unlikely that, even with a close friend or relative, you will see eye to eye on all things. If you are very keen on others seeing your point of view and taking your "side" on issues then it may be a good idea to ask yourself where this desire springs from.

Not allowing others to have their opinions or countering everything they say with "Yes, but…" will probably make you unpopular. Most of us will have little quirks or beliefs that are different to others just because of the different family set ups we find ourselves having grown up in (see Frame of Reference) If you have grown up experiencing intolerance for your beliefs, ideas and opinions you may find it hard to be tolerant of others' points of view. You may have been forced to go along with the prevailing view in your family or to have risked been humiliated or ostracised. These fixed, rigid views and opinions that we adopt as a child, are our Critical Parent at work. He/She likes to be right and often thinks there is only one way to be. As an adult this can be very limiting making you appear extremely intolerant and possibly rather poorly informed. You need to examine what it is *you* really believe not what you were told or led to believe as a child. If you really believe something, all well and good; certainly stick to your guns but remember that someone else is entitled to stick to theirs.

An easy tolerance and interest in the views and opinions of others will make sure that you become well-informed about the myriad beliefs and opinions there are and a non-judgemental view will make sure you keep your friends. No one is asking you to forsake your views and values; just remember that no one else needs to hold them, after all they are part of what makes you uniquely you.

Optimism

There are lots of good reasons for being an optimist. Chief amongst these are the research findings that optimists tend to live longer than pessimists and that they are much less likely to succumb to depression. They are also, generally, much more fun to be around.

Martin Seligman has done a lot of research into the behaviour of both optimists and pessimists in his book *Learned Optimism* (Vintage 2006). Optimists tend to view anything adverse as temporary, specific and external whilst pessimists will view an adverse situation as permanent, pervasive and personal. These two styles produce very different outcomes. Pessimists tend to become despondent quickly, give up on difficult tasks when adversity strikes and are much more likely to suffer from depression. The more optimistic style means that people will persevere for much longer, try different approaches and if they don't succeed are likely to chalk it up to "a bad day at the office" rather than something about themselves or the situation in general.

If we can adopt the optimist's style then we are likely to live longer and be happier during our lives. Without being delusional about our chances of success it has been proved that you are much more likely to succeed with an optimistic, positive viewpoint.

Negativity encourages us to focus on what could go wrong and what you pay attention to is usually what you get. Whilst it is important to maintain a good sense of reality by checking out the pros and cons of any situation, a sunny outlook will more usually result in success.

If you are generally cheerful you are more likely to get help when you need it – who wants to help a grump? Humans thrive on success and so if we feel that someone is always expecting failure we are likely to shy away from them. We do not want to be regarded in the same light as someone who always expects the worst. So if you are naturally someone who errs on the side of pessimism, start challenging your negative thoughts. Are things "always" bad or just "sometimes"? Do you fail at everything you try or are some tasks more difficult for you than others (like everyone else on the planet!)? Try to be specific when recognising your faults and difficulties as this then leaves plenty of room for things you may succeed at. Check your negative comments, they give a one-sided view of who you are.

Similarly optimists need to remember that not everything is going to work out brilliantly and someone who is constantly looking on the bright side despite all evidence to the contrary can be very annoying and will seem to be out of touch with reality. A balanced view of any situation with a leaning towards the most optimistic outcome is probably a healthy way to view most situations. Remember hope springs eternal for the optimist and hope is what keeps us going.

Overreacting

If you overreact in situations several things are likely to happen. People may avoid telling you when anything has gone wrong. People may not take you seriously when you are worried about something – after all they know that you usually "cry wolf". Your viewpoint on a situation may be discounted as people feel that they cannot trust your judgement. So how do you know it's an overreaction? If you are the only person who responds in this way and many others don't. If you cannot let the situation drop but go on and on about it after it is over. If other people seem annoyed or alarmed by your response in more than one or two situations – in some situations you may be right and they are underreacting rather than you being the one to overreact.

When we overreact it is usually through fear, so it is important to work out why your fear response is out of step with other people's. Sometimes if we have had a particularly nasty experience with a certain situation in the past then we will have an amplified response to the danger that situation poses in the present. This is understandable and takes time to dampen down. However if you were bitten by a dog when aged seven it is not appropriate to leap back from every dog you encounter in your thirties and forties. It would be reasonable to be cautious, maybe enquiring if the dog is friendly before making overtures or passing it.

If you had very over anxious parents who overreacted to situations you may have learnt this behaviour off them. However in the present day it is no longer useful and can be highly restrictive to overreact. It may stop you from trying out new things and from enjoying your life. The same is true of over-controlling parents, in an attempt to control everything they may have kept all risks to a minimum and taught you to do the same. In this situation any risk, however small, can be deemed (inappropriately) to be a threat.

Life carries risk and we need to realise that we cannot plan or legislate for everything nor would it be sensible to do so. We do need to be able to assess what is reasonable and what is over the top. If you are not sure ask around and take the temperature of what most people do in similar situations, then chose a level of safety or response that leaves you comfortable enough to try new things and enjoy your life with a minimum of restrictions.

If you have had no empathy and little response when you were frightened as a child you may have learnt to turn up the drama in order to get the response you were seeking. This is understandable but as an adult it will have the opposite affect. Far from people rushing to comfort you or commiserate with you they will be annoyed at your over response and will probably ignore you, compounding your feelings of not being responded to. You need to learn to express your fears appropriately. Maybe explaining that you have always been alarmed by dogs, thunder, wasps or whatever is the problem and that you have a slight overreaction. This will alert people to your particular fear – most people have one or two – and will elicit a more sympathetic response. However an over response to every situation will not be made better by explanation and will need a change of style.

Try to assess the immediate threat to you or others. A house fire where you live is a serious, immediate threat, a bonfire in the next door garden is not. One demands an emergency response the other does not. Although I have used a pretty extreme example there are people who have called out the fire brigade to low-level bonfires. It is important that you note other people's reactions to situations or ask advice from people you trust and like. You will then build up a picture of what is appropriate for the situation you find yourself in. In this way you can learn to judge for yourself how you wish to respond without appearing to be alarmist or completely out of step with everyone else. Once you are secure that your response is appropriate you can sit back and relax knowing that you have the ability to cope with most situations and the judgement to ask for help when you need it.

Overweight

If you are happy being overweight, skip this section. You have every right to be any shape or size you choose. The operative word here is "choose". If you feel that your weight affects you negatively then you may want to think about tackling this issue. Some people are designed to be larger than others with a heavier build but if your size is curtailing your enjoyment of life or damaging your health then it probably needs to be tackled. The body is a wonderful tool that is designed to self-regulate and heal. We will occupy our body for life and it will pay dividends if we look after it well. If we feed ourselves too much or consume low quality fuel then we start to risk malfunction. If you put the wrong fuel into a car eventually it will function poorly or will occasionally grind to a halt. Losing weight is not rocket science; eat less, exercise more is the only proven formula. However, if you are a failed dieter it is not that simple.

There are hundreds of books and programmes designed to help you lose weight. If these were successful there would not be a billion dollar diet industry. Any-one can lose weight; it is keeping it off which is the hard part. If you have dieted several times and not managed to maintain your lower weight, food and eating are probably not the issue. How can I say that? Well if you are fat and despite claims that you want to be thinner, you remain fat, then food and eating are more than "food and eating" to you.

You will need to work out what "role" food plays for you and what "benefits" you have by remaining fat. Food can be a way of comforting ourselves, a form of solace, a way of avoiding facing up to situations or confronting what is really going on. We can address our anger, loneliness, depression or hurt by eating and thus avoid having to confront the real emotional issues. Being fat is a good way of insulating yourself against the world and protecting yourself from being hurt. It also means you can avoid the risk of trying new things – "I'll do that when I've lost weight." Why not live your life now; you will never get any of the time already spent back. Unless you feel secure, healthy and happy, being overweight it is not much fun.

So how do you find out what your particular issues are which prevent you staying slim? First keep a food diary. These are very revealing. You need to note EVERYTHING you eat, how much and what it is, when you eat it and (most importantly) how you are feeling before you eat the food and after you eat the food. This will help reveal what you use food for. Is it to stave off boredom? Is it to avoid loneliness? Do you reach for the biscuit barrel instead of saying how you are feeling? Once you have done this you will have some idea what your issues are. If these are deep seated, involving abuse or neglect, I suggest you seek professional help.

Once you have worked out what your issues are – boredom, anger, loneliness, an unwillingness to confront loved ones and what food represents for you – comfort, love, treats, then you can decide to do something different. Anything involving exercise is a good choice. Go for a walk, start swimming, take up a sport or dancing. Generally set about moving more and replacing eating with some other, pleasurable activity – knitting, reading, singing, dancing; anything that makes you feel good and you enjoy. Making a decision to only eat food you really want and of the best quality, is a good one.

Take time to decide what it is you really want to eat. Imagine eating whatever you have chosen. When you have found what you really want try this exercise: For every movement involved in the eating of whatever you have chosen you need to say "I am choosing to eat a biscuit (or whatever)." "I am going into the kitchen." "I am opening the biscuit tin." "I am choosing a chocolate biscuit." "I am closing the biscuit tin." "I am going into the sitting room." "I am sitting on the sofa." "I am taking a bite of the biscuit." "I am taking another bite of the biscuit." Etc. etc. This will bring into awareness exactly what you are "choosing" to do. It is very hard (and time consuming!) to eat seven biscuits in a row if you follow the above instructions!

Once you have started to lose weight (and you will if you follow the above diary-keeping exercise, think about what you really want to eat and follow the conscious eating exercise) then you will be in a position to address the real issues. Such as how you wish others to treat you or how you are going to meet more people. You may need to work out what being fat represents for you; is it safety? Is it anger? Is it withdrawal? And then find other ways to stay safe, be angry or withdraw, ones that don't involve eating. You could take a self-defence course to increase your safety levels. You could express your anger appropriately (see Anger) and you could legitimately withdraw when you need time to yourself. You will need to find what appeals and works for you.

Using weight as a protection from the world or emotions is effective but damaging in the long term. Many people use the excuse of being overweight so that they can avoid certain situations. Being overweight can stop you from doing so many things, it can interfere with the quality of your life, shorten your life and interfere with your relationships. If it bothers you, then do something about it. It may not be easy to tackle your weight issues but it will definitely be worthwhile.

Parent

This is in two parts; being someone else's parent (Parenting) and your internal Parent.

Parenting

Being someone else's parent is a tough, hard, job that comes without a manual and may just be one of the most important things you do; you are shaping the future of another human being. Parenting is all about providing a model, scaffold and guide for your child until they are able to function independently. You need to provide security and love on an I'm OK/You're OK basis (see "IMOK/You're OK"), remembering at all times that you are the adult in this relationship and that your child is learning to be a fully-functioning human. It is important that you recognise the different stages of development so that you are not expecting a two-year-old to be toilet trained or a four-year-old to be tactful or a fifteen-year-old to be confiding.

Your child can only develop at the pace the environment allows. So if your child feels unloved, unsafe or insecure or conversely is led to believe they can do no wrong, somewhere this will show in their accelerated or inhibited acquiring of certain social and emotional skills. For instance a child who is constantly shouted at may learn to keep a low profile and therefore have problems socialising. A child who is constantly told how wonderful they are may have difficulties adjusting to school where there will be others with more advance skills in certain areas and where other children will resent someone who thinks they are so fabulous. If there are no toys, books or stimulus – a pan and a wooden spoon will do – your child cannot test the limits of his surroundings, the objects he encounters or his own abilities. A fertile environment and an encouraging carer will help nurture your child.

Most children benefit from consistency. If you are always changing your mind or you do not follow through when you have said you will do something, your child will find the world confusing. Children need constants to learn from. Until we learn what is constant in our world we are unable to extrapolate information from situations and we cannot develop abstract thought (necessary for the development of the intellect) as our world will contain no concrete "givens". This applies as much to learning about gravity by chucking a toy out of a pram as to learning that when we hit other people we will be made to do a "time out". Just as the toy will always fall to the ground, so the parent, however tedious, needs to follow through with the promised "time out". In this way the world becomes safe and secure and consequently easier to navigate.

There is much research to show that an authoritative parenting style is the most effective for bringing up pleasant, balanced, socially-functioning children. A laissez-faire attitude produces insecure, shy and poorly-socially-equipped children and an authoritarian stance produces aggressive, erratic children with a tendency to bully others. (Baumrind, D (1971) *Current Patterns of Parental Authority, Developmental Psychology Monographs*, 1, pp 1-103).

Try to treat your children as you would like them to treat others and remember that even when they are at an age where their understanding has not developed, they see and hear everything and at some level they take it in. So exposure to inappropriately violent films when they are little may not appear to affect them but has been shown in the long run to affect their behaviour. According to the Institute of Paediatrics "Extensive research evidence indicates that media violence can contribute to aggressive behaviour and desensitisation to violence… watching violent shows is also linked with having less empathy towards others." Your child is designed to pick up information from the environment and whether or not they understand what they are seeing and hearing that is exactly what they will do.

Your job as a parent is to end up with a fully functioning, well-rounded member of society. This does not mean a child in your own image. They will have their own thoughts, ideas and dreams and in some instances will not appear to be like you in many ways. The best you can do for your children is make sure that they know you love them, let them develop into their own people and equip them to get on in the culture and society they are born into. This means showing them how to be tolerant and fair, interesting and interested and that nothing comes without effort on their part. It means putting in good boundaries, showing them that when you say "no" you mean "no" and listening to them and helping them develop all their skills and attributes. They are not your best friend, a mini version of you or someone on to whom you can project all the things you wanted for yourself.

Parenting is a tough, unpaid, relentless job but most people I know with children would say it is wonderful. Children are their own reward but they are a true example of "you reap what you sow". If you are lazy and neglectful in your parenting, it will show up in your child. However with some time and effort, fun and good planning you will end up like most of us – with a "good enough" parenting style and a "good enough" child or children; it doesn't get much better than that.

Your internal Parent

I have said something about this in the introduction. This is the part of our psyche where we have stored, wholly and unedited, the messages, beliefs and views of our carers and parents. As a child we wholeheartedly accept our parents' view of the world, indeed we need to do this in order to survive. We do not have the tools when little to judge how valid or useful these beliefs and views are; it is only later that we find some of the information we have accepted as "givens" does not sit well with who we have become.

The Parent is divided into two parts, the Nurturing Parent and the Critical Parent. These are the internal voices we hear when we are unsure, under stress or facing a dilemma. The Nurturing Parent will soothe and look after us, providing we have had an example of a caring, nurturing parent to internalise from and the Critical Parent will castigate, push and drive us, if that is the example we have received as we grew up. "I can do this." Or "I need to look after myself, I am not feeling well," would be examples of our Nurturing Parent messages. "Get on with it." "Stop mucking about and bite the bullet.", would be examples of our Critical Parent. If these messages are reasonable, useful and self-enhancing then they may function well in the present. However, most people will find that they have unhelpful Parent messages that are out of date and are unhelpful but they nevertheless allow them licence to bully, harry and chivvy.

We need to check that our beliefs and views are our own and not somebody else's outdated and unchallenged views. Do we really believe "that people get what they deserve if they work hard enough?" or have we some evidence that some people are caught in a poverty trap or are victims of poor education and lousy parenting? Do we really believe that if we castigate ourselves we will drive ourselves to succeed? Only you can decide what it is you believe but make sure that your views are exactly that – "yours". If your parents' beliefs and views are sitting in your psyche uninvited, then kick them out, after all they haven't paid any rent!

If you have chiding rather than encouraging internal voices, change the tape. No more "Get on with it." Replace this with "You can do it." Or "It is perfectly fine to ask for help when you need it." Some of the unhappiest people I have seen in therapy, have relentless, corrosive voices that are left over from an unhappy upbringing and outdated views, courtesy of an over-active Critical Parent. By contrast some of the most passive people I have seen who fail to achieve at all levels and don't get anything done have an overactive Nurturing Parent. An over cautious Nurturing Parent can be just as limiting as an overzealous Critical Parent. This is the voice that continually tells you to "Be careful!" or to "Watch out, if you read too much, who knows where it may lead?" or trots out sayings such as "Too clever by half." Too clever for what, exactly? These sayings, which may have been wholeheartedly internalised by the child you, who could not judge their validity, need to be examined and if they are found to be stifling and outdated, they need to be chucked.

Although you may never completely get rid of inhibiting and critical messages, you can replace them with much more enhancing and motivational ones instead such as "You are a good person and you deserve good things." However I leave you to come up with your own versions as the whole point of this is to replace other people's expectations, judgements and views with those of your own which you consider in keeping with who you are now. You are not a vulnerable child to be imposed upon but an adult with views, tastes and judgements of your own. Now is the time to step into your Adult shoes and set your own standards, chuck out outdated views and judgements and move forward into your future.

Pay it forward

This is a life-affirming altruistic concept. This is how it works: whenever you get the chance to do a good deed to another human you take it. There is no reward, no expectation of thanks, nothing. This is done purely in the belief that at some time in your life, or your children's you will need a similar act – a favour, a loan of money, a complete stranger to trust you and lend you your fare home, enough for a phone call, the loan of their laptop or mobile etc. It's about recognising that "no man is an island", we are all connected. If you are cynical this will not appeal to you, you have to be able to understand that some people may be lying or taking advantage of you but actually you just want to be the sort of person who can lend the money or help or even give it and trust that sometimes you will be doing a really good act for another person and sometimes you will be taken advantage of. You don't do this if you can't afford to, or it causes you big trouble, just when you can and when you want to. It's about becoming the person you would want to encounter should you or your family need help. Oh, and incidentally, altruism is really good for your health!

It is a wonderful concept – like putting a deposit in the bank for humanity.

Pedantic

Attention to detail is no bad thing but this has a time and a place. Your love of detail may put some people off particularly in social situations. You may miss the bigger picture and spoil someone else's enjoyment if you are unable to focus on anything other than the details. Sometimes people will get small details wrong whilst relating a story and this is the occasion when, if you are one of life's perfectionists, you need to turn a blind eye. Does it matter? If the answer you come up with is "Yes." Then ask yourself "To whom?" The most likely answer will be that it only matters to you. Most other people will be enjoying the story and letting the small, inconsequential details pass them by.

Some people also believe that if they know something is inaccurate they must alert others to the situation. Must they? Certainly if you have been overcharged in a restaurant. Definitely if part of a safety check is not completed before you abseil over a cliff. But in the middle of someone's story? Or if your friend relates the wrong flavour ice cream that you served at dinner? These things do not matter and picking up on them can be a source of irritation to others. If you can learn to tell the difference between alerting someone to the important (maybe life-saving) details and letting little inconsistencies in someone's story go, then you, and your friends, will probably be much happier.

Permission

Whose permission am I talking about? Well, fundamentally your own. As we grow up our parents and carers give us all sorts of forbiddens and permissions and sometimes, maybes. For instance our parents may believe that being lazy is a vice. "Lazy people don't deserve good things in life; only hardworking people do." If you carry this internal belief then you may not be able to give yourself "permission" to enjoy the good things in life if you perceive (by your parent's measure) that you are (or have been) lazy. This can come out in all sorts of ways. You may have fallen into a job with very little effort on your part and be really very good at it. However your internal perception, based on your parent's beliefs, will be that you are "lazy" as you had to make no special effort to get the job. You may then "sabotage" yourself when it comes to promotions, subliminally believing that you don't really deserve them.

Alternatively you may have done something foolish when you were young, like shoplifting. You know that this was not the right thing to do. You may have made redress to the shopkeeper, apologised and even been forgiven by your family and those involved but if you don't forgive yourself, then at some level you will be carrying this around and believe certain negative things about yourself. Maybe you believe you are not trustworthy and therefore behave in an untrustworthy manner. Maybe you believe that you are not worth treating well, if this is so, people will indeed treat you less well than they should. Many of our beliefs about our self, colour our expectations and behaviour and send out subliminal messages to others about what we expect for ourselves and what we think we deserve.

It is important to check your belief system to make sure you are not carrying a whole load of old forbidden and permission messages from your parents/carers. You need to make sure that it is your judgement and beliefs that you are living by. Sometimes it takes time to work out what you do and don't hold dear, what matters to you, what your ethical principles are. This, however, is more about holding yourself to account with some outdated, internal rules that simply no longer apply.

If you have some part of your life where you fail to achieve what you want, you may find it useful to examine your beliefs about what it is you want to achieve. Do you believe it is possible? Many people grow up with messages that contradict what they are trying to achieve. For instance you may want to be the CEO of a company but you may have grown up believing that only public school children are eligible for these positions. You will sabotage yourself in the interview process if, at some level you have bought into this belief that because you were educated by the state you are somehow not in the running.

If you do believe what you seek is possible, do you believe that you deserve it? Have you grown up with messages that you are not good enough, clever enough, pretty enough, modest enough, tough enough, charming enough (add your own version)? If these messages have been passed to you as you were growing up they may be very hard to shake off. If you don't really believe that you deserve something then the likelihood is that you won't get it. Don't forget; if you do what you've always done you'll get what you've always got.

Sometimes we need to examine our past beliefs and release ourselves from them. We need to give ourselves permission to be who we want to be not who our parents, carers and teachers told us we were. This does not mean that we won't have to take the right exams, work hard or sacrifice certain things to achieve want we want. It does mean, however, that we won't be buying into a set of outdated beliefs about ourselves that are not based on facts, just on other people's belief systems which may have also, in their turn, been distorted by past generations.

Perfectionism

There are certain people who are brought up in exacting circumstances who end up believing they must get everything right in order to survive. This may sound extreme but it is certainly the belief they will have held as children. They will have been given the message by their parents that they need to know everything (how is that possible as a child?) and they mustn't get anything wrong (how alarming is that?) or they will fall short. These are life's perfectionists and if they adhere to their childhood beliefs, they will have a tough, exhausting path ahead.

Perfectionists have been led to believe there is only one way of doing things and this is the right way. This can considerably narrow down your field of experiences and does not leave a lot of room for spontaneity. It is also very tiring as you need to be constantly vigilant to make sure you don't slip up and get anything wrong. Because these people work very hard to get everything "right" they are extremely sensitive to criticism whilst not recognising how judgemental and critical of others they are when they perceive another to have got something "wrong".

There are certainly times when being a perfectionist is a plus. If you are in charge of shutting down a nuclear reactor then it will be most important to get all the details exactly right. However differentiating between a life-threatening need for attention to detail and a desire to get things "right" is a useful and necessary social skill to learn. Your childhood experiences may not have a equipped you to tell the difference. It could be that when you are asked to "perform" you flip back into your Child state where it was important (and felt life threatening) to get things right. Letting go of this out-dated belief will be hard.

If you are one of life's perfectionists it will be tough trying to stop but the benefits in the long term are huge. The probability is that, many more people will like you; you will like yourself more; you will free up energy and time previously devoted to getting things right and checking on other people. You need to release yourself from the erroneous belief that there is only one way to do something. You will need to embrace other people's experience and expertise and be willing to concede that you are not always right and that other methods are just as good as yours and sometimes (oh, yes!) even better.

You should start slowly by going along with somebody else's plans even though you think your plans (which are different) would be the "right" way to proceed. Choose a situation which does not really matter if it goes wrong; for instance, choosing the quickest route to get somewhere when you have plenty of time to spare. If the route selected by the other person turns out to be longer, you will not have lost much, maybe a few minutes here or there. If the route chosen turns out to be quicker, you gain; you have learnt a quicker route. If they are the same you will have learnt a valuable lesson – there are many effective ways to achieve the same goal.

As you test different situations you will begin to see for yourself that rigid beliefs can be self-limiting. They also stop us learning new techniques and evolving and refining better ways of doing tasks. Once you let go of the belief that there is a right and wrong way to approach tasks you will become more approachable and your flexibility will grow. Also, if you have children, you will free them from the tyranny of having to perform in a certain way to gain the approval of their parent. In this way you will not be passing down the perfectionist trait to yet another generation. Being a perfectionist is a bind, it is tiring and tiresome, self-limiting and dull. If you can persuade yourself to give it up the benefits will be surprising, didactic and life enhancing. Go for it!

Personalities

Personalities is a topic for a whole book! However there are a few pointers which will help you to "manage" certain personalities in a more productive way, rather than to clash or totally fail to understand them. It is also useful if you can identify your own "favourite" as an awareness of your particular traits can help you from falling into familiar patterns of behaviour which may not be easy for others to appreciate. We all have particular behaviours which we developed as children in order to adapt to the family and situation we found ourselves in; these are comfortable and familiar but may not serve us well as adults.

There are several distinct personality types which I will briefly outline with recommendations on the best approach and the potential pit-falls. These are loosely based on the drivers from TA, although I have added a couple of my own. Most of us will be a mixture of several "personalities" but when challenged, irritated or excited, we will definitely favour one or two as our main line of defence. If you can remember when encountering these characteristics that they are for protection it can help you to be more sympathetic towards those personalities that irritate you the most. Interestingly the characteristics we most dislike are usually the ones we fear we have ourselves!

Passive-aggressive

This is the person who refuses to engage, often mocking what is going on or seemingly uninterested. When asked their opinion they will often say they "don't mind" or "do what you want". However the Passive aggressive will add to themselves, "You're not interested in what I think." Or "You do what you want, anyway." This is a person low on trust who has decided to opt out and stand on the side lines critically appraising the rest of us. This person may appear cynical and detached.

This person longs to belong but has trust issues and doesn't know how. They often annoy others by being ambivalent but critical about ventures or issues. They don't want to join in because what you are doing is "silly" or "pointless". The worst stance you can take is to be Parental and critical. The passive aggressive will withdraw, often curling their lip in contempt. The best approach is humour or action. Teasing works very well and engages their Child who is ultimately afraid they don't belong and so always maintains that they don't want to belong anyway.

Stoic

The stoic has been taught to endure. They will very often not admit that they have any needs or wants. These people can be described as the "strong, silent type". However they are neither. As children they will have been forced to bury their own needs and will have learnt early on that what they want or need is of very little interest. Stoics do not like to be teased or made fun of. They do not want to be the centre of attention, teased for their lack of joining in. They need to be quietly appreciated and their opinion sought on a one-to-one basis. If you do not agree with their opinion you need to be open with them as ignoring their views confirms to them that their needs are of no importance. These are people who have trouble engaging, and in particular engaging the child/pleasure part of themselves. They need to feel really safe before they can have fun. So be quiet, firm and open with a stoic and only tease them gently and in private.

Shy

By contrast those who are shy are usually very well aware of their feelings and needs but they have a problem trusting anyone enough to confide in them. As children these people have learnt to hide away as they have found the world too scary. They may have had a very loud, robust family or aggressive domineering parents; whatever the cause they can be easily overwhelmed by the too dominant, enthusiastic person.

Avoid being over-opinionated or over-dominant or you will get nothing from the shy person. Smiles and offers are the best way forward. "Can I get you a cup of tea, I'm making one anyway?" One-to-one conversation, rather than groups will be less alarming. Now and again the shy person may pop up with a resentful observation, feeling they have had no chance to be heard "I tried to say what I thought but you didn't listen." In reality it is very unlikely they have volunteered something. If they have they may have started to say something and then have claimed, "It doesn't really matter." Be gentle and friendly with a shy person, don't press your friendship upon them or they will disappear into their shell. Tempt them out and when they emerge don't frighten them with far-reaching plans but go step by step, asking their consent along the way and confirming you are headed in a mutually-desired direction.

Righteous

Righteous people are usually loud, opinionated and keen to organise others. They are hiding the fact that they have grown up being castigated or ridiculed for getting things wrong. As adults they try always to be right and loathe to be criticised. They find it very hard to say sorry even when they know they are wrong as they believe that this will be used against them to prove (as when they were children) that they are lacking or inferior. They are at their best when organising others and being praised for their efforts.

If you want them to change their mind don't challenge them directly but use stealth. "That's really interesting, how did you arrive at that conclusion?" rather than "That's not what I understood it to mean." Or "How do you know that?" These people desperately want to be liked and approved of and make good friends but can be their own worst enemy in sticking to their guns at all costs. If you can acknowledge that to be "wrong" to them seems dire and go the stealth route, whilst using praise you will get the best out of your righteous acquaintance and may gain a faithful friend for life.

Dramatic

These people love to be the centre of attention and cannot bear to be ignored. They are often flamboyantly or alternatively dressed and use hand gestures and exaggerated facial expressions. Any high-profile profession will attract these people. These are people who have been feted as children and never left the egocentric stage aged about five or six or alternatively they found the only way to be noticed was to be over the top. The worst thing you can do is ignore them or disapprove of them; they will merely up the ante becoming more and more exaggerated in their behaviour. If challenged they can quickly resort to hurt, indignation or outrage.

The best way to engage these dramatic people is to acknowledge and praise them, particularly when they are falling into line and to appeal to their sense of fairness. "It's lovely that we have your ideas but now I need to hear from the others." Get them to think and you have won the battle. They have traded on looks, emotions and behaviour and have never been encouraged to think. Use your logical Adult and engage their reasoning and the *Dramatic* will start thinking about alternative, more productive behaviour in order to win attention and praise. So praise them for good ideas or ask their opinion on a problem and they will drop their annoying, attention seeking behaviour and start to contribute in ways that others find less irritating. This will help create a positive circle of behaviour and feedback which will help them to flourish.

Pleasing

Here we have someone who has been valued for how they please others. As children they will have been encouraged to see their role as helping and enhancing others. "Make mummy a cup of tea, there's a dear." "Don't be selfish, you must think of others." They have been required to attend to the needs and wants of others at the expense of their own. This is the area they have been praised for. Do not be Parental with these people or they will clam up fearing that they will be labelled as selfish or greedy. Try and engage their sense of fun and get them to explore what they might enjoy. At some level there will be huge resentment at not being allowed to pursue their own agenda even though they may not even know what that agenda is.

It will be very hard to get this person to volunteer an opinion or say what they want as they will have been programmed to second guess what others want and fall in with their plans. Try to offer several alternatives and be non-judgemental about each; then a real choice can be made. However you may need to be patient as the *pleaser* will be looking for the answer you want and may have difficulty choosing if there is no obviously preferred choice. This is the person who when you say "Would you like tea or coffee, I'm making both?" will answer "I don't mind." Or "You choose." If you are a *righteous* personality you will find this infuriating. You need to reign in your own opinion and let someone who rarely has one find out what theirs is. You may choose this person as a friend because they fall in with your plans but ultimately this is not satisfying and there will be underlying resentment on their part. As with all good friendships, try to be even-handed and non-judgemental in who chooses what you do and the *pleaser* will become confident in their own choices and much more fun to be with.

Defensive/Aggressive

This person is expecting to be wrong or to be picked on. They may have had very exacting parents or been bullied by siblings or their peer group. As adults they can often appear hectoring or bullying themselves. Because these people have been frightened and undervalued as children they learn effective defensive behaviour from an early age and find it hard to dismantle even when they like someone and want to be friends. They are often described by others as "prickly". They can be very judgemental and Parental in their own outlook as a defence against the imagined Parental disapproval in others and their own fears of being judged and found wanting.

Obviously these are people who hate to be corrected and judged and have great difficulty admitting when they are wrong. Be liberal in your appreciation and praise of these people and slow to judge or correct. When they realise you like them, they may rebuff friendship at first as they cannot understand why anyone would like them. It is worth persevering through their carapace as they make good and loyal friends although they will usually remain "touchy". If you can remember they have been hurt and undervalued as children and in contrast be gentle and friendly, your patience will be rewarded. These people usually think extremely well but are poor in recognising their and others' emotions or acting appropriately on these. If you model good emotional competence and appropriate behaviour they will quickly pick this up and will gradually become more friendly and less defensive. One of the best approaches to use when they are particularly aggressive is to ask "Are you all right?" This shows concern but also alerts them to the inappropriateness of their behaviour and allows them to change tack without being humiliated. Incidentally this is a good approach with any aggressive individual as it "wrong foots" them without showing them up.

Laid back

Unlike the other personalities outlined, this is not an uncomfortable personality to be or to encounter. However, it is the personality least likely to capitalise on their abilities and talents and the least likely to achieve anything. This person may have had so little interest shown in them as a child that they were never able to find anything they, or their carers were passionate about. They will have had their physical needs catered for but probably had no interest taken in what they thought or liked or wanted to do. Alternatively they may have come from a family with a strong interest in something that they themselves were no good at or did not find compelling. These people have decided as children that nothing they like or are good at matters overly much and, therefore, they will sit on the sidelines "chilling".

Laid back personalities are hard to engage as it appears that nothing stimulates them. This is very rarely the case and perseverance is the key. As children they will have been quickly dismissed so as adults they are subconsciously testing your staying power. Unfortunately many people cannot be bothered to invest as much interest and energy into the laid-back persona. Often the best way to reach these personality types is through something kinaesthetic such as dancing, music, cooking, pottery, writing, building etc. These may be the very people who suddenly develop a passion later on in life. Once they find something they like and are good at, this personality will drop the "laid-back" façade and become engaged and animated. On the surface these people are unargumentative, relaxed and easy going but in reality their passions lie dormant under the surface and just need a little kick start. If you favour this personality be careful you don't "chill" others into total disinterest and isolate yourself by your lack of drive and passion.

Stubborn

This person will appear "closed" and uninterested in alternative ideas and theories. They stick to what they know and feel comfortable with, rarely venturing to try anything new. New is scary and threatening. As children they will either have had very reckless parents who did not take note of their child's anxieties and fears or they will have had particularly over-cautious parents, who were themselves afraid of anything new or untried and found the world a threatening place. This is a similar scenario to the *shy* persona but instead of withdrawing the *stubborn* person decides to stand their ground, whilst losing out on the possibility of trying anything new. The stubborn persona has engaged their Rebellious Child and feels bullied or threatened if forced to change their mind.

You will not be able to persuade a stubborn personality to do anything different but you may be able to show them, particularly if you use behaviour and emotions to win them round. Say you are planning a picnic and they don't want to come, they "hate" picnics. First reassure them that they don't have to come but remind them that you will miss them and would like them to come (emotion). Keep asking them to join in whilst extolling the fun of planning the day, choosing the food, what you will do when you get there (play volleyball, swim, eat ice-cream – anything that sounds fun).

Rebellious Child personalities are very suspicious of "fun" but desperately want to try fun activities. They have resisted for so long that they often don't know how to join in or capitulate; they are wedded to their stubborn stance. Compromise on arrangements; let them come on the picnic but let them "buy" their food from a "regular" café when you get there and tell them they can bring their book and just chill. If you tempt the stubborn person and show them by example what they are missing you will soon have an enthusiastic convert.

Nervous/Anxious

This person is similar to a pleasing personality in that they want to get it right for you but the pressure this creates for them often renders them helpless. Instead of conforming to a pleasing role this person triggers a "flight/fright" response. These children will have been put on the spot as children and will have had parents with strong "hurry up" drivers (see Hurry Up). They are often deep thinkers who have not been given enough time to reach decisions and may have been bullied or chivvied or compared to more decisive siblings. When they have made a decision this will often be considered "wrong" or "ridiculous". They may have had very domineering parents who overwhelmed them and regarded them as "wimps" or alternatively parents who were careless and neglectful leaving them feeling vulnerable and scared. Unlike the pleasers they are rarely resentful, just frightened.

At best these people will just dither over situations unable to choose for fear of getting their decision wrong; at worst, they will be literally unable to decide. The *Nervous/anxious* personality appears as exactly that: nervous, indecisive and dithering. Losing patience with this person will scare them further. Helping them to make a decision will support them. By pointing out their options and then suggesting by virtue of pros and cons, which option to choose this will help engage their Adult. They will then start to realise their ability to make decisions and will be able to exercise their "choices" more and more, particularly with continued support. If you are one of these personalities, remember to breathe – no, not a joke, these people often hold their breath whilst caught in indecision and holding breath tells the body that there is a scary situation afoot which in turn floods the body with adrenaline and cortisol and can make you feel sick and anxious – a vicious circle! It is important to realise that you are now an adult and that your parents no longer hold sway. Nothing bad will happen as you start to exercise your own choices. Sure, you will make mistakes now and again as all of us do but you will gain an ability to decide what it is you want and who you are.

Anarchistic

In total contrast to the *laid back* personality this person rejects most things that society and others stand for. This personality will usually have been the child of authoritarian "my way or the highway" parents or by contrast parents whose ideas run counter to the majority and who may have brought up their children in a commune or another closed society. The third alternative is a child who has been physically or mentally abused and has seen other adults or authority figures turn a blind eye. However this person has been brought up they will have decided that society has very little to offer them and that they want no part of it. However, to survive at some level and be in contact with others they will have had to conform in some way and they will resent this.

An *anarchist* is angry. They are either angry with the way they were forced to conform as children or they are angry at the way society colludes to make rules and regulations they want no part of. At the very worst level these are people who turn against society and end up shooting lots of people and then themselves or else they turn anger in on themselves and become alcoholics or drug addicts. However at a social level this is a person who wants to belong but has such a cynical view of the world that they prevent themselves. Anarchists make poor friends and need a lot of self-examination and warmth in order to want to join in and become part of the society they believe is corrupt and doesn't want them. These are people on the outside looking in with contempt and anger. I would suggest that until they have laid their own ghosts that *anarchists* are best avoided and that if you feel you may have this personality trait more often than is comfortable that you seek some sort of counselling. This person displays the IMNOK/YNOK (see OK) position to the hilt and can be very lonely. However if they want to relinquish this position and get help suddenly the world will seem a lot more promising and other people a lot more inviting; it may be a long haul but it will be worth it.

These "personality" definitions are not fixed and they are not who we are; they are expressions of our deepest insecurities that come to the fore when we are pressured. However if you find yourself behaving closely along the lines of one or more of the above personality definitions more often than you (or others) would like, I would suggest that something is out of balance and that you need to alleviate some stressors. It goes without saying that none of the above fall in the IMOK/YOK category and that they are all "flip back" positions either into Parent or Child. Until these characteristics are pointed out to us, these are merely unconscious defensive positions that we adopt when we feel threatened or challenged. However, an awareness of the personality positions that we like to occupy means that we can choose to behave differently and aim towards an IMOK/YOK position. When we recognise these personality traits in others we can adopt a less judgemental and more forgiving stance, recognising that we all have certain behaviours that are unattractive to others. Taking a proactive role in your response to your own personality traits and those of others is something that is likely to leave you feeling much less stressed and instead you will hopefully feel more happily balanced.

Personal Space

All humans have a defined area of personal space around them. Depending on our culture, experiences and upbringing this will be different for each of us. This is not a problem as long as we recognise this and act accordingly. You will definitely be unpopular if you stand too close to someone. You need to gauge their reaction to where you position yourself. If they back up, then you are too close. Don't move into the space they free up or you will begin to move around the room like a couple of dancers. Alternatively if someone is constantly moving closer to you or putting their hand on your arm they may wish you to come closer – lovely if you are on a date with someone you like. Not so great if they are someone who is intent on invading your space!

Try to drop kind hints if the person gets too close. "I get a little claustrophobic at these events" or "There isn't much space here is there?" can alert the other to your need for personal space. If you like the person and they continue to invade your space you may have to tell them straight that you need more space. This shouldn't arise if we all pay attention to the cues others are giving. Most of us have very similarly defined personal space dimensions and it becomes obvious if someone doesn't share this view. Watch for discomfort i.e. backing up or feeling their neck or hugging a drink or bag protectively in front of them; these are all clues you are too close. Be sensitive to others and as a last resort let the other person know, in the kindest way you can, if they are getting too close.

Pleasure

Humans are designed to be receptive to pleasure, both physical and cerebral. Pleasure enhances our lives in many ways. If at all possible, try to build some of each kind of pleasure into your day. Experiencing pleasure releases all sorts of hormones into our system which prevent us from getting depression and may even guard against certain illnesses. We know that eating certain pleasurable food, such as chocolate, can release serotonin in the brain and that sexual intercourse or stroking our pet can increase dopamine. Exercise can create endorphins which give us a lift. Listening to certain music can lower our blood pressure and heart rate as can a massage or stroking our pets. Certain smells can calm or arouse us; indeed aromatherapy is based on that principle.

Going back to the Balance chart, (see Balance) try to build some pleasure into your Me Time slot. It can be something simple like having strawberries for breakfast or listening to your favourite CD in the car. Remember you have five senses and they are all programmed to register pleasure so give the senses you usually overlook something to experience. If you're not big on touch then make some bread with your hands or have a bubble bath or book a massage. If you don't usually listen to music get some CDs out of the library or tune into a different radio station until you find something you enjoy. Visit a museum or art gallery and see some beautiful or unusual objects. However, you need to acknowledge the pleasure you are getting for it to have any positive affect. So up your awareness of the particular things in your life that enhance your day and bring you pleasure and try out some new activities to expand your repertoire.

Power

All relationships contain an element of power struggle. From the parent and child, where the struggle is between freedom and autonomy on the part of the child and safety and compliance required by the parent, to the power struggle between romantic partners where each will want to establish dominance in certain areas of the relationship. There are myriad relationships in between where the power ratio needs to be worked out in order for the relationship to continue and function.

Most people think that power runs along the lines of "I win, you lose" or "I lose, you win". A much healthier option all round is the "Win/win" situation. This is based on the recognition of each person's role in the relationship. It will be different dependent on all sorts of criteria but it is obvious that a working relationship where you are the employee is different to a relationship between you and your children, where you are the parent. That said, all power relationships need to recognise that if there is a "loser" the relationship will be damaged. So be alert to the other's need for control and autonomy and build that into any negotiations for a power relationship.

In our society we have some acknowledged power differences that most people are willing to accept in order to keep the status quo. Most of us will recognise the authority and power of a member of the police force to stop us and ask questions. Most of us recognise that the Inland Revenue can demand invoices, access to bank statements and personal information that we would be loathe to let others have. However these societal restraints and power balances are not often a problem as they are long established and accepted by most. It is the personal relationship power dichotomy that causes problems at home, at work and socially.

It is important to establish whether it is legitimate for you to want power, what you will gain if you get it and also what you will lose. Where you are someone's employee, it should be obvious that the main power base lies with the employer. However any good employer will know that in order to keep staff happy and productive they need to have some autonomy within their role, even if they are ultimately answerable to the employer. Any employee should recognise that if they make an attempt to gain too much power and start to show up their boss, the end result will probably be that they will lose their job. This is common sense in power relationships at work. When you work for someone, you work for someone. The real problems usually lie within our social relationships both romantic and platonic.

In social relationships it is important to establish some ground rules, this really goes back to personal boundaries (see Boundaries) where if you have good, solid, visible boundaries there should be very little jockeying for power. It will be obvious as the friendship develops what will and won't be tolerated by each person and what can be negotiated. Everyone will have their deal-breaker. As long as dialogue is open and each person expresses their needs and wants in a reasonable way, a status quo in the power relationship will be established with very little difficulty. This is also true of romantic relationships but often past experiences and entrenched beliefs lead us to vie for power, in both romantic and platonic relationships, even when it is not in our best interests and may disenfranchise the other party causing resentment and difficulties.

It is important that you realise that each person will want a certain amount of control over events. This is a normal, human requirement which some people will have to a greater degree than others. If you try to wrest total control from another party, be it toddler or teenager, colleague or lover, you will ultimately come unstuck. Listen to the other person and their needs and requirements will become apparent, hopefully they will be listening to you, too. When you lay out your requirements, try really listening to what you are asking of the other person. Is it reasonable? Does it encroach on their sense of self? Does it directly oppose something they hold important? Are some of your requirements left over from previous relationships and nothing to do with this one? These are important questions that you should be asking yourself. This will help ensure that your relationships requirements are reasonable and mainly Adult; some Parent and Child needs will inevitably sneak in there and you will need to keep a check on these.

If you constantly need reassurance because as a child you were neglected this is something you really need to address for yourself in order not to bring it into a new relationship and impose it on your friend or partner; this is a left over Child need. If you find yourself wanting to be right in every argument you have, then take a step back. What will this cost you? What is it like for the other party never to be allowed to be right? Where does this desire to be right come from? It is probably left over in your Parent and will have been ingested whole from your experiences as a child if your own parents were always wanting things to be just so. So check what your needs are and whether they are reasonable and with some self awareness you should be able to ascertain which are "here and now" needs and requirements such as "I want you to be honest." "It's important to me that you're on time; when you keep me waiting I feel discounted." If you can keep to the present and meet the other person half way, trying hard to see the other's point of view (yes, including your toddler and teenager!), your negotiations should go well and the power ratio in your relationships should remain balanced and harmonious.

Preparation

Preparation will save a lot of soul searching, disappointment and ultimately failure. "Failing to prepare is preparing to fail." This does not mean you cannot be spontaneous or cannot do things on the spur of the moment. What it does mean is that if it is important, will have a long-term effect or reflects on who you are as a person, then you should probably think about how you wish to come over and prepare and rehearse how you will be and what you will say.

If you are one of those people who has a strong "hurry up" driver then you may not realise that you can save time in the long run by preparing well. If you take time to think about whether you do or don't want to do something before you agree to it, you will save so much time that is needed to back track and extricate yourself later out of something you wish you weren't doing. If something is important to you it is worth taking your time and thinking about how you wish proceedings to go. Do you want to take the initiative, or do you want the other party to do this? What do you need to know and ask before you can proceed? How comfortable do you feel with how things are progressing? If you think about these questions in advance of an interview, meeting or social situation you will be ready to deal with them more effectively and get the outcome you want.

One of the key issues, of course, is to actually know what it is that you want. You can't prepare for something if you don't know what you wish the outcome to be. If you are not sure, take time to think what outcome will suit you best. With a job interview – Do you want this job? Would you like a different job, but in this firm? I once heard some friends of mine were forming a book club. I couldn't understand why they hadn't asked me. Everyone knew how much I liked to read, that I was a single parent who didn't get out much and would have enjoyed the social situation. I would really like to be in that I told my closest friend, without thinking about it. We've got optimal numbers, she told me but I'll think of you if someone drops out. Someone did and they asked me to join. Oh dear! I didn't like the books most people chose, I didn't want to read books that I didn't like and I certainly didn't want to discuss books that I hadn't chosen, read or liked! Oops. If I had just thought what a book club really meant I would have known it wasn't for me. It was difficult and embarrassing to extricate myself and I felt bad because my friend had gone out on a limb to get me invited. Had I prepared (just thought about it, in this instance) I would have got over the initial feeling of being "left out" and realised that perhaps my friends understood me better than I did. So a little bit of thought and preparation can go a long way in not only helping you decide what you want and then making sure that you get it but in making sure you don't go after things you really don't want or wouldn't suit you.

Procrastination

"Procrastination is the thief of time" – Edward Young. By the time you have wasted time not doing whatever it is you need to do, you probably could have done it. However, what is interesting is why you haven't settled down to just "get on with it". Now and again we avoid getting on with tasks because we just don't like them, or they're difficult or time consuming. However if these are regular chores that come up time and time again or part of our everyday job or existence, we are going to have to address what it is that is holding us up.

Procrastination can be a good indicator that you are on the wrong path. If time and time again you find yourself avoiding a task, you need to ask yourself what it is that you are really avoiding? Sometimes we avoid doing things that we are afraid we will get wrong or be no good at. This is a normal fear but one that needs addressing. What's the worst that could happen? Is it better to stay safe, never trying anything new, never extending your skills and experiences? Or is it better to give things a go, ask for help if you need it and see mistakes and failures as information towards a more successful, future attempt? However sometimes we just keep avoiding a task or confrontation because we are not really invested in it. This can be true of your job, a relationship or any situation where you find yourself circling the issue.

It is important to take note when you feel reluctant as sometimes the issue is choice. It can be a "flip back" to Child, where we were made to do things we didn't want to and we now have an inbuilt resistance to being made to do those things again. If you feel your resistance is irrational but persistent then I would suggest that you ask yourself "Does this make sense?" This is an Adult question that cuts through the Child prevarication and resistance and brings you into the here and now. Sometimes although we don't want to do something or we feel a resistance then checking out whether it is sensible and will benefit us, enables us to get on with the task.

For instance if, as a child, you were always made to take out the rubbish then you may have an inbuilt resistance to doing this now. However if you live alone and your rubbish bin is overflowing then in order to avoid a health hazard it will make sense to take your rubbish out regularly. However if you are in a house share it would be worth swapping a task you loathe (and often fail to do) for one you don't mind and can complete competently.

Procrastination breeds procrastination. Try not to indulge in it. Instead work out where your resistance comes from and address it in the most practical and Adult way you can. In this way, you will free up a lot of time to do more pleasurable activities and find yourself with a lot more energy to pursue things you truly enjoy.

Questions

How you ask a question will determine the answer you are likely to get. I would urge you to drop the question "Why?" in all but a very few situations. A "why" question puts the person being questioned in a position of having to account for themselves; of almost having been accused of something. After all, why are you asking "why?" if you don't think that there is something amiss in what they have done? If it's in the pursuit of enquiry then why will lead to a dead end. Why comes from a very Parental position and may often put the other person in the position of feeling like a child when asked "Why?" If they are a child it can make them feel resentful and disempowered. "Why?" will often close down a discussion and put the questioned on the defensive.

A much better approach which leads to an opening up of discussion is to ask "What happened?" Or "How do you think this happened?" This allows the other person to explain their thinking, beliefs and emotions behind an action they have chosen which may have seemed incomprehensible or just plain stupid to you. It will open up a whole different perspective and allow you to see the reasoning behind the event, or indeed, how an accident happened. When you are in an authoritative position as either an employer or a parent, then this also allows you to explore alternatives. Once you have established what or how something happened then you can go on to ask. "How do you think you would proceed now, knowing what you do?" "Or, what do you think you could have done differently." Or even "Was this the result you were expecting?"

Quite often people get themselves into trouble by following a line of behaviour which doesn't make sense. By asking the less accusative question of how or what, instead of why it allows them to see for themselves the mistakes, errors or assumptions they have made and to adjust next time. If you simply ask why, you miss this opportunity for learning and also close down the lines of communication, possibly causing the other person to feel under attack and to view you as the enemy. As a parent, employer or teacher this change in questioning is absolutely invaluable; please try it and you will reap the rewards from the moment you change your questioning style.

Quirks

We all possess myriad differences and individual quirks which make us the unique people we are. A society that tolerates "difference" well, gains from the variation it embraces. Nevertheless if you can help your child to "fit in" whilst growing up they will have a much easier path. I don't mean by this that you seek to change your child's character but in some instances to moderate their behaviour. Part of parenting is to help your child fit into the society into which they are born and to help them recognise other people's needs and rights as well as their own.

Children on the autistic/aspergers spectrum will need help to learn specifics for communication such as eye contact and not holding forth for too long on subjects that may only interest them. However all children need to learn this skill to some extent, some just find it easier than others. If you help your child to empathise with others and to recognise that they have similar needs and feelings, then social behaviours will naturally emerge. If you allow your offspring to follow their own agenda to the exclusion of others' feelings and desires they may find themselves unpopular and largely ignored by their peer group.

It is also important to encourage your children to recognise that we are all different and that little quirks in their friends' behaviour or appearance are part of who they are not differences to be pounced on or ridiculed. Children learn their attitudes largely from the adults around them so try to be accepting yourself of others' individual characteristics whilst developing empathy and good social awareness; your child will then follow suit. If we all adopt an embracing attitude towards difference, our society will be more balanced, diverse and less judgmental; something which will benefit us all.

Rabbit Thoughts

These thoughts are so named because they multiply as fast as rabbits do! These are the sort of thoughts that begin, usually when you are dropping off to sleep, "what if?" Once you have begun along this track it is very hard to get off and the thoughts will go round and round in your head, multiplying and increasing your anxiety. It goes without saying (although I am going to say it!) that these are completely pointless and futile. However, it is a very rare human being that never suffers from rabbit thoughts.

Once you recognise you are mentally "rabbiting" you need to stop. Change tack and do something else, even something as mundane as repeating your times tables can help. Weaning yourself off rabbit thoughts is about breaking the habit. By changing tack in the middle of "what if" thoughts you break the neural pathways that have got used to following a particular pattern. The more you break the habit the less likely you are to suffer from rabbit thoughts.

The only person that suffers is you and they are a tremendous waste of time. After all you are not able to respond to something until it has happened so why imagine it might. If you have done something or agreed to something that causes rabbit thoughts to go into overdrive, then you need to examine that stage of the process – the decision. Either you shouldn't have agreed to something as it really is a bad idea or on balance, it was fine you agreed to it in which case relax. That is really the stark choice – once you have decided on a course of action then you must believe it is the right one until it is proved otherwise, otherwise change your mind. Worrying about things that haven't happened is exhausting, time consuming and futile; it will also infuriate those closest to you. Try and put down your rabbit thoughts as humanely as possible and stop torturing yourself with what ifs! As I say to my children when they ask me "What if such and such happens?" – "Then it does." And when it does, and only then, is when I'll deal with it.

Racket Feelings

These are identified by Stewart and Joines in their book *TA Today*. They are up there with rabbit thoughts as a completely futile exercise and waste of time; But also up there as a completely human response to certain situations. Rackety feelings are manufactured by us and are recognisable, as when we express rackety feelings they leave a situation unfinished. Real feelings by contrast are in the here and now and are an entirely appropriate way of solving an incident which helps finish a situation for us. I will do my best to précis Stewart and Joines excellent chapter on racket feelings in order that you can recognise them for yourself and avoid the futility of indulging in them.

Authentic feelings of anger are for solving a situation in the present. Someone is talking loudly behind me in the cinema, I ask them to whisper. They don't and I get angry, turning round and snapping "You are completely ruining the film for me, please be quite or I will get the manager." They fall silent. My anger has solved the problem, been effectively and appropriately expressed and dissipated once the situation is resolved. An inauthentic expression of feeling would be to get angry and then to mutter to my companion through most of the film how it was being ruined for me by the talker. I might even carry on being angry about the situation and tell several people about it later. This is rackety anger; it solves no problem and allows me to chunter on complainingly for a long while, stoking and sustaining my "anger", whilst not solving the problem and not being in the here and now.

As humans we tend to do this a lot. We mutter about long

queues whilst not asking that another server open a check out. We complain about our child's teacher whilst not going in to see her and talk over the problem. We complain about the dustmen strewing litter in the street on dustbin day but we don't contact the council or speak to the men themselves. This is rackety behaviour and its only use is to sure up our feelings of righteousness. It doesn't solve any problems and allows us to spend an awful lot of time and energy out of the present.

People racket in order to receive positive recognition from others. You want people to agree how awful the queue is or what a terrible teacher year five has and then you can have your view of the world confirmed. However the downside is that nothing will get resolved and the authentic feelings you have about the situation become buried and go unrecognised. This is how we get into the habit of repeating rackety behaviour as we are trying to resolve the real underlying feelings; we just do it in a familiar way that is always going to be ineffective.

So, first recognise that if your feelings do not solve a here and now problem they are rackety; then tackle the racket. Rackets, according to Stewart and Joines are built on three elements: Beliefs and feelings, Reinforcing memories and Rackety displays which include internal experiences, observable behaviours and fantasies. In order to stop manufacturing inauthentic feelings and the behaviours that go with them we need to stop at any one of the three above points. So you can start to challenge your beliefs and feelings; for instance, the man in the cinema isn't just a yobbo designed to ruin your evening, he is another human being that doesn't realise how loud he is being. This will alter your view of how you can tackle the situation in the here and now.

Alternatively you could tackle reinforcing memories that you have, these are a collection of memories which reinforce your belief about situations and allow you to express inauthentic feelings. For instance you could believe that most people don't like you. You will have memories that confirm this, even though those memories may be able to be interpreted a different way. You will look for negative reinforcing evidence that people don't like you and ignore any evidence or "forget" evidence that proves that they do. You need to challenge this so that you do not express rackety feelings of "anger" about how everyone always ignores you or how people never listen to you. Start looking for evidence that people do like you or even (more realistically) that they don't have any strong feelings one way or the other.

Rackety displays are those which are designed to get the desired response from others but usually cover a genuine feeling which is never explored or discharged. For instance I might get angry whenever I am challenged. I have decided that whenever I feel threatened or defensive I will get angry, instead of recognising that I feel fearful and put on the spot. In this way I never have to deal with my feelings of fear and rejection (left over from childhood) I just bluster and get angry when challenged and frighten people away from me – ultimately confirming my belief that I will be rejected! Brilliantly flawed, Child logic which keeps me from dealing with situations in the present and keeps me stoked up against perceived slights and hurts. I might have internal experiences which go with this such as feeling sick or getting a headache when I find myself in conflict situations. And finally I may fantasise about ultimately being rejected even though this is not a reality. I may fantasise that I will get so angry that I will stab someone and be locked away for ever (the ultimate societal rejection).

It is therefore important to recognise inauthentic rackety feelings and then challenge them in any of the ways outlined above. You will get better and better at not indulging in fruitless displays of fake emotion and in turn will be able to express real emotions and deal with them as they occur, in an appropriate manner. One of the most helpful techniques I have found is in practising Mindful Meditation, which is all about recognising the here and now and staying in it, however difficult this first appears to be. There are many tapes and classes in Mindful Meditation and I suggest that if you are a particular fan of the rackety feelings described here that 1) You read Stewart and Joines brilliant chapters on Rackets and Stamps and the

Racket System in *TA Today* and that 2) you take up Mindful Meditation. In this way you will gain more energy, start to work through your real feelings and needs and begin to form more meaningful relationships built on who you really are and what you really want.

Radiators/Drains

People are usually a mixture of behaviours but their interaction style usually falls into either radiator or drain. A radiator is someone who gives off warmth and when you have spent time with them you often feel energised and renewed. A drain, by contrast, is someone who exhausts you, wants your energy and ideas and will often leave you feeling slightly depressed without really knowing why. Of course anyone of us can have a "drain" day when we need support and ideas from others and are not capable of generating help and progress for ourselves. Indeed if you are having a bad patch you may be exhibiting more "drain behaviour" than usual and need extra support. But if someone you know constantly behaves like a drain you need to avoid them or explain that you need them to exhibit some "radiator" behaviour in order to balance up their demands with a more generous style. This does not include people with depression who are not capable of exhibiting "radiator" traits until they are on their way to recovery. Indeed someone exhibiting constant drain behaviour may be depressed and in need of help or a referral to someone who can help.

However, someone who is well and has become stuck in this behaviour pattern is not a healthy person to keep company with. You will know who these people are as they often leave you feeling tired and fed up and in some cases you dread their phone calls or feel reluctant to see them – there's a good reason for this. They are people who use others' energy, ideas and warmth but fail to generate these themselves. By contrast radiators are the friends we seek out, look forward to seeing and whose company we enjoy. They are often energetic and engaged and have interests and goals of their own. They boost others and themselves. Make sure that the majority of your contact is with radiators and not drains and try to ensure that you limit your own drain behaviour for times of need.

Relationships

Relationships by their very nature can be tricky and they can also be wonderful. I am referring here to relationships between two or more adults in order to form friendships or partnerships, not parent/child or sibling or family relationships. Relationships begin as a complex set of negotiations as the parties involved start to reveal their needs, boundaries, frames of reference and ultimately, their deal breakers. When we first meet someone we are attracted to, we will put out a variety of feelers to gauge the response we get and whether it fits in with our view of how a relationship "should" be.

Good relationships don't just "happen" they need willing participants who are prepared to be considerate of each other and give the relationship time and energy. If there is nothing that you enjoy doing together you are going to struggle, whether you are seeking a friend or a lover. I would suggest that you feel your way slowly into a relationship being very clear about your expectations and also about what you are prepared to give and concede on. If you are from very different backgrounds (see Frame of Reference) you may initially be attracted by each other's differences but these will need careful and kind negotiation between you both in order to find the middle ground where you both feel heard and responded to.

In his book *Making Marriage Work* John Gottman suggests there are four behaviours which will destroy a relationship and make it unsustainable. I believe these are very valid and that if you are aware of these at the beginning of a relationship you can "nip them in the bud" should they start to creep in. They are contempt, criticism, stonewalling and defence. I would add a fifth, which I consider absolutely essential to keep out of a relationship as much as possible, and that is dishonesty or deceit.

If you are contemptuous of your partner or friend then essentially you are not "giving them the benefit of the doubt" which is vital to all good relationships. If you love or care for someone you must, by that very definition, believe that they have the best of intentions until there is evidence of otherwise. Criticism, I take to mean, unconstructive and designed to hurt, not flagging up when you feel the other person has made a mistake or let you down, which I consider perfectly valid when done in a measured and kindly fashion with a desire for change and not as a point-scoring exercise. Stonewalling is an absolute killer and at the risk of sounding sexist, is in my opinion a largely male behaviour. It is the shutdown of communication and the refusal to discuss an issue at any level; how can a relationship progress if the hard things cannot be discussed? Discourage your partner from adopting this behaviour using emotional language to get through. "I feel shut out and hurt when you won't discuss (whatever) with me." "Is there a better time/place/way to talk about this with you?" Do not accept stonewalling or you are on the slippery slope to collecting a herd of "elephants in the room". Defence is where you or your partner adopts a defensive position. This by its very description means that you are armed and ready to do battle in some way. Why? What are you defending yourself from? This is really the issue; why you feel you need to defend yourself from your partner? This is about trust and a willingness to appear vulnerable in front of the other. Obviously this develops with time over the relationship but if it isn't there, then you are more than likely in trouble. With no trust there can be no vulnerability and with no vulnerability there can be no intimacy; if you cannot be intimate with your partner, do you really know each other and have you any sort of partnership at all?

Although you may be looking at the bigger picture and "in love" or captivated by a new friend, attention to detail will stand you in good stead. Small things matter in relationships as well as the large controversial issues. It matters who is doing the cooking or driving, who will travel to whose accommodation and who pays for what. These things need talking about as the relationship progresses and I would suggest that dishonesty at any stage of a relationship will lay waste to a bright future. If you build your relationship on falsehoods or misunderstandings somewhere along the line you will come unstuck. This includes misrepresenting yourself and who and how you are.

If you feel that the other person doesn't like aspects of you, you need to talk about this. Maybe you don't like those characteristics you possess either and if this is the case, any criticism will doubly hurt, having a seed of underlying truth. You need to be honest "Yes, I know I am overly critical, I'm working on it and if you could help me be more aware I'd really appreciate that." Also if the other person does not like traits in you that you do, you need to be firm but willing to compromise. "Actually I quite like my directness, I think it clears the air; how would you like me to tell you when I am unhappy with something?" If you find that you are constantly having to adapt to someone else's expectations, you will eventually find that either, you have merged to become two halves of a whole or that you deeply resent the changes that you have been asked to make. Neither of these situations is sustainable in a healthy Adult to Adult relationship.

The first example, where you merge with another, is the example of a symbiotic or co-dependent relationship, which is not healthy for either participant. There are, of course exceptions. If I am ill with a fever and disorientated and my partner comes and smooth's the covers of my bed and tells me "Don't worry, the sickness will pass, I'll be right here." I will feel taken care of and my inner Child will be looked after by their Adult and Parent, whilst mine are decommissioned by my illness. However if they are constantly "Adulting" or "Parenting" me in other situations where I am perfectly capable, they are discounting (see Discounting) my ability to look after myself and this is inappropriate symbiosis; even if I may be enjoying being taken care of.

The reason symbiosis is not usually healthy between two adults is because of the feeling of one or both of the parties that if the other moves out of the symbiotic relationship the remaining partner will be unable to survive. It is this "dependence" and co-dependence which should be avoided. Each person in a relationship needs to be an entity in their own right as well as a voluntary part of a pairing. The relationship, in order to be healthy, must not be formed out of need and fear with an obvious power imbalance as these kind of relationships cannot be sustained without a huge cost to one or both of the people involved. This really describes the second kind of relationship where you find yourself being asked to change and adapt to suit the other.

It is possible to "change" within a relationship in order to suit each other without any damage occurring to either person but you need to be careful. Negotiations over behaviour and appropriate ways of being are part and parcel of a relationship but being asked to change when you don't want to or you like how you are, is detrimental to a relationship unless you are both changing, through awareness, parts of yourselves that you think could do with improvement. In some relationships it is the good example of one of the parties which encourages the other to become their better self; because they want to, not because they feel they have to in order to get the other person to stay with them. That is the fundamental difference. So be careful about "adapting" to another adult's requirements as this is what we tend to do when we are children and it is not appropriate or sustainable in a long-term adult relationship.

So go slowly, with care and concern for both yourself and your partner. Relationships are not always easy but with attention to detail and open loving negotiations you can form a wonderful union. However this is not something you do once, this is an ongoing situation which requires nurturing and attention, good will and staying power. If you are willing to put in the hard work, you will certainly reap the rewards which will then go on to enhance your life in all sorts of other ways. Good relationships improve health and well-being, confidence and tolerance to stress, whilst poor relationships have the reverse effect: Tend your relationship well and you and it will flourish.

Resentment

Resentment is a corrosive behaviour. Someone said it is like swallowing poison and waiting for the other person to die. In other words the only person damaged by resentment is the person harbouring it. If you have the choice between feeling resentment or guilt, always choose guilt. As humans we live with guilty feelings and they are not particularly damaging to us. Resentment, in contrast, can make us ill. In his wonderful book, *When the body says No* Gabor Mate talks about behaviours that lead to serious illness and resentment is one of them. So say no to things that you think you will resent being committed to, instead live with the guilt, which is part of the human condition rather than toxic to it.

Responsibility

Taking responsibility for your actions and words and the impact that they have on others is a fundamental part of being an adult. It is absolutely vital that you realise the connection between actions and consequences and that you take responsibility for yours. Hopefully as a child you have been taught that your behaviour impacts on others and that you need to be aware of this and take responsibility for the outcomes. However, some people are not taught this, as evidenced by the people who allow their children to disrupt whole carriage trains or entire cinemas with no rebuke or consequence. So if you are under any illusion that you are not responsible for what you do or say and the impact this has on others, don't be – you are.

This means you need to cultivate an awareness of how others are, too. If someone is particularly shy or introverted, or in contrast, excitable and extrovert, you will need to temper your response accordingly. If you don't, you need to face the fact that there will be consequences and that these are partly your responsibility. Only partly your responsibility, however, because the other person in this equation is responsible for their own behaviour and responses, too. If all adults were to take responsibility for their own behaviour and reactions then there would be a sharp learning curve in the resulting consequences and a correlating change in behaviour. However there is not such a level of awareness in the wider world.

Having an awareness of yourself, however, will greatly improve your communication skills and mean that you can gauge what to expect back when you behave in certain ways. It also means that you can be more in control of a situation. Accepting responsibility for what you do or say will also make you much more careful in your actions and much more likely to get the response that you want. If you are tempering your behaviour to the situation you find yourself in and also recognising that how negotiations develop is, in part, your responsibility, then, you are much more likely to handle even the trickiest people and situations well. So being personally responsible for all that you do or say will greatly improve your communication skills and the knock on effect from that can be immense.

Rumination

Rumination is all very well but only if there is a purpose to it. Purposeful rumination, where you go over events in your head, working out what went well and what didn't, acknowledging what you could change next time you are in the same situation, is productive. Rumination which engages your Critical Parent (that nagging, critical voice in your head) is pointless and engenders guilt, which is also pointless unless it spurs you into changing things for the better.

Going over and over an event that has already passed and blaming yourself for the outcome is a pointless, exhausting, self-punishing exercise. Calling yourself stupid, or an idiot will undermine you and have consequences for your next encounter where similar issues arise. A much better idea is to engage your Adult thoughts and analyse what went wrong (if it did) how you could have avoided what happened (and maybe you couldn't). Then review the situation and recognise what you would like to change about your responses and behaviour. Remember you cannot change other people's behaviour but taking responsibility for your own may cause them to respond differently to you. Good questions to ask yourself are "What happened?" "How can I get a different and preferable outcome next time?"

If you are someone who has a large internal Critical Parent then you will need to be kind to yourself and start to use phrases such as "I did my best but I forgot to ask the right questions." Or "Given my level of experience I did OK." Doing OK is absolutely fine. We cannot always be expected to perform to our very best, particularly in unfamiliar or scary situations. Try to talk to yourself as if you were a child of six or seven or as if you were talking to your best friend. Would you call them an idiot and go on and on about past mistakes – unlikely; so don't do this to yourself. Instead, be kind to yourself, ask for help if you need it and recognise that that old, scolding voice is unproductive and detrimental to success. With time and effort you can change an internal Critical Parent into a supportive Nurturing Parent which will support and sustain you and eliminate pointless, undermining, guilt trips.

Sadness

Sadness is one of the four human emotions. The others being happiness, fear and anger. Sadness is a valid and useful emotion which alerts us to how we need to treat ourselves and also how we want to be treated by others. I am not talking about long term sadness or as Lewis Wolpert calls depression "malignant sadness" and certainly not talking about grief. Here I am talking about the feeling of sadness that can be experienced when someone we like or love is unkind to us or we see or experience something poignant or we experience some loss or hurt. These feelings will not last weeks but also they will not be transient. It may feel like a temporary shadow has passed across your feelings.

Some people have real difficulty identifying this emotion as we live in a culture which values "positive" emotions above many of the more negative ones. This is a mistake because as humans we need the full range of our emotions to be in working order in order to be able to respond appropriately to our own needs and those of others. As sadness is not always acceptable in our culture and many people are uncomfortable witnessing another's sadness, it can often be covered up by anger.

Often when I feel angry at something someone has said to me, when I check the underlying emotion it will be sadness or fear. You can check your true feelings by asking yourself what made you feel angry. Your answers will reveal your true feelings. "I felt angry because he was rude about my family." Then ask yourself "What does it mean to me when people are rude about my family?" Maybe it means you feel attacked, or that you have parented badly – this could cause feelings of fear that you are inadequate or sadness that you haven't done a good job and that your friend thinks badly of you. I don't know what you will come up with but if you are interested in your authentic feelings in order that you can respond appropriately to them, then you can uncover what you feel by keeping asking the same question "What does it mean when (fill in whatever they said or did)?"

Once you have identified sadness then you need to be able to respond appropriately to this emotion in yourself and others. First, allow yourself to be sad. You don't have to be "up" or "positive" all the time. If you feel sad explore the feelings and find out what you need. You may need to talk to a friend, have time to yourself or to work through your feelings and accept them. When you respond to others who are feeling sad you may just need to be with them, not rejecting them whilst they feel sad. It is okay to ask them "What do you need right now?" Sometimes the experience of having someone sit with you whilst you experience previously unacceptable feelings can be very healing.

Whatever your own experience of sadness, remember it is part of being human and allows us to recognise and value the contrast between feeling happy and feeling sad. We need these contrasts in order to recognise our own vulnerabilities and those of others and also in order to appreciate our gains and losses. The ability to recognise and respond to your own and others' emotions will stand you in good stead. It will mean you are more likely to understand others and that they are more likely to understand you. Try to embrace all the emotions you have at your disposal, even the ones that may seem "weak" or "shameful", after all these are what allow you to experience life at its fullest and ultimately they are part of what make you human.

Secrets

Obviously if someone tells you something in confidence it is not a good idea to pass it on. You will be betraying their trust. Similarly if you are organising a surprise secret lunch or birthday treat for someone that is obviously a good sort of a secret. However I am not generally in favour of keeping secrets or having secrets for the following reasons. Generally, I would want to know, if something is secret, why is it? Is it too shameful to reveal? Does it say something about us that we don't want most people to know? Are you sneaking around behind someone else's back? Secrets resemble icebergs; there is a lot about them that lies hidden under the water, unidentified and potentially dangerous.

It is important if you are part of a secret or supporting someone else's secret you know why. Also you should realise what you are portraying about yourself if you are keeping a secret. Are you colluding with a deceitful act because you want to support a friend? Does that make you deceitful, too? Are you protecting someone and if so, are you sure that this is the right course of action and you are the one to be able to help them the most? If keeping a secret causes you to feel uncomfortable then you have your answer. You are not obliged to collude with someone else if they are choosing to construct a secret, however friendly you are with them, if by collaborating you are sacrificing something of your own integrity. Unless, of course, you think the friendship is more valuable than your own ethics and morals. If this is the case I would question your friendship which essentially requires you to distort who you really are.

If this all seems a bit heavy, then it is. Secrets in my opinion, generally lead to some sort of deception, misunderstandings (purely because there are hidden aspects to a situation) and you are rarely party to the agenda the perpetrator of the secret is running. Sometimes there are very good reasons for temporarily keeping something under wraps, however, make sure you find out what these reasons are before you become party to something which may taint others' view of you and which may require you to distort your values and beliefs.

Sensitivity

If you are very sensitive and find yourself easily hurt by others then you are probably not giving off enough signals about your boundaries. If this is the case others will not be aware that they have upset you or that anything is wrong. However, if you find yourself at odds with others who genuinely cannot understand what you are objecting to, then it may be, due to your upbringing or past experiences, that you are unusually sensitive. This is no way means that others have a right to upset you but it does mean that if you want to get on well with a majority of people, rather than a minority you may have to adjust your sensitivity meter. This is not easily done.

You will need to raise your awareness of what is considered an acceptable "norm" with regard to things you find difficult. In most circumstances you will be able to identify if you are being overly sensitive and would do better if you didn't respond to certain provocations. However, in other instances there may be no "acceptable" norm for you. Maybe you never want to hear jokes with sexual innuendo – this is your right and it is not okay for others to force their own idea of what is amusing onto you. However if you work somewhere where these behaviours are considered the "norm" then you may want to think about whether you are in the right job, or whether, indeed, they are overstepping the mark and their behaviour is not acceptable anywhere. This is up to you. A good way of combating differences in what is and isn't acceptable, is to use humour: If people are constantly telling inappropriate jokes you could try saying "You know what? I think you need to tell those jokes in the toilet; they're pretty grubby." Or "Save it for the playground, please."

Alternatively you may find yourself particularly sensitive to criticism or personal remarks. It is important to remind yourself that it is only one person's opinion or judgement and that if you ask for details when being criticised you open up the dialogue and can often find out what it is that is worrying or annoying others. For instance if someone thinks your work isn't good enough, what does that mean? Try asking "Could I have some specifics, after all I've been in the job five/six/seven years, I can't be doing it all wrong!" or ask "What do you mean; what would you like me to concentrate on specifically?" By asking for details you can often pinpoint the small thing that may be causing a problem and then you can choose to alter it or not depending on what you think.

A word here, too, about being kind and more sensitive to others who are sensitive; If you know someone is particularly sensitive or doesn't like a particular form of banter, then why do it? If you continue, you are being crass and insensitive and saying to the other person that you don't really care what their feelings are or that you think their feelings are invalid. The same is true if you need to correct someone or point out a fault. Be kind. Think how you would like to be told similar information. If the person is particularly sensitive, pave the way and let them know what's coming. "I need to talk to you about your management style." Or "I need to pass on some comments from your team, not all of them good, I'm afraid." This is not pussyfooting around, it is acknowledging the different sensitivity levels that we all have and taking them into account in order to get the other person to understand. If you pave the way the other person will be able to hear what you say and will not be able to ignore it. If you just launch in with a complaint the other person can become dismissive, not hear what the complaint is, and chalk up the conversation to you "just having a go." So with a little subtlety, you can get someone sensitive to really listen and not take offence: probably worth it.

Sex

Sex is how we express intimacy through action. It is also a form of play and bonding which can benefit most relationships. However not everyone has been brought up to view sex as a pleasurable and enjoyable activity when taking place between two (or sometimes more) consenting adults. An unanxious, non-judgemental approach will benefit most sexual relationships, as will the realisation that this intimate act should be full of fun and joy. If this is not the case and you have serious reservations about whether sex is to be enjoyed or you have some physical bar to taking part, then you should probably seek some professional advice; there is a lot out there so start with a sympathetic doctor.

There is a myth that we should all be "good" at sexual relations which is odd since it is learned, as other sports are learned, through participation and practice. Read, learn, practice, experiment and enjoy and remember to be kind to each other, listen to each other and respond accordingly to each other sexual needs. The only things off limits are the things that you as a couple have decided are not for you but, equally, don't dismiss new ideas out of hand; after all you have no idea what you might be missing. Like learning other sports, sex is very different depending who you are playing with. Each partner will be completely different and if you can bring an open mind, expectation of enjoyment and exploration and non-judgemental approach to the bedroom you should be half-way to achieving fun and pleasure.

Although published in the 1970s *The Joy of Sex* is as good a place to start as any. It is a celebratory, step-by-step manual on "how to" make love and although the illustrations are pretty outdated the text is as valid today as it's even been. It is a completely Adult book, non-salacious but detailed in explanation of techniques to enhance your own and your partner's sexual pleasure. If the thought of using a manual for sexual information is off-putting try to remember that it is a learnt pleasure and in order to learn we need good information. Don't deny yourself the pleasure of improving your sex life because of a few prejudices and myths circulating about how "real" men and women automatically know how to please each other – this is plainly tosh.

Sexual health

It is important to look after your sexual health as certain infections, once caught, cannot be cured and can easily be passed on. It is absolutely essential to know your partner's sexual history as you will be, effectively, sleeping with all their previous partners. Practice "safe sex" using barrier methods, such as condoms, and for extra protection for the woman the diaphragm until you have both been to the doctor's or clinic and had a sexual health check and received the all clear. There has been a huge rise in sexually transmitted diseases (STDs) recently. It seems post-AIDS that everyone has "forgotten" that there are some very unpleasant STDs out there. There is no cure for genital herpes, which can be very unpleasant and is easily transmitted, there is no cure for HIV which can develop into full blown AIDS and, obviously cause death. Some of the less-serious diseases cause infertility and if left untreated can spread to other parts of the body.

Your sexual health is your responsibility. Do not be persuaded into giving up barrier methods until you are completely sure of the other person's health. If you have something you must be honest and let a partner know before a sexual encounter takes place. The best idea is obviously to prevent yourself from catching anything in the first place but if the worst happens and you catch something, if you are lucky it will be curable and will have done no long-lasting damage. If you are unfortunate enough to catch something that, as yet, has no cure, it is perfectly possible to have a good sex life using barrier methods and precautions.

Sexuality

Many people do not settle on their sexual identity until they are past puberty. We are still experimenting and forming our psyche and our sexual image until we are well into our twenties. Your sexual inclinations, preferences and habits are your business and yours alone until you engage a partner. Once you are part of a relationship then you need to be clear, as in all communications, what your boundaries are and be careful that you don't misrepresent who you are sexually.

If you are very flirtatious and give overt sexual invitation through your body language, then you must expect to draw sexual attention from those you are targeting. You cannot act outraged or surprised if that is how others see you when you have portrayed yourself in that manner. The same is true of your sexual inclinations. Either keep them to yourself or, if you make them overt, expect to attract the sort of attention you are inviting. If you behave in an overtly camp manner or target people of the same sex, others will assume that you are interested in a same-sex relationship. If this is not the case then don't mis-advertise who you are. I would suggest that there is a certain amount of sense in keeping your sexual interests relatively private until you think you have found a partner. Then you both need to explore what works for you and your partnership. In this way you can avoid misunderstandings and hurt and you will end up with someone who suits you. You need to be kind and careful in all sexual encounters as this can be an area in which many people are sensitive and can be easily hurt. Try to treat others as you would like to be treated and you won't go too far wrong.

Siblings

Very few people feel indifferent about their sibling relationships. As with our relationship to our parents, sibling relationships are formative. They are our first experience of how we are perceived by others and where we practice our interaction skills. However there is a distinct difference in that some siblings also perceive themselves to be rivals for parental attention and affection which they believe, often erroneously, to be limited. It is this parental attention and affection which matters. So although many people may dislike their siblings and blame them for their negative experiences of growing up it has been found in numerous studies that it is the perceived parental relationship which has a much greater impact on our self esteem and perception. "For children, on most things the reflected appraisals of their parents may matter much more than those of their siblings. In general these studies find that parental support and encouragement, responsiveness and use of inductive control are related positively to children's self-esteem." (Gecas and Seff 1990)

It is also interesting that in childhood studies much of the blame for teasing and bullying was attributed to the siblings involved and that the parent's role in mediating or preventing this behaviour was rarely mentioned. However there is evidence that hostile or bullying behaviour by siblings does impact later in life. "Early adolescents who grow up with a sibling who has been unfriendly or hostile and aggressive in the pre-school years are more likely to show worrying, anxious or depressed behaviour or aggressive behaviour than those whose siblings had been friendly and affectionate." (Dunn, J and Kendrick, C (1982))

Although it is of fundamental importance to your sibling relationship how you treated each other, it is the response of your parents which will influence both your experience of your sibling and your perception of yourself. If you have an aggressive sibling who resents your arrival it will be the responsibility of the adult to mediate and show that there is enough love and support for as many children as are in the family unit. When needy or poorly-parented parents (ie parents who have poor parental role models themselves) are involved, this is when sibling rivalries begin and continue as there is a belief by the children (which is often borne out) that love, support and encouragement (and in some cases resources such as food, clothes and toys) are in short supply.

Therefore, I would point out that, if you have a particularly poor relationship (or none) with a sibling, you both started out as defenceless, vulnerable children who needed support from your parents. If this was not forthcoming or was only available for one child, then an imbalance in your relationship with your brother or sister will have been on the cards from the moment you were born. This can lead to a lifetime of resentment and alienation from the person (or people) who most closely shared your formative experiences. That is quite something to lose or turn your back on.

It is never too late to try and resurrect a lost relationship. It may be that you don't want to but it is very rare that you can't. A poor sibling relationship will often have developed as a result of a lack of parental checks and balances, rather than deliberate malice by one sibling to another; this is worth bearing in mind. A good sibling relationship provides huge support. Often these people know you very well, your little idiosyncrasies and what makes you tick – that is rare and of course they have first-hand knowledge and experience of environment you were brought up in although it is important to recognise their perceptions may be different. This can be a huge support when parents become difficult, get old or die. No one else has been there from your beginning except another sibling.

So if you have a good relationship with one or more of your siblings, look after this as it is a precious commodity. If you have a poor or non-existent relationship with your sibling(s) then it is never too late to hold out the olive branch and start again as Adults. This is hard because when we reunite with our parents or siblings we are mentally transported back to the time when we were young and our behaviour can change accordingly. Your will need to stay in your Adult persona, behaving reasonably and logically and not responding on the spur of the moment to historically old issues. You will also need to allow that a brother or sister may have a different perception or interpretation of events than you do; this is okay you can agree to differ whilst respecting each other's view. You will also need to refuse to adopt the role you had when young. So now you are no longer the "annoying younger sister" or the "bossy older brother" or the "brilliantly-talented older sister". Parents are quick to label us when we are young as lazy, clever, sporty, shy etc. and it is up to us as adults to throw off these uninvited titles and demonstrate through our actions and words (in Adult) who we are now. If you can do this with your siblings you may be able to mend fences and form new adult relationships. The pay-off will be enormous; for there will be very few people in your life who understand your origins and subsequent development as well as someone who was in there with you from the beginning.

DUNN, J and KENDRICK, C (1982) *Siblings: love envy and understanding*, () Harvard University Press
GECAS, V. and SEFF, M.A. (1990), *Families and Adolescents: A review of the 1980s*. Journal of Marriage and the Family 52, 941-958

Sleep

Enough sleep is absolutely essential in order to function well. Insomnia, as I have mentioned in the Balance section, is one of the main indicators that your life is out of balance and that something needs readjusting.

There are obvious steps to take in order to get a good night's sleep. Your room needs to be quiet and cool, without electronic equipment. If you have to store something electronic in your room, make sure it is turned off at least two hours before you have to sleep. Interaction with electronic equipment keeps our alpha waves functioning which keep us alert; we need beta waves to be predominant as we prepare for bed. We need to slow down, take a warm bath, read a book and avoid stimulants. This means no caffeine, no loud television or electronics, blackberries, computers or phones etc. Ideally, no nicotine and very little alcohol, too, as these both disrupt sleeping patterns. Remember, also, that some medicines can have side effects which disrupt your sleep; so if you take regular medication you need to find out if that could be impacting on poor sleep. Also keeping erratic hours will not work. Your body loves regulation, so going to sleep one night at ten and the following night at one will not work. You're effectively introducing a jet lag situation when you keep irregular hours and we all know how awful that can be! Regular habits will establish a good sleeping pattern.

Try to avoid medication if you can. Most sleeping tablets have side effects and almost all are habit forming if taken over a period of time. However three or four nights on medication to re-establish a good sleeping pattern could be effective so take the advice of your medical practitioner. There are many herbal remedies which can be effective, including valerian, hops and avena sativa which have been used for thousands of years. To see what might suit you consult someone with expertise in this area.

Lack of sleep is miserable and affects all areas of your life so it is worth spending some time addressing your sleeping habits and behaviour in order to minimise disruption and regulate your body clock. Treat your body well and persevere, sometimes bad habits have been dominating for a while and it will take two or three weeks of going to bed at the same time and getting up at the same time to re-regulate, however, it will be worth it for the renewed, refreshed feeling that comes after a restful night.

Smile

Smile! Not inanely at any passing person but generally. This means when going about your business, to work, to the shops, walking the dog etc. that you keep yourself available for friendly contact. Walking around with an mp3 player plugged in or looking at your feet or constantly on your mobile cuts your chance for friendly interaction with other humans. Most people's lives can be improved by a friendly nod and smile and if you're feeling particularly brave, a "Hello". Obviously some common sense needs to be employed and if you feel uncomfortable acknowledging some people, or, indeed, unsafe, then by all means look at your feet. However most of the population welcome some form of non-intrusive, gentle interaction.

Thirty years ago it would have been considered extremely rude to pass another human and not at least nod in recognition. We have lost this art, I think to the detriment of fellow feeling and general connection. Try to start up this habit in your neighbourhood, after all you never know when you might need a hand with something and this is much more likely to be offered in an area where the people feel connected to each other.

Stamps

These are really grudges; injustices or slights that you hang on to in order to store up ill feeling or a sense of righteousness against another person or persons. They are referred to as "stamps" by Transactional Analysts as they are similar to the saving stamps that you can collect in a book and then cash in. It is this cashing in that needs to be avoided.

Saving stamps or harbouring grudges means that when something you don't like happens to you, you do not address the situation immediately. If you are able to shrug and let the incident go, then this is not a problem. However, if you then hang on to the incident and use it to engender ill feeling about the perpetrator(s) then you are collecting stamps. The other person, of course, has no idea that they have offended you and you are able to feel hard done by in your own mind with no real justification. After all you have not told the other person(s) how they have offended you or what you would have liked done differently, so they have had no chance to put things right, apologise or change how they behave – this is a lose/lose situation for both parties. You walk around with a load of ill feeling and they walk around behaving as they always have not knowing that this is not okay for some people (namely, you!). If you are of the persuasion that people who love you or care about you "should know how you feel" and act accordingly, please disabuse yourself of this notion – since when have any humans possessed telepathic powers?! If you want people to change how they behave towards you then you need to let them know how you are affected by their behaviour.

This does not have to be immediate. It may be inappropriate to address something the moment it happens, particularly if there are other people around or you are in a work situation. However, it is appropriate to let the other person know that there is a problem with what happened and to seek to come to an understanding with them. This means that you don't collect "enough evidence" in order to strengthen your case. It means that as situations occur, you address them within a reasonable time frame. Storing up hurts is not useful and can lead to an explosive confrontation which is not conducive to solving the issues that have arisen. Pick a good time (ask!) and lay out your concerns in as an unemotional manner as you can manage, trying to stay with the facts and letting the other person know how you were affected. Use the "I/You" method which is to state "When you do (whatever it is), I feel (whatever you feel)." This is very good at getting people who sometimes dismiss others' concerns over their behaviour to focus on the fact that it does not work for the other person, regardless of whether they think their behaviour reasonable or not.

So do not hang onto old hurts. Usually the only person seriously affected by this behaviour is you. This is what we mean when we use the phrases, "chip on the shoulder", or when we refer to someone having "a lot of old baggage". Life is tricky enough without lugging round old hurts and this behaviour means you remain stuck in old patterns, never resolving issues which matter to you and that will help you establish good boundaries. People need to know what does and does not work for you, so tell them.

Stupidity

People are not stupid; they behave stupidly sometimes. Of course, sometimes people choose to behave stupidly; they indulge in a behaviour which they know is risky or foolish. However no person is stupid, we just have differing abilities and knowledge.

You are not stupid if you don't understand something – you may not have the education skills or experience to understand a certain concept. There is a nasty belief that has crept into our society that only certain people are "clever" and by contrast, those who do not share their abilities (often gained via a privileged education, or fortunate life experiences) are stupid. It is my belief, having worked with people with special needs, small children, restaurant staff, management consultants and disabled individuals, that there is no such thing as a stupid person. I have been taught things by all of these groups, things they know and I didn't. How to manoeuvre a wheelchair into a small space and up a ramp at speed, how to make a cat's cradle, the perfect temperature for a soufflé, what GNP stands for and the signing alphabet. The fact that I didn't know these things did not make me stupid, just unskilled or unknowing. Any one of the individuals concerned could have chosen to say "You're really stupid. Don't you know how to…?" These are comments I see increasingly used by some people to put others down; people who hold different knowledge to them. This is not OK behaviour, just one upmanship. Don't accept it from others and please don't perpetrate it yourself.

Suicide

Suicide is usually the result of despair and the belief that nothing can change. It is the ultimate I'm not okay/You're not okay life position (see OK). Nothing is good about how you are and nothing is good about your situation in the world. This, coupled with the belief that nothing can change, can lead to a belief that suicide is an option. Suicide is a permanent solution to a temporary problem and the big downside is its very permanence and the fact that there is no room for other options.

If you are feeling suicidal I urge you to seek help. Nothing is permanent, not even when you have a terminal illness or have been sentenced to twenty years in prison. Time and perspective change even the most trenchant of beliefs. Suicide is often the product of depression and this can be addressed if help is sought. Trite though it is "All things come to pass".

I am not of the belief that you do not have the right to take your own life. I just believe that there are so many other options available and that suicide is usually a poor one, chosen in despair and under duress. Many people who have contemplated suicide find it very hard looking back later to see why they would have taken that option. There is a particular mind set that takes hold where we convince ourselves that this is the best choice available. Often we do not let anybody else know what we are thinking as we do not want to be dissuaded from our planned route. How many other life-changing decisions would you take where you would not run it past a couple of friends and maybe an expert or two?

A quick dispatch is not the only kind of suicide. There is the slow, ugly, descent towards an ignominious death that comes from alcohol or drug abuse or sabotaging behaviour such as drink driving or extreme neglect of the self or continuing to live with an abusive and dangerous partner. These behaviours need addressing in the same way as they are indicative of despair and of having given up.

Please let someone know how you are feeling. Shame goes with suicide but there is no shame in feeling this low; it often goes with some form of mental or physical illness and is a symptom, not something you can control or decide upon. I believe that when a human contemplates suicide their mind balance is altered where rational thought and reason are unavailable to them; after all it is usually the case with humans that we strive to stay alive at all costs. So I urge you to talk over this enormous decision, to feel the impact it would have on your nearest and dearest and for you to realise what you would be giving up. It may be the more courageous and harder route but there is always another choice and that involves facing your demons and deciding to live.

Please remember that if someone you know or love commits suicide that this is an act that has nothing to do with you and everything to do with them. I don't mean in any way to belittle the impact of a suicidal death on the nearest and dearest but to state quite clearly that if someone is intent on taking their own life then they will find a way to do it regardless of any interventions or lack of them. Often people contemplating suicide are in such an unbalanced state that the people they love are left out of any deliberations that they have. Many people who contemplate suicide truly believe at the time that their family and friends would be much better off without them.

If someone close to you, particularly a parent, has committed suicide, I would suggest that you need to talk this through with someone in a professional capacity. If left unexplored and unresolved this can go on to infiltrate and distort almost every aspect of some people's life – if this sounds like it might be you, please get some professional help.

Support

As humans we are most fulfilled when we are both able to receive and give support. Quite a lot of us are, however, lopsided in that we either receive a lot of support or give a lot of support, but are poor at balancing the two. If you are constantly giving support to others at your own expense, eventually this imbalance will impact negatively on your life. Either you or the other, unsupported members of your circle will begin to feel neglected. It may be that you got or get a lot of recognition for being selfless and this is your "normal" way of behaving. But the very word "selfless" should flag up warning signals; when we pay less attention to ourselves then we are in a poorer position to support others.

It may be that you are naturally "a giver" or that is where you got your praise when you were growing up. "Oh, he's so helpful." Or "She always thinks about others first, she's so kind and good." Certainly these are traits that are welcome but not to the exclusion of one's self. Remember there needs to be a balance, where you also receive support when you need it. If the support route is a one-way street, you need to examine how this has occurred and start to rebalance the situation.

It is perfectly normal, for instance, to be doing everything for your children when they are babies or toddlers, however, as they grow up we need to rebalance this situation and encourage them to flourish and do things for themselves. So if you are still running round after children who are fifteen, sixteen, or seventeen or dropping your leisure pursuits at a moment's notice in order to fetch or carry for them, then there is an imbalance. The same is true of a friendship or partnership. If your friend/partner has a particularly stressful period, of course you will want to support them and may give up some of your own time, pursuits or desires in order to support them. In due course, though, this will not be sustainable and as they get back on their feet you need to return to your own routines which support you. It is important, therefore, that you do not give up everything, however needy the person you want to support is. If you do, there will be no "normal" life to return to, as you will have given it up. Meanwhile the person you have supported will no longer need your support and will happily return to their routine leaving you flat.

So by all means support someone else but not at too high a cost to yourself, as this then this becomes a parasitical relationship which cannot be sustained.

The second type of support relationship is one where you are constantly seeking support. Maybe you grew up with parents who did everything for you and you are used to others running around after you. As you mature you will need to realise that in order to function as an adult you need to be able to do the majority of living and working tasks for yourself. It is perfectly reasonable to ask for help if you feel out of your depth but don't hand over the whole task or responsibility for something to another, however out of your depth you feel. If you do this, you disenfranchise yourself and learn nothing. Get the other to show you what it is they do in this situation that is supportive and then gradually take over the task yourself.

If you have been encouraged to be "needy" and have had too much done for you, then this will be hard. Remember, though, that the whole time you are being "supported" by another then you are not truly autonomous and will never have complete control of your life. In a partnership this control is something that has to be sacrificed to a certain extent because there are two of you in the situation but this is negotiated, usually, to the benefit of both partners, not at the expense of one.

Balance (as so often is the case) is the key. In any long term relationship, there will be a give and take of support. At certain points during the relationship one person's needs will dominate but in a normal relationship the pendulum will swing back the other way and the supported will become the supporter. If this does not happen, the relationship changes to a parasite and host situation which will become unsustainable. It is this that we need to watch out for and guard against both in order to support ourselves and to support the other person within a functioning adult relationship.

Telepathy

If you are someone who believes that humans have telepathic abilities, then now is the time to let go of that belief. Too numerous to count are the times I have heard people in and out of my therapy room say "If he/she knew me/loved me they would know that I like/want/need… (whatever it is)." Oh really? How's that then? Did you tell them? "But they should know." goes up the wail. Once and for all – no one can know what you want unless you tell them. Please do not believe otherwise as this is the cause of much misery and huge misunderstanding.

The people who buy into the belief that their nearest and dearest "should" know what they want are often people who as children had their needs overruled, ignored or contradicted. In this way they learnt to hide their true needs and fell in with what was offered in order to get something from their carers. These people have "adapted" to the situation they found themselves in as children and have not really grown up. If when you were little you said that you were cold and the response was "Nonsense, it's a lovely warm day." Then you had your true experiences ignored and rewritten by your carer. If when you were sad or angry you were told "You're just making a fuss, don't upset yourself so." Then you were led to believe that your feelings were invalid and that you were in charge of dealing with them. As a child it is our parents who model how to deal with emotions. If the modelling you receive denied how you felt or was poor in its coping strategies then you will be poor at taking care of your own needs or even recognising them. It is important in order to function as an Adult that you find out what it is you really need. This starts with acknowledging what it is you really feel.

If you are used to covering up your real feelings in order to "adapt" to those around you then it will be hard for you to recognise what you do feel and as a consequence of those feelings, need. You will have to start listening to yourself and taking care of your own needs. This will be hard; after all you are the person who expects others around you to tell you what it is you want or guess and if they get it wrong the "rebellious child" inside of you will resent them. Taking care of yourself means eating when you are hungry, resting when you are tired, not telling yourself or others you are fine when you are not, not abusing yourself with nicotine, alcohol or stimulants and generally listening to what it is you need.

The emotional implication of this means not overriding your feelings. It means that you cry when something evokes sadness and that you ask those you are close to for help or comfort when you need it. You are allowed to exhibit anger, if it is appropriate and be happy when you are. This may be alien and for some people; overriding their childhood habits may take many years and a deal of hard work. However, the goal is authentic interaction and with that comes true connection, one of the most rewarding things for humans. Connection with other humans enhances us and gives us meaning and value. So no more belief in telepathy! Own up to your own responsibilities for yourself and start communicating clearly what it is that you need; only then will you start to get it.

Terminal Illness

Being diagnosed with a terminal illness for which there is limited treatment is a harsh blow to withstand. You will need support and comfort in coming to terms with your own mortality. Most people will need to grieve before they can get on with living the best life they can under these circumstances. An acknowledgement of what you are losing and how that affects you and your loved ones will take time. It is quite usual to be in denial and to look for a "cure" against all odds or simply to refuse to accept that you are dying. This is not to say that you shouldn't thoroughly explore your options and take a second opinion. Just be careful not to be sucked into an unproved therapy or treatment which may impact negatively on the time you have left.

I don't know what it is like to be told that you have limited time left to live but I have supported several people who have been given this diagnosis. All I can offer is the support and suggestions which seemed to help. Be open and tell people what is going on for you. If people know what it is that you are going through they will be better equipped to support you. Tell your friends what you need. They don't know and can withdraw through embarrassment or ignorance not because they don't care. Some people will not be able to respond in ways you want them to; this is about them and not a reflection on you. It is quite common to lose some friends along the way as they simply do not know how to be with you when they know you are dying. It is also on the cards that you will make new friends and that some people will surprise you with their ability to support you.

You need to make plans for your death. Do you want to be at home? Are there people you want to be present? What sort of treatment do you want? Where do you want to be buried? Do you want a church service? These are things you may want to think about and consider. Alternatively you may not be able to cope with these aspects of your situation and may want to ask someone close to you to think about these arrangements.

In the West we are not particularly good at addressing death. However, it is a guaranteed part of being a living being and recognition of this can bring some measure of peace and acceptance. I urge you to find out all you need to know about your condition, how you will handle it and how you want to die. In doing this you are exerting some control over your dying and death. Ask for help and support and if some people are unable to give it, move on and ask for what you need from others. Plenty of people will rise to the situation and your limited time can be hugely enhanced by informed, loving, support.

If this is the diagnosis you have received, then I am truly sorry. You are, however, alive and need to wrest some control over how you will live your remaining time. The quality of this remaining time will be determined largely by you, so dig deep and do your best to support yourself, ask for what you need and live the rest of your life as well as you can.

Timing

Good timing is something that can be learnt, although for a lucky few, it seems to be innate. There's a very useful phrase about "knowing when to stop digging". This means when the situation is bad, and whatever steps you have subsequently taken have either made things worse or changed nothing, that you recognise this and abandon the task of rectifying the situation. You can return at a later, more propitious time and tackle the situation if needs be but when you are making poor progress or exacerbating an already poor situation, good timing is about knowing when to withdraw.

Equally knowing when to tackle a situation is also a very important skill. When tempers are frayed or time is short are both examples of a poor time to tackle a problem. Also when the event is actually taking place can be a bad time to tackle what is bothering you. For example if your partner does something in bed that you don't like, saying it then and there can be crushing. However in the aftermath of lovemaking when you are close you could bring it up carefully, explaining that you know he/she wants to please you, as most of the time this is the case but that (whatever) just doesn't work for you. This is not manipulative but kind. Think about when and where you would like to be tackled about your mistakes or perceived flaws and try to employ this information when dealing with others.

Often long-term arguments, disagreements or feuds are

exacerbated or left unresolved due to poor timing. Picking a neutral time and place can make all the difference, as can not capitalising on a power imbalance. If you hold all the cards it is not a good idea when seeking resolution to make this fact overt. The other party will have recognised this already. Good timing is about choosing the time when the other party is most receptive to what you are saying not about wielding power in order to get what you want. Good timing coupled with charm is a fairly unbeatable combination so it may be worth studying the properties of both. If they do not come naturally to you, study someone who is good at these behaviours and then follow their lead. And remember when you treat people as you would wish to be treated you will often end up with a happy result all round.

Tolerance

This means being able to hold your own views and beliefs alongside those of other peoples without wanting to impose your version on anyone else. It is a "live and let live" philosophy. What sort of beliefs are valid and a good example if they are about making other people conform to a certain set of values? Who sets the standard and the rules? It is important that individuals are allowed to choose their own beliefs according to their religion, culture and upbringing without interference from other people, however well meant. Would you like someone to try and change your mind on something you hold dear to your way of living? It is really quite rude to assume that other adults do not have the same abilities as yourself to decide what they will and won't believe. You are not the arbiter of morals, ethics or good taste; all you need to do is stick by your own standards and leave others to take care of their own.

If you can "mind your own business" in the most literal sense then you will be taking care of what is relevant to you and your life whilst letting others do the same. It is hugely patronising to assume that others have not thought about the implications of what they believe in and frankly, if they haven't, then it's none of your business anyway.

Tolerance, however, is more than just letting others be, although that is a good start. It's about embracing the diversity of ideas and beliefs that different humans hold and recognising what we gain from such a mix. After all many of the ideas that we hold dear and accept as normal within our culture come from other cultures all over the world. We have geometry originating in Egyptian times, our numerical system is owed to Arabic culture, we enjoy pasta, originally from China and now from Italy, tea from Asia and books and films from all over the world. Many more instances can be found throughout our daily lives of other cultural influences from across the globe. We need to recognise that we no longer live in a world where there are more than a few insulated cultures and that many of these miss out on the benefits of shared knowledge and ideas which benefit the more cosmopolitan societies that exist.

We owe much to the international pool of knowledge and if we can remember this when we encounter an individual who does not share our views or beliefs then it will stand us in good stead in developing a tolerant and accepting outlook. This in turn will make us more approachable and open to other possibilities which could enhance our understanding of ourselves and extend our knowledge to our benefit.

Trauma

What is traumatic for one person can be something that is coped with well by another. If you have repeated flashbacks of an event and physiological symptoms as well as emotional ones, it may be that you have suffered some form of trauma. However it is normal after a terrifying or extraordinary perilous event, where your life or that of others is at risk, to feel physically and emotionally distraught for several weeks. However, if this continues, disrupting everyday life, concentration, sleep and eating patterns then you may need some specifically tailored trauma counselling or intervention.

There are several interventions available and there are Post Traumatic Stress Disorder therapists who specialise in this sort of therapy. You definitely need someone who has experience of dealing with people who have been exposed to trauma as this is very different from other forms of mental disturbance.

There is a relatively new therapy called EMDR which stands for Eye Movement Desensitising and Reprocessing, which is used for accelerated healing of emotional trauma. It should only be delivered by health-care professionals in conjunction with other traditional psychological approaches. Clinical research studies have shown it can accelerate the body's own natural adaptive information processing of memories and that the effects are usually long lasting. It is relatively new, since 1989, and many people do not know about it so you may have to use word of mouth or the internet to find recognised practitioners in your area.

Although any traumatic event can be extremely destabilising many people find their own coping strategies will see them through. Each of us will deal with an event differently and there is no one method of coping. However, it is normal to expect physical symptoms of anxiety to last for several months after an event and also for similar experiences (loud noises, people rushing towards you) to set off an anxiety response. This will result in heightened cortisol levels, sweating, nausea and a flight or fight response. Even though these symptoms are unpleasant to experience, they will subside and over several weeks or months become weaker and weaker. Make sure you let people know what you need – sympathy, support, to talk about things, not to talk about the event etc. Your friends will want to help but may feel at a loss to know what to do; let them know and you will both benefit.

Remember that you have been through a life-threatening event.

You are entitled to feel and respond in the way that you do. You will need help and support and it is important that you find the support that suits you. Many people find that they have a deeper appreciation for all that they have after such an experience and that their life returns to manageable proportions after they have acknowledge just what an impact the trauma has had on them and their loved ones. The people who can experience the most difficulty are those whose trauma is unacknowledged, either by themselves or others. Denial is not an effective remedy for any form of emotional disturbance and trauma is not an exception.

Minimising or discounting (see Discounting) behaviour by others, towards you, belittles your experience and the feelings you have attached to that experience. Most people respond in this way through ignorance or embarrassment; they simply do not know what to say as what has happened to you is so far out of their own experience that they have nothing to compare it with and no coping skills available; this is where support groups can be empowering and help validate your own experience. People who have been through the same trauma or a similar one will identify with your feelings and help normalise your experience. It is then that you will be able to start to make sense of what has happened to you and to go forward with your life. However what has happened to you will always be part of your history and who you now are; if you can acknowledge this but not make it central to your existence you will be well on the road to recovery.

Truth

In any intimate relationship truth is essential. However not all of your relationships will require that degree of intimacy. There are occasions when it is unwise to be completely or unkindly truthful. If a friend, for instance, has already had a haircut that you consider unflattering, there is no need to tell him/her. If asked for your opinion you could reply that you thought the previous haircut suited them better – there is nothing to be gained by telling them you don't like it. One, they've already had the cut, two, they might like it, three, your opinion is only *your* opinion and not a fact – other people could think that the haircut is much nicer or suits your friend better. Sometimes people who considered themselves very truthful "I always tell it how I see it.", are negligent of other people's feelings and don't consider the implications of what they are saying on the other person. Also, what exactly is the truth – the truth may be that you don't like something but as I have said above, that does not make it a fact, just an opinion and we need to be careful when playing the "truth" card that we register this. We are entitled to our opinions but we do not necessarily need to share them. Think to yourself, "Is this kind? How will this improve the situation?" before expressing your point of view.

In intimate relationships that matter to you, I would consider always telling the truth. You do the other party a great disservice when you withhold the truth. You don't allow them to really know you or to understand what you do and don't like. You will fail to outline your boundaries and needs both of which are essential information in a close and loving relationship. This does not mean that one partner has to pander to the needs and demands of the other. It is a process of laying your cards on the table and then negotiating to the satisfaction of both parties on each issue. When you let an issue slide, it is very difficult to return to it later as the other person thinks that you were OK with what occurred. If you don't like the way your child/friend/partner speaks to you, treats you or responds to you, you need to say so then and there (in a careful and considerate way) otherwise you have created a lie between you. Your loved ones are not telepathic so help them out. They do not always have to understand why you like certain behaviours and not others, neither do they have to agree with you but for intimacy and true knowledge of each other and for love, regard and consideration to blossom, they do need to know what is and what is not acceptable to you.

It requires a certain amount of bravery to let people know what does and doesn't work for you. Short term it can be uncomfortable and you will not always be popular but you will do away with a lot of unnecessary baggage. The long term gains will be far reaching and your relationship will be much less arduous. Left over baggage and resentments will be cut to a minimum (no one's perfect and you won't get it right every time). Using kindness and subtlety, try to give an authentic, consistent, reliable portrait of who you are and what you can tolerate to the other person, whether it be your mother, your child or your lover and you will reap the benefit with an open, tolerant, loving and largely functioning adult relationship. Believe me, in a decade of psychotherapy, this has a value "above rubies".

Try too hard

Please don't. Try too hard that is. When you try too hard it shows and unfortunately it smacks of desperation. Trying too hard usually stems from a childhood where your efforts were either not rewarded or were not regarded as ever good enough or you perceived yourself to be undervalued or unappreciated. Humans can work like a wolf pack when in groups and if they get a sniff of desperation they will either ostracise the perpetrator or target them unkindly. If you are someone who finds it hard to make friends easily or feels that you are on the outside of a group, my advice would be not to try too hard.

Certainly, exhibit friendliness and willingness to join in or have a joke but try not to mind too much early on whether you are included in group activities or not. If you hear about a group activity or it is mentioned to you say something like "That sounds like you had fun" rather than "Oh, I would have liked to do that". The latter comment can be perceived as you looking for an invitation whereas the former comment is merely an observation. Rather unfairly, the less desperate you are about being included the more likely a group or potential friend is to invite you to do something with them.

The same goes for personal relationships. Try not to look for an exclusive relationship with someone, even a potential partner. Most well-balanced humans will have other interests and other friends as well as family. This is not a threat to your relationship, rather the sign of a well-rounded and popular person – somebody good to go out with or be friends with. However needy you feel try to remember that you too need a variety of relationships and that one person, however much you like them, cannot supply all your needs, nor should they be expected to. If you are very needy and have not addressed childhood issues of being unloved or unappreciated then it is very unlikely that anyone will be able to address all your needs; you need to do this for yourself.

As adults we need to be able to minister to ourselves. To self soothe and to support ourselves are grown up tools that we need to have acquired before we can be in a relationship with another. Of course it is lovely to have someone who empathises with us, supports us and soothes us but if we cannot do it for ourselves we become overly needy and desperate and that is when relationships (of any sort) start to go awry. So if you feel you want something from somebody, particularly a relationship with another, rather desperately, try to pull back and go gently as this will be far more attractive and be much more likely to yield results. If this is a really hard "ask" then you need some help in learning how to minister to your needs and how to nurture yourself and should maybe seek counselling. Once you have learnt these skills, all relationships will become much easier, particularly the one you have with yourself. And once you have a good relationship with yourself you will find you become much more attractive to others and that relationships become much easier and more pleasurable for everyone involved.

Ultimatum

If you issue an ultimatum be sure that this is your intention. Ultimatums are all or nothing behaviour and will elicit a similar response in those they are directed towards. They are very rarely necessary. If you do issue an ultimatum then you will need to be ready to follow through with the promised reaction should the person this is directed to ignore your threat. Be absolutely sure you are prepared to do this before issuing one or you will have shown yourself to have poor boundaries and to be a person who does not deliver what they promise. If you push someone to the edge by saying if you do (whatever)then I'll (stop your allowance/never see you again/cut you out of my will) then you are taking someone to the edge and you shouldn't be surprised if some individuals think they have so few choices left that they jump!

That said, I think there are many other ways to resolve issues rather than an all or nothing approach. Try to remember an ultimatum response is usually a result of when two people's Frame of reference (see Frame of Reference) lie on opposite poles. Try to work out what you do have in common and if possible what's in it for the other person as well as what you stand to gain; then make both of these goals clear. If they have nothing to gain then they are not going to play ball, ultimatum or not.

Work out what end result you are after and what part the other party plays in helping you to achieve the end result. For instance if your child is always out late and doesn't let you know when they are coming back then issuing an ultimatum won't help "Next time you don't tell me when you're coming back then I'm going to ground you." Well maybe you are, however a more profitable approach would be to explain the situation "When you go out and I don't know where you are, then I worry. If I do know where you are and you are responsible for telling me for the next few weeks then maybe we could negotiate a later Friday night curfew. At the moment I can't do that because I feel that you're not trustworthy." In this way the other person can see how *their* behaviour not yours is driving the situation and hampering any progress for them. By all means follow this up with an ultimatum if the behaviour doesn't improve; then an ultimatum is appropriate as other avenues and reasonable negotiation have already been explored. But try to add a "get out clause". Let the other person know that after the consequence (in this case grounding) then you are willing to go back to negotiation after a period of probation from the other party which shows an improvement in attitude and behaviour. If you leave no up-side for the other person then there will be very little incentive for them to comply with what you want.

Where an ultimatum is wholly appropriate is when someone has overstepped a personal boundary that you have already made clear to them. For instance, if you have asked someone not to behave in a certain way to you and explained why you don't like it, then if they continue it is completely appropriate to offer an ultimatum – one which you must be prepared to carry through. "If you continue to belittle me in public, then I am not prepared to go out in a group situation where you have been invited." This is a very clear statement of intention and makes entirely evident your feelings on the matter. Not many people will ignore such a message but some will, so you absolutely have to be prepared to carry out your promised actions otherwise you and your words carry no weight and your boundaries are shot to pieces.

So my advice would be to avoid an ultimatum unless you have been pushed to the edge of a personal boundary or an issue which you can no longer tolerate (see WAM WAM WAFM) and then be very clear about what actions you are prepared to take and make sure you know the consequences for yourself and the other party; sometimes the consequences of an ultimatum can punish you more than the person it is directed towards. So plan, negotiate and use with care but in some situations an ultimatum is the only weapon of choice as long as you treat it with respect, are aware of the consequences and use it sparingly.

Umbrella

Why have I put the word umbrella here? Is it because I can't think of anything to put in the "U" section? No, of course it isn't. A compliment umbrella is something that we put up when we believe, either that the person is giving us a compliment just for the sake of it, or, when we believe that the compliment does not apply to us. It is also something that will be unconsciously erected if we are in the "I'm not Okay" position (see OK).

Because of the way we were brought up or the experiences we have received we will have a certain view of ourselves. We will have taken on some of the labels given to us by other people and this can narrow our potential in that we believe we are a certain way and cannot change. "Oh, I just can't help myself." Well actually, you can – you may just believe you can't or you may actually feel comfortable in the role you have been given. One of the things you can do to widen your horizons and increase your potential to be whatever it is you want for yourself, is to be aware of when you erect your umbrella against compliments.

Some compliments may ring true and you will acknowledge and accept these. Perhaps you see yourself as very efficient so that when someone says to you "You ran that project very well, congratulations.", you will have no trouble accepting such a compliment. However you may not have such a good view of your physical attractiveness and so when someone says "Oh, have you changed your hair? You look really pretty that way", you will have erected your "compliment umbrella" and the compliment will bounce right off and not go in. You will believe that you are not pretty and will, therefore, dismiss such a remark as "just being kind" or "trying to butter you up" or any other belief that allows you not to accept such a compliment. You will have seen others do this, maybe remarking, "That's very kind" when they have been paid a compliment. They believe the person is being kind, or polite but they have not accepted that there is any truth in what is being said.

Once you are aware of what compliments you easily accept, which ones you like but don't sit comfortably and which ones you long for, you will have a pretty good idea of what you think your attributes are. You may have always been the "reliable one" or the "pretty one" or the "clever one". However, you are so much more than the labels you were given as you grew up. Once we get to adulthood and move into a wider social circle we will come across people who view us on face value and not with our childhood baggage and in our Child frame of reference. These people have the ability to see many different facets and abilities that may have not been recognised by or were simply not acceptable to the people who brought us up. If we allow these compliments past our umbrella and allow ourselves to accept that we may be beautiful or clever or kind or funny, we expand our possibilities of who we are and how we might be.

The compliments that you easily accept will be those that sit with the character you think you are. The compliments which you like but don't sit well with you will be attributes you may suspect you have or abilities you have been praised for in the past but that you are not sure are "really" you or you have some doubts about or even that these attributes were not acceptable in your family and so you feel uncomfortable acknowledging that you have them. The compliments which you yearn for are those you were denied as a Child. You may have longed to have been thought of as "pretty" or "clever" but were never acknowledged as such. This does not mean you are not those things! It means that the environment in which you were brought up and the people who were your main carers did not recognise the possibility of you being any of those things. However, as an Adult you will need to realise that your Child situation can be very narrow and restrictive and because of the baggage adults around us are carrying they are not always able to give the child in their care what he/she needs. So it is entirely possible that you are beautiful and clever and funny but that your adult carers were unable to acknowledge this; thus helping you to erect an umbrella against such compliments. Once you have recognised this you can chuck your umbrella away and judge compliments for yourself, as an Adult.

Of course some compliments will be false but the great majority of people do not bother to say nice things about people they encounter unless they are thinking them. Certainly an uninvited compliment by a stranger is almost certainly heartfelt and authentic – why else would they bother to put themselves out to comment on you or something you are wearing? They don't know you and have nothing to gain by such an action, therefore they must just have been struck by how nice your hair/coat/shoes etc. is. People who know you may have an ulterior motive but on the whole giving a compliment is an effort and most people do not give them out uninvited unless they wish their compliment to be a small acknowledgement of something nice about the other person.

Once you are more used to accepting and believing compliments – "Thank you" is all that is required to accept these – then you will also be in a better position to issue compliments. Based on all that I have said, make sure that these are true and that you view the giving of compliments as a life enhancing behaviour. Once you are giving and receiving authentic, well-meant compliments your horizons on who you are and the possibilities you have for personal growth will expand. So, please, remember umbrellas are only to be used for rain.

Undercurrents

If you do not say what is on your mind, what preoccupies you or what is bothering you, then what you do say will carry undercurrents. The same goes for others when they are speaking to you. This can lead to misunderstandings and crossed conversations which is where neither of you is talking on the same wavelength and you only discover this some way into the conversation. This is where the term "Freudian slip" originates. Something that is preoccupying you or your real belief will "slip" through into your manner or your conversation.

The cure for this is to say what it is that concerns you. As mentioned before in the "Elephant in the room" and "Timing" sections, you need to pick a good time and remain in Adult saying what it is that concerns you with as little accusatory or emotional language as you can. You also need to listen to the other person. These tips will help you to iron out misunderstandings and also to avoid muddled conversations. Another important tip when you want to find out why someone behaved the way they did is not to ask "Why?" but to ask "What happened?" or "What was your thinking?" see "Questions" section.

Walking around with a whole lot of unanswered questions simmering away inside or a whole lot of things you haven't said but would like to, is a sure-fire recipe for undercurrents to thrive and where undercurrents thrive misunderstandings and resentment grow. So say it straight or it will come out in distorted behaviour later which will mean it is impossible for you to have authentic or intimate relationships with the people you feel you cannot be honest with. If you are frightened to tell people what you think or fear they will not like you, try to remind yourself that the relationship you currently have is invalid as one or both of you is not being honest with the other, so you have very little to lose by being truthful and much to gain.

If it is your usual style to store up hurts and resentments to use against others later, remind yourself that the long term loser is you (see Stamps). For every time you do not say what it is you need and want, what it is you like or don't, you distort the other person's view of you and who they believe you to be. You also distort who you are and this helps you to continue with behaviours which stop you being close to people and being your true self. It is a vicious circle and one that is hard to get out of. If you recognise this behaviour in yourself gradually, starting with small incidences, start to tell people (politely) how you feel. It is true that some people will not welcome this (they will like the status quo) – after all they might have to change a few habits but gradually they will come to accept your preferences and boundaries and you will be much happier with better and more solid relationships which are relatively free of undercurrents.

Undermine

Try not to undermine others plans or ideas. If you think they have got something dramatically wrong and that the course of action they are planning on is a huge mistake there are other, more subtle, ways of letting them know this. Rather than saying "That sounds like a bad idea." You need instead to start to ask questions that will reveal the flaws in their plan that you are worried about. "How will you finance that?" "What sort of experience do you have in that field?" "That sounds interesting; I didn't know there was a market for porcelain pigs in…" An all-out campaign of undermining remarks can make the other person feel unsupported or got at and leave you appearing mean. In contrast, a series of useful questions will either reveal to you that they have done their homework and your fears are groundless or will reveal to them that their idea is not as sound as they thought.

The other way that we can undermine others is by continually comparing them and their efforts to others. Try not to do this as it has a detrimental effect on the person who is always being compared to another rather than judged on their own merits. This is a particular trap which parents fall into. Either they compare siblings or cousins within a family with each other or they compare one child's achievements with those of others in the same school or class. Both sorts of comparison are completely pointless; two siblings are never going to be the same – even identical twins can have big differences in abilities and interests. Comparing your child with that of another in the same class or school lets your child know that they are 1) in competition, 2) you are the one doing the comparing and 3) It doesn't matter to you how well they are doing for themselves or their own abilities what matters to you is where they come in comparison to others in a similar situation – OUCH! This is very undermining and will lead a child to believe they are not good enough and have very little chance of being good enough unless they are top of everything – not very realistic or very nurturing. This is also true for adults but to a slightly lesser degree as they have more perspective and maturity to bring to bear. In my opinion, the road to hell really is paved with comparisons and they achieve virtually nothing other than to make the compared feel undervalued and undermined. Instead focus on the individual, their achievements and their abilities and you will help their self-esteem which in turn will enable them to flourish.

Utopia

As humans we tend to be aiming or striving for something – our perfect life; our Utopia. Of course there is no such thing. We will not eventually "arrive" and "have it all". As humans we are always in a state of transition and experience and if we miss this, then we miss life. This is not to say that having ambition and wishing to achieve things is a mistake; it isn't but it can be if we don't enjoy the process along the way and merely focus on the end result.

If we are always waiting "until" then we are very rarely in the present enjoying what life has to offer. As mentioned in "heads up" it is important to recognise what you have when you have it, in order that you can enjoy this. This particularly includes things that are elusive rather than concrete. By this I mean good health, good friends, a stable job, a good neighbourhood, parents, siblings, colleagues. By focussing on the quality of your life and your well-being rather than what you have in terms of commodities such as a house or a car, your life will become more experiential and you will be what you are supposed to be a "human being" not a "human having".

Most of our happiness comes from shared experiences with other humans who are close to us. The excitement of a new coat, car or television wears off very quickly whereas the memories of a wonderful shared experience, whether this is an afternoon in the sandpit with your children or a romantic holiday with your partner will linger in your memory and can be recalled at will. Accumulating commodities such as hifis and games consoles will not engender a feeling of well-being for most people, or if it does it will be temporary and fleeting. However, remembering how you felt when your child took their first steps or when you first saw your new puppy will be easily recalled with a reminiscent smile.

The very nature of the society in which we live means that we need to forward plan and take note of the future but whilst doing this for practical reasons we still need to remember to live here today. All we have is now and if we don't savour this we are left with an idea that we will "arrive" if only we strive hard enough – this is the Utopian illusion that we are tempted to buy into – resist for your own quality of life and happiness and don't say you weren't warned!

Violence

Any form of violence towards another human or their property is totally unacceptable. It is very rare during our everyday lives that we encounter serious violence, either towards ourselves or another unless we are involved in an abusive relationship or encounter a very unlucky one-off situation such as being mugged. Violence is usually the end result of a behavioural style that has become out of control. Somewhere along the way people will have colluded with this person by turning a blind eye to such behaviour. Maybe toddler tantrums were allowed to end with the smashing of toys. Maybe throwing things was acceptable as this person grew up. Maybe there was an adult modelling violent behaviour within the home or at school. Violence at any age should never be unchecked.

There is a belief by the perpetrator that this is the only behaviour which will make others sit up and take notice. It is often the last resort of a person who feels they are unheard; nevertheless this is not an acceptable means of communication whatever the reasons that lie behind it. Under no circumstances accept any sort of violent behaviour towards yourself unless in an extreme situation where to challenge the behaviour may put you in even greater danger. If you are the victim of a violent attack report it and prosecute; nothing else will persuade the perpetrator that this is unacceptable behaviour.

If you are someone who believes that your violent behaviour is acceptable then you need to seek help. There are many really good anger-management courses and Cognitive Behaviour Therapy (CBT) is very effective in managing and eliminating this behavioural style. Violence is the ultimate weapon of a bully who wants to "make" others do what he/she wants – this leaves no room to acknowledge the other person, the victim, who not only doesn't get heard, or get what they want but gets injured, too. It is a weapon of the desperate and needs to be stopped as soon as possible. If you can't tackle this yourself get help as there is a belief by therapists that violence left unchecked will either end in the hospital, the court or the morgue. Whatever your situation, do not under any circumstances leave violent behaviour unaddressed.

Volition

When you do things by your own volition, this means that you have chosen to do something. To choose to do something is so much better than having something imposed upon you by another. There is plenty of research which shows that autonomous people live longer and have less illness. Obviously, as humans, we cannot always do what we want. However you can play a trick on yourself and take a reductionist argument which goes something like this… "If I have agreed to do this job then when I am asked to do things I don't like doing within the scope of this job, effectively I have already chosen to do these things: therefore it is my choice and not something that has been imposed upon me." The same goes for the other roles you have which are sometimes less than rewarding for example being a spouse, being a parent, being a carer.

Once you buy into the fact that by having children/being a carer/getting married you are responsible, in some part, for them and for all the tasks that this implies, then it becomes easier on days when you seem to move from chore to chore to acknowledge that somewhere this originates from a choice and is of your own volition. Everything that you do or don't do involves making a choice, including doing nothing. Ultimately this means that you have agreed to do all that you do. Or at least you see the sense and worth of following that route for the time being. This is a much healthier attitude and stops a build up of resentment and a belief that you are not getting to do what you want. Of course it is important to balance this up with things that give you genuine pleasure and pursuits which are just for your benefit; these can be simple things such as having a bubble bath or going for a walk or reading your book.

Once you convince yourself that all your actions are within your own choice then you will start to feel calmer and more in control. This in turn allows you to consider what you will and won't do, where your boundaries lie and what steps you need to take to eliminate tasks that you really hate from your life. Effectively you champion the Adult part of you and stop the Parent and Child parts warring with each other. The Child is the part that doesn't want to do duties and chores, the Parent part is the one that says you should/you ought/you must. Once you stop their argument then you free up a lot of energy in Adult which can be used to concentrate on organising your life so you get to do mainly what you want and start to do things of your own volition.

Volume Control

We live in a busy, noisy world. Too much noise can be damaging to our health and so we need to be aware of how we, personally, add to the volume around us. Be considerate of others and try not to impose your standards and needs on everyone else. In public places turn your mobile phone to vibrate, keep your conversations short and factual and keep your voice down. This is common courtesy of which some people appear to have no knowledge. It is very rude, extremely disturbing and totally unnecessary to have chatty conversations on public transport or in public places because you are bored; these discussions can wait.

There is nothing wrong with talking to a friend or friends in public either but watch your noise levels. Other people do not want details of your conversation and will be having conversations of their own, reading or listening (quietly!) to music. Do not talk in the theatre or cinema or concert during the performance, except for the smallest whispered comment – musicals, pantomimes and comedy turns are not so serious and a few comments and chat are much more acceptable. If you have an MP3 player invest in good headphones and be polite and comply if you are asked to turn the volume down; you are not at home and cannot do as you please. It is essential you consider the other people around you.

Parents need to be aware of the impact their children are having on others, too. It is not OK for one or two small children to dominate and drown out others in public places. Children need to be taught consideration for others and as parents this is your responsibility. If your child shouts or screams in church, at the theatre, in the cinema, at a restaurant it is your job to remove them and explain that they cannot go back until they behave, talk nicely or sit still (whichever applies). Children are very fast learners and will respond avidly to praise and rewards and once the lesson is learnt you have produced delightfully aware citizens who are considerate of others for life.

This is really a matter of basic consideration and politeness. When you are not in private you need to take into account the others around you and the impact that you and what you are doing may be having. Respond politely to people who ask for your consideration in the hope that others will respond in a similar manner to you when you have such requests.

Vulnerability

Many of us are brought up with the belief that to show any vulnerability is a huge weakness which will be pounced on by others. It is certainly true that there are a few individuals who look for other's vulnerabilities and then use these to gain their own ends. However the majority of humans do not. I am not suggesting that you go round wearing your heart on your sleeve; in many situations this would be wholly inappropriate. However, part of being human is that we have flaws and vulnerabilities and in good friendships and intimate relationships a sharing of these vulnerabilities will solidify and enhance a relationship not detract from it. It is a question of trust.

When you are embarking on a relationship or friendship it is important that you get to know the other person well and that you check out the other person's trustworthiness before imparting too much personal information. However no one wants a perfect friend or partner who seems completely invulnerable and has no weaknesses. Someone like that is very hard to warm to or live with. It is fine to gradually let down your defences and let the other person see who you are, complete with all your flaws and weaknesses. Any long-lasting relationship needs to take into account each other's imperfections and accept these, or decide to have a less honest, less intimate relationship. Either relationship is fine just so long as you know which one you are in.

If you think you are in a completely honest relationship and the other person is not up for this then there will be a serious mismatch where there is the danger of the other person flagging up any weaknesses you have revealed. However in a trusting, accepting and intimate relationship you accept each other's vulnerabilities and live with these, accommodating them into the relationship. In this way you allow each of you to be yourselves, accepting each other's humanity. This is what makes us unique individuals and valuable for ourselves alone. If you can reach this understanding with another then you have reached a form of love and the only way you can achieve that is to reveal your vulnerabilities. This is not a decision to be made lightly and not one that everybody will want to make. As I have said, it involves good judgement about the relationship, is not without risk and involves a strong element of trust but I believe it is the only way to experience the full range of love and nurturing that we are capable of as humans. So do not buy into the belief that vulnerability is a weakness; it is part of what makes us human and that very humanity allows us to love each other, flaws and all.

WAM, WAM, WAFM!

This little acronym was taught to me by a lovely therapist that I know, called Mark and was originated by Claude Steiner. It stands for "Wait a minute; wait a minute; wait a f**king minute!" It is used to judge when someone has overstepped your boundaries and you need to say something. It is useful as an internal register. So the first couple of times you encounter something unpleasant from another person you may be prepared to just think to yourself "Wait a minute. I'm not really happy about this. What is this person up to?" However, by about the third time this has happened with this person you will be registering a level of unhappiness that reaches the WAFM scale. This is when you need to step in and say something. You need to let the other person know that they have overstepped your personal boundary. You need to let them know what this is, how this offends you and state that you don't want them to do it again. This is done using the "I" "You" method I have outlined throughout the book. "When you do (whatever), I feel (whatever it is you feel – angry, outraged, hurt). I would like you not to do that again." This is a very clear message, explains your feelings on the matter and if it is ignored then you have every right to be angry and act on that anger.

When you create boundaries for yourself the WAM, WAM, WAFM measure lets you know when they have been breached and at what level. At the WAM level you may not wish to say something but by the WAFM level then you need to say something. In this way it becomes very clear to everyone around you what you will and won't tolerate and in this way people are aware of the sort of person you are. You will then be treated how you wish to be treated. This is truly how to want what you get and get what you want.

What (or how) not Why?

I have mentioned this in various sections throughout the book but it is worth mentioning again in case you skipped the sections that this appears in, as this little adjustment in questioning technique can and does transform relationships. When we ask why about something someone has already chosen to do, this subliminally implies criticism or a parental judgement. "Why did you do that?" Is not a helpful question and is not likely to get a straight answer. However, if you ask "What happened?" or "What was your thinking when you decided to do that?" this gives the other person a chance to show what went on and how their decision was made, often giving you an insight into how they view what happened. Alternatively you can ask "How did that happen?" which is much less accusatory and parental.

Switching from Why to What or How really does change the dynamics of a relationship. No one likes to have their actions criticised but if they can see that the line of enquiry is questioning and seeking information, rather than accusatory they are more likely to accept when they have made a mistake or be open to alternative views. I have found that this is particularly useful with adolescents who seem to loathe having to justify actions. Equally, if you are in a supervisory role this method of enquiry seems to go down much better. Try it and see.

eXcitement

If you have no excitement in your life you will need to ask yourself how risk averse you have become? Fear and excitement are very close neighbours and you may be mistaking one for the other. If you are naturally cautious and that suits you and you feel content with your life, all well and good. However if you think your life is dull or lacks purpose then perhaps that is because you are too cautious. You may have been brought up by anxious, careful parents who tried to impart their fears to you and who partially succeeded. Check that your fears are reasonable – it is fine to avoid holidays to war zones but not fine to avoid holidays to areas with diseases that we can vaccinate against. Avoiding any sort of holiday because of a fear of the unknown would be extreme. By all means check out the risks and dangers of anything you plan, take out insurance and ask people who've had similar experiences but don't avoid situations just because they cause you to feel some apprehension; some fear of the unknown is reasonable and just needs to be acknowledged and lived with otherwise you risk missing out on some exciting highs that life has to offer.

In contrast, it is foolish to believe that life is one big exciting journey. Quite a lot of life can be exciting, exploratory and new but a lot of life, once you become an adult involves repetitive chores to keep yourself clean, housed and fed. This is normal and it is why we pursue hobbies and sports that add a little spice to our lives. If you had parents who thought life was a laugh and were minimally responsible, often happy to live in chaos, you could believe that any sort of regular routine kills creativity and is stifling. However, it is part of an extremely Child-ish mind set to believe that you can live comfortably and avoid all responsibility. It is possible for a while but not really sustainable long-term and there are many things you will have to forfeit. We all know about one or two fifty-year-old hippy surfers who are "free, man" but also lack family, community or any solid roots. This is absolutely fine if this is what you want. But don't buy into the belief that a regular life is boring or mundane just because you have a routine going. It can be the very support that allows you to pursue exciting activities or provides the contrast to the more exciting pursuits you enjoy.

I view excitement as a wonderful feeling involving anticipation, maybe some apprehension and some childlike wonder at what will take place. It is an integral part of being a curious, eager human but it is not a never-ending roller-coaster ride. So build pockets of excitement into your life and try to keep pursuits fresh and new. Try not to become jaded and remember some of the things you may view as mundane or boring are what in reality sustain you in order that you can pursue more exciting activities – balance is all.

eXistentialism

Okay, this is cheating but I really did need something else under X and although many people think the concept of existentialism is arty-farty I think it is fundamental to all humans and enhances our lives if occasionally we embrace the question of our existence and what purpose we have.

Existentialism is all about realising our lives are finite and that we will die. We have limited time to make our mark on the planet and then we will no longer exist, be relevant or matter. This is what causes us to ask the bigger questions such as "Why are we here?" and "What is our purpose?" and even "Who am I?" I am not suggesting that you spend your whole life questioning your existence but it is a good idea to check out now and again that you are pursuing a path that you want to; that you feel happy with moral decisions that you have made and are making and that essentially you like yourself. Sometimes, through necessity, we will be unable to pursue the path that we would like or that expresses our view of ourselves in the best way but if we have this in mind then we can be alert to opportunities to align our dreams and wishes with how we live.

Not everybody will be able to become a politician or a philanthropist or a musician but we may be able to thread small pieces of who we essentially believe ourselves to be into our existence. For instance if you are a nursery school teacher but wished to be a concert pianist and feel that fundamentally that is your raison d'etre, then you may be able to introduce music into your classroom and engender a love of all things musical in several of your pupils. In that way you can marry up necessity (your job as a teacher) and your existential desire to express yourself (your music) with each other in a way that enhances and validates you as you see yourself and sits well with the job you need to do.

If we get too far away from who we believe ourselves to be this is when we become depressed or hit a mid-life crises or in a more minor way just believe ourselves to be living a life with little worth. We need to ask ourselves what we consider to be a valuable life. I personally consider the fact that I have brought up two reasonable, functioning, responsible children, largely by myself, to be of the utmost worth and this thought gives me pleasure and purpose on a regular basis. You can ask yourself what you are adding back to humanity and how you have contributed to human worth. Big questions, indeed but it has been shown that people who act altruistically for the good of others and take part in their community are usually healthier, happier and more optimistic than those who don't. So a little thought about your existence, your purpose and what you are doing may well contribute to your overall health as well as benefitting humanity in general. For an arty-farty subject, that can't be too bad.

You/I

I have mentioned this throughout the book. This is the You/I statement that allows you to express to another how their actions affect you without being critical or accusatory. Phrased in this way it is also much easier for the other person to hear and take on board what you are saying. Here's how it goes: When somebody does or says something that you don't like or that encroaches on your boundaries then this is how you can most effectively address them. "When you say (insert whatever it is) to me, I feel (whatever you feel). Instead I would like you to (whatever you want them to do instead which still allows them to express themselves)."

It is important that you express how you "feel" about what it is they have said or done. Your feelings cannot be denied as they are yours and what you "think" is opinion based and may cause an argument because you have different viewpoints on what is or isn't acceptable (see Frames of Reference). Also offer an alternative, acceptable behaviour. This shows you are not closed to any criticism or difference of opinion just opposed to the way you have been addressed or the language used. For instance: "When you shout at me in front of the children I feel belittled and unsupported. I would like it if we could discuss our differences after they have gone to bed and work out together how we can address these."

By avoiding an accusation "You make me feel" we also take away the power of the other person. After all another person doesn't "make" you feel anything; you are choosing how you respond and generating those feelings accordingly. However another can undoubtedly upset you by overstepping your boundaries or being disrespectful or hurtful. You have every right to be spoken to respectfully and have your concerns addressed. This really is one of the most useful, non-confrontational ways of resolving issues that bother you and can be used anywhere. It is also a very useful method to teach your children. Try it, this is one of the most popular, painless changes that my clients tell me bring almost instant results.

You (It's not all about You)

Of course, your whole life is essentially about you. However (and here comes the "but") most outcomes and occurrences will have very little to do with you. In the Western world we very much believe in our own autonomy and our ability to influence our environment and our lives. That said, most of us grow up acknowledging other people's impact, influences and needs as well as recognising that the world we live in can be unpredictable. If, however, you grew up with unacknowledged needs you will, more than most, like to be able to control your environment and this can lead to problems. When you are confronted with situations where you have little control you are likely to revert back to your Child behaviour, that of being egocentric and referencing all outcomes and occurrences back to your own views and opinion and emotions, regardless of outside events or other people. At an extreme level this produces a narcissistic personality disorder but at an ordinary everyday level it produces a person who finds it very difficult to see another's point of view or acknowledge a difference in opinion.

If our parents do not meet our needs we may stay more egocentric than is good for us and overreact when we do not get the outcomes that we want; this is our way of keeping control over the situation. When we were little we did not have that control and so when we become adult we make sure that we have it. This, however, can lead to a belief that you control events much more than you do. For instance if you make a request of a friend and they refuse you, the more egocentric you are the more you are likely to believe that you are the cause of the request being turned down. You are not likely to factor in that the other person may have been too busy, had other commitments, felt too tired etc. etc. This can lead to a slightly paranoid outlook on life and an overreaction when things do not go according to your particular plan. You need to develop the ability to recognise what you do and don't influence and the wisdom to realise that a lot of outcomes are not within your control. That is not to say you can't influence events and give yourself the best possible chance of getting what you want, just that you don't take rejection too personally or try to control situations too rigidly.

The other side of this egocentric personality, as mentioned above, is an inability to see any other point of view but your own, or to be unable to factor in that others have completely opposing viewpoints or desires whilst still remaining OK people. This will make you an uncomfortable friend, partner or relative to have. If you can be more accepting of others' needs and desires and can adopt an ability to compromise, life will become much easier. For instance if your friend is about to get a kitten and you hate cats, there is absolutely no need to tell your friend – after all your dislike of cats is entirely irrelevant; if you think it isn't, then you need to work on being a little bit less self-obsessed!

If in the main, life seems to be all about you, then be kind to yourself. You probably had parents who either didn't notice your wants and needs or just ignored them. Make sure that you attend to your needs and are forgiving towards yourself when you become dogmatic or insistent. Gradually you will be able to relax and let others have their own way some of the time as well as adopting a live and let live attitude which will make you much easier to befriend and much more fun to be around. After all it is very tiring to be the "opinion police" and to insist on your own way all the time. It's much more fun to let someone else take control and hop along for a free ride.

Youth

I believe we have a responsibility to the young in our society. After all they will be the adults of the future and without good examples, encouragement and a feeling that they are valued and belong they can easily become disenchanted and disaffected. When this happens and they feel they have no say and therefore no investment in their community, then the young act out and can become destructive rather than constructive. We need to give our young something to aim for and some share of the future. Don't forget none of us drop from the sky fully formed and adult; growing up can be painful and difficult.

The first important thing therefore, is to listen to them properly. Often young people will express themselves differently, using slang or taking a while to get to the point. We owe it to them to listen and afford them the same courtesy we would give to anyone else. The biggest complaint from my two teenage sons is that adults who don't know them make assumptions about them. We wouldn't like that, so please don't lump all young people together, either good or bad. Young people often have a different "take" on something and will think outside the box, coming up with novel ideas that can add insight to old problems. When they are included in decisions, they have the energy and drive to see tasks through, particularly if they are praised and encouraged.

In order to get the young people that we want, we need to invest in our youth and value them. They need to know this. They need to be acknowledged and appreciated as well as guided and educated. If we take our role as adults seriously, whether or not we are parents, then we have a lot to give to the young and in turn we can learn a lot from them. It's very clichéd but children are our future and you get what you put in. So try to treat younger people courteously and generously without always trying to "teach" them something and they will probably surprise you in that you will be the one who learns something valuable.

Zeal

Enthusiasm for an enterprise or idea is always welcome but expecting other people to feel similarly enthused or to hold the same ideas or values will lead to disappointment. If we become over-zealous about something we are in danger of becoming dogmatic and wanting others to buy into our point of view. One of the very important lessons about getting on with other adults is allowing them to hold their own views however contrary they are to yours.

No one likes to have their own views or beliefs criticised or found wanting and so it is important that we don't behave like that towards others in our enthusiasm for an issue we hold dear. It is perfectly possible to be friends with someone who holds opposing views to your own, providing that you respect each other's rights to hold any views that they want and do not believe that this in any way encroaches on you.

If you had a parent or carer who was always wanting you to align your views with theirs or a parent who made you feel inferior for holding views that were different from their own, then it will be hard for you to feel entirely confident about holding your own views whilst another holds theirs which are opposing. This is the conflict you need to overcome in order to be comfortable with who you are and what you believe whilst allowing others this same courtesy. However this is the hallmark of a reasonable, confident and harmonious adult human being and will make your life so much easier. After all if you believe your views are valid and sacrosanct then why shouldn't someone else believe exactly the same of their views? Think about it.

Zest

Zest is the spicy enjoyment of life. Adding a little bit of zest into your everyday existence can help make the more mundane aspects of life easier to experience. If you have the chance to try something new then do so. Whether it be a completely different film, entertainment, food or drink or just an idea to go indoor skiing or visit an art gallery, getting outside your comfort zone and experiencing something new in a wholehearted manner will add spice to your life. If you haven't tried something then you can't possibly know whether you would like it or not and you are narrowing your experiences without giving yourself a chance. Even with routines, try not to get stuck into a rut so that you lose the novelty and enjoyment of what you are doing. This can include your sex life, reading to your children, your tennis game – add something new or different, try something out but don't take it too seriously. If it's a flop it doesn't matter; it is something you can cross off as having tried and not wanted to do again. Remember you are only here once so try to open yourself up to new and interesting experiences and try not to narrow your field of interests.

You need, too, to be careful that you don't project a closed, uninterested view on novel things or people will be discouraged from asking you to the quiz evening or the wine tasting as they'll assume (maybe quite wrongly) that it is not your thing. If you are too prescriptive about what you do then you may miss out on some new and fun things. The same goes for meeting new people. You need to be approachable and open, whilst obviously maintaining your own safety. A friendly comment or smile can often start a conversation with a stranger and you will find that someone else's point of view and interests can add a different perspective and maybe introduce you to something you hadn't experienced or thought of before. To miss out by narrowing your options is a shame. Be brave and remember that trying something and not liking it or being good at it is not a failure; it's a learning curve and an experience. After all your life is only a sequence of different experiences and if they are not all that different then you may have a much narrower life. If you aren't willing to try novel ideas then you may lose out on the richness of new and previously untried events which it would be a shame to leave the planet without trying. Think of it as a banquet – you only have to have a little nibble and if it's not for you, you can leave it.

In the Zone

Being "in the zone" is when you have achieved an integrated Adult self. By this I mean you have come to terms with how you are with regards to your upbringing and experiences and have the Parent and Child parts of yourself under your Adult's control. This means you understand what triggers your different behaviours but do not necessarily choose to respond to them or if you do respond you choose only to respond in ways that do not damage you. This does not mean you won't experience Child and Parent behaviours it just means that when you have Parent-like behaviour you will (ideally) use this for the benefit not the detriment of who you are. Therefore you do not use your Parent information to castigate and cajole your Child self into doing things when you are too tired or that will not benefit you. In turn you do not use your Child knowledge to override the Parental safety aspects. For instance if you are having fun at a party you do not drink to excess, lose control of yourself and end up unaware of your surroundings and unable to look out for yourself. That would be de-commissioning your Parent and Adult so that your Child could play without supervision (usually Rebellious Child behaviour). You may acknowledge a fleeting desire to rebel and then (because you understand yourself) reject this idea because your past experience lets you know that this is not a good route for you to take.

When you are "in the Zone", all the parts of yourself work to enhance and support each other and all come under the control of your Adult who is the overall judge and supervisor of what is good for you based on your values, boundaries and beliefs. In this way your behaviour matches who you are and who you want to be and this is projected outwards so that it is very clear to others who know you what you will and won't tolerate and how you expect to be treated. When you make mistakes (and you will) you are able to forgive yourself, pick yourself up and learn from your errors and in this way you can steadily improve your learning curve.

I believe that Integrated Adult is the ultimate goal for human happiness. It means you have to acknowledge your experiences throughout life and assess what works well and what doesn't and then make serious choices. You cannot have everything and may have to sacrifice a part of yourself that you find difficult to let go of. You might like the image you have of "party girl" but realise this is a way you got attention in the past and that the morning after is never good for you. You will need to consciously choose a more beneficial way of getting attention in order to give up the negative attention seeking behaviour. If you do not replace your negative behaviours with ones that get you what you need in a productive and beneficial way you will not be able to give them up. This is because you will not get your needs met and explains why addicts find their addiction so hard to give up. They are usually unable, due to their addiction, to replace their negative behaviour with anything beneficial and therefore it is exceptionally hard to let go of the one thing that appears to be fulfilling some of their needs.

You will need to examine internal beliefs and messages that you have "adopted" as you have grown up. Some of them will be outdated and unhelpful and be a poor reflection of who you are or who you want to be. We often take on beliefs and views from our parents and peers as a survival mechanism when we are dependent on those adults around us. When we look at some of these later we can see that often we have been given "mixed messages" such as "Be clever but don't outshine other people." That's quite a balancing act to achieve. We may need to replace other people's messages and views with ones of our own that sit well with how and who we are becoming. Some, of course, we will value and want to hold onto but in order to sort out which are beneficial and which are not we need to do some fairly conscientious self-examination – hard work but definitely worth it.

To achieve Integrated Adult and land "in the Zone" is a conscious ongoing project which requires hard work, awareness, dedication and a good sense of humour! You are not going to get it right all the time. However it is the awareness of what you are aiming for and the recognition of how you might get this by making small changes to your behaviour which will enable you to go from strength to strength. Acknowledging the Child and Parent parts of yourself and employing them for your own benefit is the route to take and will allow you to get what you want and want what you get. Believe me there is very little else that will benefit you more and not just you but everyone you come into contact with. I make that win/win.

Top Tips on how to make yourself and others really miserable

1. Look for someone to blame for every event in your life; never think about your own part in circumstances or how you could make things better.
2. Never, ever commit to anything wholeheartedly, be cynical. Don't believe in anything completely, yourself included.
3. Go over and over events, how they should have been, how you should have behaved, how others should have responded. Remind yourself how you blew it. Especially dwell on events that are in the past and that you can't change.
4. Catastrophise or minimise anything and everything. Events are "nightmares" or "nothing". People are "ghastly or wonderful". Don't be moderate or slow to judge about anything.
5. Don't tell anyone how you are feeling. Expect others to know. When your feelings boil over shout a lot and use words such as "always" and "never" when describing others' behaviour.
6. Talk about other people behind their back. Spread gossip about others and don't check out the reality of events or worry about anyone's feelings.
7. Blurt out how you are feeling anywhere, any time, any place. After all your feelings are your feelings.
8. Don't set limits on how or when people can speak to you. Let them interrupt what you are doing, swear at you and complain to you publicly. Never confront them about how they are treating you.
9. Do everything as quickly as possibly especially when dealing with tricky situations involving others. Don't ask for extra time or think about how to approach things.

10. Take everything personally. Hold grudges for as long as possible. Don't tell the people involved what it is they have done. Build up your resentment as much as you can, stoking it up with reminders of past hurts and injustices.

11. Be as hard as you can on yourself and others. Find yourself lacking. Tell yourself what an idiot you are. Remind yourself that you'll never amount to anything and no one likes you anyway.

12. Chuck this book in the bin or give it to a charity shop. No one ever got good advice from a book – after all a leopard can't change its spots.

13. Be as grumpy as possible. Don't acknowledge other people if they say hello or thank you and definitely don't smile or respond to any friendly overtures. Be suspicious.

14. Don't accept compliments. The person doesn't really mean it they just want something or are passing the time of day. Just grunt or shrug. Don't be gracious otherwise they might compliment you in the future.

15. When life is stressful, eat rubbish, smoke and drink and certainly don't take any exercise or relax – you simply haven't got time!

Top tips on how to make life easier and better for yourself and others

1. Remind yourself we're all sharing the planet and everyone has difficulties. Ease up on yourself and others.
2. Be generous with time, energy and compassion – it will never be wasted.
3. Take your time. You don't have to give an immediate answer to an invitation or a request for help. "I'll get back to you. When do you need to know by?" or "I need to think about that" are perfectly reasonable responses.
4. Resolve situations as they arise. Don't let issues linger; deal with the problem and then move on. If it didn't turn out how you wanted it to you've learnt something for next time.
5. Retrain your inner voice to be kinder. Erase "You idiot, look what you did" and replace it with "How can you make sure you don't do that again." Employ this technique with your children.
6. Tell people how you feel if situations bother you. Use the formula "When you (do whatever) I feel (whatever you feel)", For instance "When you swear at me, I feel hurt and angry." Ask them to think of something different they could do.
7. Let people know how you expect to be treated. Firstly, by treating others as you wish to be treated and, secondly, by letting others know when you find their behaviour/language or timing inappropriate. Offer a preferred style e.g. "It doesn't work for me when you approach me about work difficulties in the canteen… could we schedule a meeting instead?"
8. You don't need to be right. Hammering home your own agenda or beliefs is tiresome and alienates people. Insisting you're right

and that everyone agrees with you is a definite no-no. Recognise that others are entitled to believe whatever they want even if you don't agree – you are not the opinion police!

9. The past is the past. Don't hang on to old past hurts, either address them or drop them. Old hurts are highly corrosive, usually only to the people who are hanging on to them. A good, enjoyable life is the best antidote.

10. Choose your battles. Some things don't matter. Learn to recognise important issues as oppose to small stuff. Ask yourself will this matter in a week, a month or a year. You don't need to pick on everything and often people don't need to know what you think, either. Learn to let the little things go. You will be astonished by how much energy you free up.

11. Pay attention to your health. Eat well and schedule regular exercise and relaxation. If you have a problem, get it checked out by your doctor. Attend all your regular health checks.

12. Do things you have agreed to wholeheartedly, cheerfully and with good grace or alternatively say "No".

13. Count your blessings. Enjoy small, free everyday pleasures: The sunshine, rainbows, a good movie, a chat to a friend, your new sweater, a hot shower, a comedy on TV, a hug from a friend or your child.

14. Smile at others – not an inane grin – just a friendly smile. It helps the world go round. Accept compliments graciously. Give others compliments if you are thinking nice things about them.

15. Say please and thank you. Apologise if you get something wrong or you upset someone.

And remember – if you keep on doing what you've always done, you'll get what you've always got!

Bibliography

BAUMRIND, D (1971) *Current patterns of Parental Authority, Developmental Psychology*, Monographs 1 pp 1-103

BOSMA, H, MARMOT, MG, HEMINGAY, H, NICHOLSON, AG, BUNNER, E, STANDFIELD, A, (1997) Low Job Control and Risk of Coronary Heart Disease in Whitehall II Study, *BMJ* Vol.314; 558-65

COMFORT, A (Ed) (1978) *The Joy of Sex: A Gourmet Guide to Lovemaking*, Quartet Books Ltd, London, Melbourne, New York

GECAS, V and SEFF, MA (1990) *Families and Adolescents: A review of the 1980s.* Journal of Marriage and the family 52, 941-958

GOTTMAN, J and SILVER N (2000) *Making Marriage Work*, Orion Publishing Group Ltd

HARRIS, T (1969) *I'm OK/You're OK*, Harper and Row

JAMES, O (2007) *Affluenza*, Vermillion

KÜBLER-ROSS, E (1969) *On Death and Dying*, Macmillan, New York

LEE, H (1960) *To Kill a Mocking Bird*, Philadelphia: J B Leppincott & Co 1960

MASLOW, A H (1987) *Motivation and Personality*, 3rd Edition, New York: Harper and Row (first published 1954)

MASLOW, AH (1973) *The Farther Reaches of Human nature* p.45, Harmondsworth: Penguin

MATE, Gabor, (2003) *When the Body Says No*, John Wiley & Sons Inc., Hoboken, New Jersey

ROSENTHAL, R and JACOBSON, L (1968) *Pygmalion in the Classroom*, New York, Holt, Reinhart and Winston

SELIGMAN, MEP PhD, *Learned Optimisim: How to Change your Mind and your Life* 1990, Random House Inc., New York

STEWART, I and JOINES, V (2002) *Personality Adaptations: A New Guide to Human Understanding in Psychotherapy and Counselling*, Lifespace Publishing, Nottingham and Chapel Hill, North Carolina USA

STEWART, I and JOINES, V (1987) *TA Today: A New Introduction to Transactional Analysis*, Lifespace Publishing, Nottingham and Chapel Hill, North Carolina, USA

TONES, K and TILFORD, S (1994) *Health Education: Effectiveness, Efficiency and Equity*, Chapman and Hall, London

WEISS, R.S. (1974) *The Provisions of Social Relationships*. In Rubin, Z (Ed). *Doing Unto Others: Joining, Moulding, Conforming, Helping, Loving*. Englewood Cliffs, NJ: Prentice-Hall Spectrum Books, 17-26